AMERICAN LABOR AND CONSENSUS CAPITALISM, 1935–1990

AMERICAN LABOR AND CONSENSUS CAPITALISM, 1935–1990

Patrick Renshaw

University Press of Mississippi
Jackson

First published in 1991 in the United States of America by the
University Press of Mississippi.

Library of Congress Cataloging-in-Publication Data

Renshaw, Patrick, 1936–
    American labor and consensus capitalism, 1935–1985 / Patrick
Renshaw.
        p.   cm.
    Includes bibliographical references (p.   ) and index.
    ISBN 0–87805–536–3. — ISBN 0–87805–537–1 (pbk.)
    1. Trade-unions—United States—History—20th century. 2. Labor-
–United States—History—20th century. 3. Capitalism—United
States—History—20th century. I. Title.
HD6508.R39   1991
331.88′0973′0904—dc20   91–13034
                                                              CIP

Printed in Hong Kong

*To the memory of Philip Maynard Williams (1920–84),
my tutor, mentor and close friend for thirty years*

'You remember the workingman? You used to write an awful lot about the workingman. He's turning into something called organized labor. You're not going to like that one little bit when you find out it means that your workingman expects something as his right and not your gift. Charlie, when your precious underprivileged really get together – oh, boy, that's going to add up to something bigger than your privilege, and then I don't know what you'll do.'

Jedadiah Leland to Charles Foster Kane
in the movie *Citizen Kane*

Contents

Contents

Editors' Preface

Mention the United States and few people respond with feelings of neutrality. Discussions about the role of the United States in the contemporary world typically evoke a sense of admiration or a shudder of dislike. Pundits and politicians alike make sweeping references to attributes of modern society deemed 'characteristically American'. Yet qualifications are in order, especially regarding the distinctiveness of American society and the uniqueness of American culture. True, American society has been shaped by the size of the country, the migratory habits of the people and the federal system of government. Certainly, American culture cannot be understood apart from its multi-cultural character, its irreverence for tradition and its worship of technological imagery. It is equally true, however, that life in the United States has been profoundly shaped by the dynamics of American capitalism and by the penetration of capitalist market imperatives into all aspects of daily life.

The series is designed to take advantage of the growth of specialised research about post-war America in order to foster understanding of the period as a whole as well as to offer a critical assessment of the leading developments of the post-war years. Coming to terms with the United States since 1945 requires a willingness to accept complexity and ambiguity, for the history encompasses conflict as well as consensus, hope as well as despair, progress as well as stagnation. Each book in the series offers an interpretation designed to spark discussion rather than a definite account intended to close debate. The series as a whole is meant to offer students, teachers and the general public fresh perspectives and new insights about the contemporary United States.

CHRISTOPHER BROOKEMAN
WILLIAM ISSEL

Acknowledgements

This book has been written at intervals between research and teaching in other fields. Work started in the United States in the academic year 1981–82 on a research fellowship awarded by the American Council of Learned Societies. The ACLS has sponsored generations of scholars from all parts of the world, in every aspect of American Studies. In expressing my personal thanks, I salute the ACLS for the part it has played in deepening foreign understanding of America.

The Department of History at Sheffield University granted study leave so that I could spend a semester at the State University of New York in Binghamton. The History Department there provided congenial surroundings for study, and I benefited from contact with Professor Melvyn Dubofsky, Professor Charles Freedman, Leslie ('Pepi') Levene and others at Binghamton who showed much kindness, and sympathy when family bereavement cut short my stay.

Sheffield University granted further terms of study leave in 1985 and 1989 which enabled me to continue and complete research in both Britain and the United States, while the Foreign Travel and Research Funds helped with transatlantic fares, subsistence and typing costs. Small grants from the British Academy and the cultural Affairs Office of the American Embassy in London also reduced those out-of-pocket expenses which academics, unlike businessmen, are expected to pay themselves while working for their employer. The New York State Industrial and Labor Relations Library at Cornell University, with its vast holdings and helpful staff, the incomparable Franklin D. Roosevelt Library at Hyde Park, New York, and the Hagley Collection at Eleutherian Mills, Wilmington, Delaware, all deepened my understanding of the subject I sought to master, and made long hours of desk consideration a pleasure.

Finally I must record a special word of warmest thanks to Philip Mason and Warner Pflug at the Walter P. Reuther Library of Labor and Urban Affairs at Wayne State University, Detroit, Michigan. Their award of a Kaiser Travel Grant in 1989 enabled me to spend a profitable month in the ideal surroundings of a unique archive collection, redolent of the history of the UAW and the CIO.

Sheffield University Inter-Library Loan Service, the British Library, the Bodleian and Nuffield College Libraries, Oxford, and the libraries of Cardiff and Hull universities were all helpful in enabling me to read other material not readily available.

While working and travelling in North America I was shown hospitality by people too numerous to mention, but I must name Lucinda and Jeremy Jackson, Nancy and Francis Calhoun, Pat and Irving Nyman, two of my oldest friends, and Carol and Stan Oakleaf, two of my newest, who also enabled me to fulfil a boyhood ambition to meet 'a gal in Kalamazoo'. Many friends and colleagues at Syracuse University, New York, always made me welcome when my itinerary took me to upstate New York.

In the 22 years I have worked at Sheffield, its history department has become one of the best in Britain, and it is a pleasure to thank colleagues for the stimulus they have provided over the years to research and writing. In particular, I wish to name Richard Carwardine (a distant kinsman of one of this book's major protagonists John L. Lewis), Richard Thurlow, Stephen Salter and John Stevenson, and two of my graduate students, Michael Woodiwiss and Steven Swann, for help and encouragement. My brother Geoffrey Renshaw corrected errors in my economic statistics. My greatest intellectual debt, recorded in the book's dedication, is to Philip Williams, Fellow of Nuffield College until his death on 16 November 1984, a teacher who inspired students from all over the world. That this book has taken so long to write is indicative of the impact the so-called 'Thatcher revolution' has had on British universities, forcing academics to devote increasing time and energy to administration, cost cutting, fund raising, promotional work and union agitation, rather than to the teaching and research their contracts of employment require. Future labour historians will find the story of industrial relations at British universities in the 1980s instructive.

All historians learn from, borrow from, dissent from and use the work of contemporaries and predecessors, but I wish to make a special acknowledgement here to those whose work has proved most helpful. Melvyn Dubofsky and Warren Van Tine collaborated to write *John L. Lewis: a Biography*, the finest life of any American labour leader, a study which grows more impressive the more one learns about its subject and his times. Professor Dubofsky's revision of Foster R. Dulles, *Labor in America: a History* was also invaluable in providing narrative links to the analysis attempted in the following pages. Mel's relentless eye will spot the joins and, I hope, recall Oscar Wilde's remark about imitation being the sincerest form of flattery.

Professor Van Tine's *The Making of a Labor Bureaucrat*, though set in an earlier period than mine, influenced my own approach. Professor Nelson Lichtenstein, *Labor's War at Home: the CIO in World War II* was a pathfinding book about the 1940s, while Howell J. Harris, *The Right to Manage*, which I had the pleasure and good fortune to examine as an Oxford D. Phil dissertation, transformed everyone's picture of the employer's side of industrial relations in the 1940s. Irving Bernstein, *Turbulent Years* is still the most complete narrative history of labour in the 1930s, while Joel Siedman, *American Labor from Defense to Reconversion* is an important pioneering study. Harvey Levenstein, *Communism, Anti-Communism and the CIO* is a dispassionate account of an emotive topic on which chapter 5 of this book relies heavily for its narrative and conclusions.

Finally David Brody, the most gifted interpretative labour historian of his generation, whom I first met when he gave the Anglo-American Lecture at Sheffield in 1989, will see ideas from his essays scattered throughout my text.

My first three chapters include material which first appeared in different form in essays published in the *Journal of Contemporary History*, vol. 21, no. 1 (January 1986), in Stephen Baskerville and Ralph Willett (eds), *Nothing Else to Fear* (1985) and Stephen Salter and John Stevenson (eds), *The Working Class and Politics in Europe and America* (1990). The author and publishers thank the publishers, respectively Sage Publications, Manchester University Press and the Longman Group UK Ltd, for permission to use this material.

Though I still use fountain pen and two-finger typing, this is the age of the touch-typed word processor. Thus Freda Brayshaw worked on early drafts with the same patience and perception she shows when partnering me at bridge, Susan Sharman delivered later drafts while Kath Wright typed the whole of the final draft with speed and skill in deciphering an untidy manuscript, and tolerance towards its many changes. Andrew Green and Mareen Smallman helped compile the bibliography, and I must thank Vanessa Couchman, who commissioned this book for the series, her successor Vanessa Graham, and the series' editors, Christopher Brookeman and William Issel for their advice, encouragement and patience. Keith Povey was the best copy-editor I have worked with in a lifetime's writing experience.

None of the people listed above bears responsibility for errors which remain, and all opinions expressed here are my own. Since books on contemporary history cover questions which have a bearing on current political controversies, I should add that I have voted for the British Labour Party in every election since 1957.

My first and last debt is to my wife Mary, who as usual sacrificed her time and much more so that I could spend more of mine working on this book. I owe her everything I most value in life, and her only consolation is that at last I have written about events which took place during our marriage.

Sheffield, Labor Day, 1990   PATRICK RENSHAW

Author's Note on Spelling

The text follows standard English spelling, as in the word labour. Quotations of course are in standard American usage where the source is American, as in labor, program and cigaret. All American institutions, such as the Defense Department, follow American spelling in the author's text.

Abbreviations

AAA	Agricultural Adjustment Act
ACTU	Association of Catholic Trade Unionists
ACW	Amalgamated Clothing Workers
ACTWU	Amalgamated Clothing and Textile Workers' Union
ADA	Americans for Democratic Action
AFL	American Federation of Labor
ALA	Alliance for Labor Action
CGT	Confederation Générale du Travail
CIO	Congress of Industrial Organizations
CP	Communist Party
CPA	Communist Political Association
FE	Farm Equipment Workers
FO	Force Ouvrière
GE	General Electric
GM	General Motors
ICFTU	International Confederation of Free Trade Unions
ILA	International Longshoremen's Association
ILGWU	International Ladies' Garment Workers
ILWU	International Longshoremen's and Warehousemen's Union
IWW	Industrial Workers of the World
NIRA	National Industrial Recovery Act
NLRA	National Labor Relations Act
NLRB	National Labor Relations Board
NRA	National Recovery Administration
NWLB	National War Labor Board
SWOC	Steel Workers' Organizing Committee
TWOC	Textile Workers' Organizing Committee
UAW	United Autoworkers
UAW-AFL	United Autoworkers faction affiliated to the AFL
UE	United Electrical Workers
UFW	United Farm Workers
USW	United Steelworkers
WFTU	World Federation of Trade Unions

Introduction

This book's epigraph is taken from the 1940 film script, by Herman J. Mankiewicz and Orson Welles, of *Citizen Kane*. A song written about the same time by left-wing clothing workers satirised American labour leadership. With capitalism in crisis during the Great Depression, and Socialism alone apparently capable of resisting the threat of world Fascism, the Jewish radicals who wrote the lyric attacked company unions and 'labour fakers' – men like Sidney Hillman, David Dubinsky and Norman Thomas, the Socialist Party candidate for President in 1932. The song, in its entirety, ran as follows:

> The cloakmakers' union
> Is a no-good union
> It's a company union
> By the bosses.

> The right-wing cloakmakers,
> And the socialist fakers,
> Are making by the workers
> Double-crosses.

> The Hillmans, Dubinskys and the Thomases
> Are making by the workers *False Promises*.

> They preach socialism
> But they practice fascism
> To preserve capitalism
> By the bosses.

The epigraph reflects capital's fears about the power organized labour possessed to change the world. The song expresses labour's contempt for the way their leaders used that power to betray them. My book tries to explore the ground which lies between these two positions: fear of change and fear of betrayal. American labour did change the world. But far from overthrowing the system, as some hoped it would, unions transformed it so that it worked more efficiently and successfully. What evolved was consensus capitalism, which made America more powerful and helped it dominate an increasingly prosperous Western world.

The rise of organized labour, argued the historian Arthur M. Schlesinger, second only to the two world wars, was what most profoundly shaped the history of the West in the first half of the 20th century. This phenomenon was common to all major industrial nations. But it occurred earlier on the European continent, in Britain and in such English-speaking countries as Australia and New Zealand than it did in the United States. Yet though comparatively late, expansion of American labour unions, once properly underway in the 1930s, was of unprecedented speed. As the celebrated labour intellectual J. B. S. Hardman put it, 'In a matter of only a few years American labor unionism emerged organized, invigorated . . . The amazingly rapid growth of unionism and its power goes beyond anything ever known. Between 1933 and 1938 union membership tripled from under three to more than nine million.'[1]

Paradoxically, the Great Depression of the 1930s was a major agent in this expansion. At its depth in 1933 the United States, hardest hit of all industrial economies by the Great Depression, appeared to be a helpless giant, its working class devastated and demoralised, its labour unions destroyed. Faced with this moral challenge, the nation elected Franklin D. Roosevelt President and embarked upon a sweeping programme of reform known as the New Deal. During the next 12 years Roosevelt, in peace and war, showed himself to be the greatest democratic leader in American history, and a key figure in world history in the 20th century.

No one, least of all Roosevelt, had any idea what the New Deal would mean in practice. It turned out to be a sweeping programme of reform based upon the idea of 'bold, persistent experimentation'. Such coherence as it had was in the field of political strategy rather than economic theory. Roosevelt knew where the votes were, and the Federal government threw its authority for the first time behind the right of the working class to organize and bargain collectively. So labour unions formed part of the Democratic Party's new coalition of liberal, urban reform which set the political agenda for a generation.

But by a process of trial and error, the New Deal also came to embrace the ideas of the British economist J. M. Keynes. The Depression had been caused in general terms because America's capacity to produce goods was tending to outstrip its capacity to consume them. Keynes and some others were struggling to find the answer: use Federal government spending not just to stimulate growth, create more jobs and end unemployment, but also to manage and control the economy. The key to prosperity, on this argument, was raising aggregate demand. So powerful unions, bidding up pay and thus consumption, would play a crucial part. This doctrine of salvation through high wages was naturally seized upon by organized labour, since it rationalised what they wanted to do anyway.

Thus the New Deal greatly strengthened labour's power to organize and bargain collectively, while accelerating acceptance of the high wage economy. This whole process – Federal economic management on Keynesian lines, deficit spending, stronger unions, rising demand – was enhanced by the Second World War. With labour scarce, government and management had to court organized labour to win its support, and make unions joint partners in managing the war economy. By 1945 union membership, at fifteen million, was five times what it had been in 1933. More than two-thirds of production workers in manufacturing industry now came under collective bargaining. In transport, coal and metal mining, steel, automobiles, meat packing, rubber and other basic industries unions had organized between 80 and 100 per cent of the workforce. Labour formed a vital part of the Democratic Party coalition. It had firmly entrenched itself into law, industry and economic and political life.

When the war ended in August 1945 America had emerged not just victorious but commanding a position of world dominance, perhaps without precedent in history. In 1933 capitalism had seemed at the point of collapse: Bolshevism or Fascism had seemed like the wave of the future. By 1945 Fascism was vanquished and Bolshevism, though menacing in Eastern Europe, had paid a terrible price for its victory over Nazi Germany. America by contrast, alone among the belligerents, had suffered no domestic damage during the war, experienced a wartime boom, enjoyed a monopoly of the atomic bomb, and now dominated the world's economic, financial and political arrangements. She would use this plenitude of power to shape global affairs for a generation. She had won this unique position largely because of her industrial might. This in turn rested on the productive capacity of her industrial working class. In the aftermath of war, Henry Luce, proprietor of *Time* magazine, spoke of 'the American Century'; Henry Wallace, running as Progressive candidate for President in 1948 and bidding for labour support, saw 'the Century of the Common Man'. In a sense, as the historian Steve Fraser has argued, American labour was caught between these two centuries. Yet what is sometimes called the Keynesian revolution had occurred and labour had been transformed by it. Sometimes in collaboration, sometimes in conflict, government, labour and management hammered out a new foundation for American economic life, which was to shape events for the next thirty years.

The main feature of this relationship was consensus. Each party recognized the right of the other to exist and exercise its authority in its own sphere of influence. The adversarial relationship which had characterized the violent conflicts of the 1930s, and to a lesser extent the war years too, was replaced by management's acceptance of the workers' right to organize unions and of management's right to manage. Increasingly unions were expected to discipline the workforce, while government provided economic conditions which would stimulate greater productivity, profits and pay. In the Red Scare hysteria of the postwar years the unions purged all Communists. Moreover, labour leaders were the most enthusiastic supporters of America's Cold War foreign policy of containment and confrontation with Soviet Russia and Communist China. On this basis American labour enjoyed unparalleled power and influence in the 1950s.

The breakup of this Keynesian consensus was equally important. In answer to a question about the long-run implications of his ideas, Keynes once replied, 'In the long run we are all dead'. It was a revealing response. It meant that Keynes only hoped to plan for a generation, no more. For thirty years Keynesian thinking provided the basis for greater prosperity, more equitably distributed, than at any time in American history. But in the 1960s and 1970s the system began to break down. America no longer dominated the world economy but faced increasingly severe competition from Germany and Japan, the nations it had helped defeat in 1945. The inflationary effects of the Vietnam War, the rising costs of oil and other raw materials, de-industrialization and many other social changes, such as discontent and unrest among black Americans and women, all began to undermine the system developed after 1945. When Ronald Reagan took office in January 1981 he promised the people to 'get the government off your backs and out of your pockets'. It marked the end of that New Deal, social reforming, consensus approach to government, which flourished between the 1930s and the 1960s, in which organized labour had prospered.

Although the United States was still, by most yardsticks, the world's leading industrial nation in the 1980s the American working class has rarely received the attention it merits, except from labour historians. Few movies, novels or plays concern themselves with the working class, though the 1950s musical *The Pajama Game* was about the shop-floor politics of the garment industry, while later films included *Blue Collar*. Historians focus on ethnicity and race, religion and culture, rather than on social class, and praise British historians like E. P. Thompson for his analysis of the making of the English working class between 1770 and 1840. In the mass affluence of American society since the 1930s it was almost as if there was a conspiracy to the effect that the working class, like poverty, did not exist in the United States. Yet it was the working class who had done more than anyone to create that affluence, and who were most likely to suffer from poverty when the market place failed them.

Everything manufactured and consumed in America was made, and partly consumed, by them; indeed the growing importance to modern capitalism of working people as *consumers* is a linking theme of this study. Moreover, the importance of working-class voters in helping create the economic and political reality of modern America is central. In recent years, the fashion among labour historians has been to write less about institutions and labour leaders, more about the daily routines and realities of working-class life. This new labour history has focused less on unions and strikes, more on workplace environment, family life and leisure, women, mothers and children. Some fine work has unearthed important facts and insights which have greatly enhanced understanding of the working-class experience. Yet this book is unashamedly written in the style of the old labour history. It concentrates on unions, strikes, politics, the law and the macroeconomic background. While seeking to cover the main events of American labour history for readers new to the subject, it aims at integrating this story into the wider context of the nation's political and economic life since the Great Depression, in the belief that labour history must be judged by its impact on the larger community.

1. Labour and the Great Depression

I

The major themes of this book were far from being the dominant themes of labour history as late as 1933. American trades unionism, never very strong hitherto, appeared near death in the depths of the Depression. The history of labour unions had begun in the 1830s or earlier, when wage earners' attempts to found unions to protect their members had met only limited success, and involved, for the most part, limited groups of largely skilled workers, artisans and craftsmen concerned to defend craft interests. Some organizations, like the National Labor Union in the 1860s, the Knights of Labor in the 1870s, or the Industrial Workers of the World in the first two decades of the 20th century, had sought to combine the immediate purposes of trades unionism with the ultimate ambition of transforming American society. In the end, the American Federation of Labor, founded by skilled craftsmen in 1886, emerged as the only permanent, national focus for the political struggle of the American worker, largely because the AFL scorned wider goals and concentrated exclusively on wages, hours and conditions. Samuel Gompers, its leader until his death in 1924, was a Dutch-born Jewish cigar wrapper, whose careful conservatism, vigorous anti-socialism and overriding concern to protect craft interests left an indelible mark on the AFL.

Historians often explain this 'business unionism', and American labour history, in terms of the doctrine of American exceptionalism. Ethnic diversity, race, the large agricultural sector, the Western frontier, better opportunities, great equality, a higher standard of living – all of this and more inhibited the growth of class consciousness and the rise of labour unions. Yet the working class which

American unions sought to lead was much the same as in other lands. It consisted mainly of wage-earning, manual workers, skilled, semi-skilled and unskilled, usually hourly-paid and lacking much job security. It worked in basic industries, such as mining, iron and steel, or the huge lumber trade, and in manufacturing, transport, construction. Part of the working class was white-collared, part uniformed, like railwaymen. This non-agricultural labour force, as historians usually call it, numbered some 30 million as the Great Depression deepened in 1930, larger than the still vast agricultural sector and about half the total workforce.

II

The greatest number worked on the railways, in basic extractive or manufacturing trades, and in construction. Yet with the transition of the American economy from a capital goods to a consumer goods phase in the 1920s, increasing numbers were found in motor manufacturing, the electrical industry, radio, rubber, chemicals, textiles and clothing. The major industrial States of New England, New York and the Great Lakes area from Pennsylvania to Wisconsin, where the nation's industrial and business heartland had been planted in the 19th century, still contained the great bulk of the proletariat. Yet by 1920 a majority of Americans were living in urban surroundings, and every town and city had its working class. Rail and transport workers, of course, worked all over America, mining often occurred in remote areas, but the South was still mostly without major industry or unions while in other sections big industrial centres stood out like islands in a rural sea. The continental size of the United States, its Federal structure and its agricultural background, had long kept the working class from uniting as readily as in Britain or Germany. But other things complicated the picture. Though immigration had been severely restricted in the 1920s, the American working class was still ethnically very diverse. Successive waves of immigrants since the 1820s had established an elaborate ethnic hierarchy, where workers' places on the ladder were largely determined by the date when their ethnic group had first arrived in strength.

Thus the British stood at the top, followed by Dutch, German and Scandinavian descendants. The Irish arrived in millions during and after the potato famine of the 1840s. Disadvantaged by desperate poverty, their Roman Catholic religion and the crude prejudices these aroused in the native population, their sheer numbers, command of English and political experience in the cause of Irish nationalism nevertheless gave them strength. Moreover they arrived in America as industrialisation and urbanisation were really taking off and so became a powerful new element in the working class. By the 1870s they were prominent in early unions and running the politics of such cities as Boston, New York and Philadelphia. So by 1900, while white Anglo-Saxon Protestants exercised effective economic power and Germans provided a solid middle class, Irish urban and union influence helped the Irish organize later large immigrant populations from Eastern and Southern Europe, who came to maturity in the workforce as the Depression struck in the 1930s.

Black workers were almost totally excluded from this picture of unionisation, though they formed an increasingly important part of the American working class by 1930. Freedom from slavery after the Civil War had been followed by steady relegation to second-class citizenship and the most vicious racist exclusion. Nine-tenths of the black population of the United States still lived in the South in 1900, four-fifths of them in rural areas. The great shift in the black working population came after 1914. European war had cut off supplies of immigrants while boosting the demands of American industry to supply Allied war orders. This vacuum sucked in black workers, and between 1915 and 1918 about 500 000 moved from rural South to urban North in such cities as Chicago, Cleveland, Detroit and New York. This was the start of a steady movement of blacks, so that by 1930 more than two million had left the South and by 1940 nearly a quarter lived in the North and West.

Blacks who moved North improved their lot. Denied the vote in the South, they could now participate in politics, while on the economic front wages, job choice and acceptance were better. But they still fell victims to white racism, which fuelled several bloody race riots in Chicago, St Louis, and elsewhere. They were crowded into evil city ghettoes and trampled on by recent immigrants, such as Italians, Slavs, and Poles, in the struggle for jobs, housing, schools and welfare. In this conflict they received virtually no support from labour unions, who generally expressed the prejudices of their white members, prevented them from joining and used their power to keep them out of traditionally white trades. A few black unions, such as the Brotherhood of Sleeping Car Porters, provided union leverage. Yet by the 1920s segregated, excluded and exploited, black workers made little headway during those prosperous years, and were hardest hit of all by the economic collapse after 1929. 'The reason the Depression did not have the impact on the Negro that it had on the whites', explained a black intellectual, 'was that the Negroes had been in the Depression all the time'.[1]

Like blacks, women also played an important part in the workforce, but were generally excluded from unions and faced barriers or prejudice. Young women, prominent in certain industries such as textiles, clothing manufacture and the service sector, on marriage commonly dropped out of the labour market to devote themselves to child-rearing and home-making. With cooking, washing, cleaning, ~~blacking~~, scrubbing, and responsibility both for children and household finance, their lives were hard and with few consolations. During the labour shortage of the First World War they had, like blacks, taken on an invaluable role in war industries, but were rapidly replaced when men returned from the fighting forces on peacetime economic conversion, a pattern of gains snatched away to be repeated in the 1940s. In any case women were (again like blacks) nearly always poorly organized and lacking influential leaders. They had finally won the vote in 1918, and the more fortunate benefited from wider educational opportunities, greater social emancipation and the spread of electricity and consumer durables to lighten household drudgery. Yet these same gadgets were reducing jobs in domestic service for the less advantaged.

Such ethnic, racial, gender and social division clearly weakened the American labour movement. The demands of the war economy between 1914 and 1918 created acute labour shortage which brought the AFL more influence and members. But this proved short-lived. Crushing defeats for steel and other groups of workers struggling to start unions in 1919 were a prelude to a vigorous employers' offensive. Trades like carpenters, plumbers, building workers, engineers and teamsters still dominated the AFL, yet the coal miners were strong enough for their secretary-treasurer, William Green, to become AFL president when Gompers died in 1924. Green, capable and decent, was also conservative and unimaginative. So the prosperous 1920s, when employers launched aggressive campaigns to spread the open shop and welfare capitalism, proved a disastrous decade for unions. Total membership, which had peaked at about five million, or some 20 per cent of the non-agricultural labour force in 1920, had fallen below three million, or about 11 per cent of an expanded working population, in the early 1930s.[2]

Political activity was equally divided and ineffective. The white, skilled craftsmen of British, German and Irish descent who led the AFL looked to unions to defend their trades rather than advance the wider interests of labour as a whole. They had fought off the efforts of Socialists and the syndicalist Industrial Workers of the World to influence the labour movement during the Progressive period before 1914. Then the war divided the left and the IWW and stimulated the Red Scare. The Bolshevik Revolution in 1917 led to further factionalism and created the American Communist Party which outflanked the IWW and the Socialists on the left. Finally, the apparent success of capitalism in the 1920s made the socialist alternative seem increasingly irrelevant and contributed to its irreversible decline.

Hostile to Socialists and Communists, with their talk of revolution and millenial promises, labour leaders accepted the capitalist system and sought only to sell their labour at the highest price. Fearful that government intervention would reduce rather than advance their freedom, they followed a policy in politics of 'rewarding friends and punishing enemies', voting Democratic, Republican or Progressive as seemed best according to time, place and candidate. But beneath the surface a quiet but decisive shift in the voting habits of the American working class was taking place. Easy Republican victories at the polls after 1916 masked the fact that the Democrats were actually winning a steadily increasing share of the urban vote. In 1928 the Democratic candidate for President, Al Smith, won a small but significant majority in America's dozen major cities. What this meant is now clear. After 1929 the sons and daughters of the last great wave of newcomers to reach American shores, before unrestricted immigration ended in 1921, were seeking their first job and casting their first vote as the Republican politics of prosperity were crumbling to dust.

So all the ingredients for a massive realignment of the American working class – ethnic, racial, sexual, regional, occupational – were in place as the Great Depression struck. No aspect of the nation's life – economic, political, social, cultural, diplomatic – was untouched by the changes stimulated by the events of that era. For no group was this more true than labour unions and the industrial working class. Though historians may call the 1930s the decade of the New Deal, for those who lived through it the 1930s was the decade of the Great Depression; and again, for no group was this more true than the working class. Despite this, for organized labour this was also a decade of astonishing progress. Labour unions began the 1930s in weakness and defeat and ended them in strength and victory.

In the dark days of 1933 there was little sign that this was to be the pattern of the future. Indeed, organized labour appeared to be on the brink not of expansion but extinction. The AFL had established itself before and during the First World War and, for the most part, its leaders accepted capitalism as slavishly as employers. Yet in the 1920s, its years of greatest prosperity, AFL membership fell, as we have seen, steadily to 3.4 million in 1929 – less than it had been in any year since 1917. The AFL still believed deeply in the benefits of free enterprise, fierce competition and rugged individualism. Yet, seduced by the prosperity of the 1920s, the AFL had slumped in union membership, while the open shop, company unions and welfare capitalism had flourished as never before. President Herbert Hoover rashly promised the abolition of poverty in our time, which would seemingly be accompanied by the end of trades unions.

Then came catastrophe in 1929 with the sudden collapse of the stock market followed by four years of terrifying economic decline. The story is familiar, but the facts bear summary to emphasise the gravity of the crisis. Manufacturing output fell by half in four years, farm prices by 40 per cent, exports by a third in value. The deficit on corporate enterprise was some 5.7 billion dollars, national income had collapsed from nearly 83 billion dollars in 1929 to just over 40 billion dollars in 1933. Even more devastating, unemployment rose inexorably and in seemingly geometrical progression, from two million in 1930 to four million in 1931 to eight million in 1932 to fifteen million in 1933.

This was more than one quarter of the workforce. Such a sudden, steep fall in demand could only drive the economy down in a tighter, deeper vortex. Lacking any system of Federal unemployment insurance, the chronic jobless had nothing to fall back on but State, local or private charity, or their own meagre savings. President Hoover obstinately opposed any idea of Federal relief for the unemployed. So during their long and increasingly hopeless search for work, the jobless found themselves driven from home and family, queuing in breadlines or at soup kitchens, living in the desperate tar-paper shanty towns, ironically known as 'Hoovervilles', which sprang up on the outskirts of countless cities. Unable to keep up their dues, workers fell out of union membership, which after the disturbing decline of the 1920s fell still further to less than three million. Industry had virtually ceased, agriculture was devastated, banking, business and finance were at the point of collapse by 1933.

III

So the country's wage earners stood by helplessly in face of the Depression. At a series of industrial conferences in Washington in the early 1930s, employers may have piously promised to uphold wages and maintain employment. But there were no collective bargaining agreements in the mass-production industries – steel, automobiles, electrical equipment – to compel observance. Pay packets grew gradually smaller and then were all too often replaced by blunt notices of dismissal. The whole programme of welfare capitalism, so popular in the 1920s, was abruptly abandoned as employers were forced to withdraw benefits which in prosperity had often been granted in place of wage increases. Profit-sharing schemes, employee stock ownership, industrial pensions, and even workers' health and recreational projects were rapidly discarded. Welfare capitalism had been essentially fraudulent. Circumstances forced retrenchment, but in some cases it was carried out at the expense of the workers while full dividends were still being paid on common stock. Company unions were powerless to protect their members' interests. Reliance upon the promise of capitalism had proved to be a delusion. As David Brody has put it, what had made the promise credible was the performance of American capitalism in the 1920s.[3] In other words, welfare collapsed when most needed.

Still, as American labour leaders came out of their storm shelters to survey the catastrophic consequences of the economic tornado which had stripped the land, they seemed bereft of ideas. Most of them – William Green, president of the AFL, 'Big Bill' Hutcheson, king of the carpenters, Dan Tobin, tsar of the teamsters – were still prisoners of the conventional wisdom which had served labour so badly in the 1920s. For example, not until the end of 1932 did the

AFL, fearful of government intervention, finally drop its opposition to unemployment insurance. When the Senate Finance Committee met in February 1933 labour leaders for the most part agreed with the glum advice employers and financiers gave about the overriding need to balance the Federal Budget – precisely the opposite of what was needed.[4] Taken with the Pecora investigation, which had revealed the duplicity of banking, business and financial leaders, the hearings were not very encouraging. Clearly the wizards of American capitalism were essentially ignorant tricksters, as wizards usually are. Yet with the whole economy on the verge of breakdown the danger was quite clear. Talk of the 'coming revolution' was widespread, at least among intellectuals. In fact, mass unemployment broke the spirit of the working class and resulted in a mood of sullen apathy in which fewer than 200 000 workers were involved in all strikes in 1933.

Labour leaders were equally passive. Their economic conservatism was matched by conservatism in politics – and it was in politics that the crucial decisions had to be taken. The AFL under William Green's leadership was still pursuing its traditional policy of rewarding friends and punishing enemies – endorsing individual candidates of either party but not endorsing anyone for President – pretty much unchanged since the days of founding AFL president Sam Gompers in the 1890s. His successor Green had made a half-hearted attempt to endorese Robert La Follette, Progressive candidate for President in 1924. But other labour leaders, like Hutcheson or the miners' president John L. Lewis, mostly voted Republican in the 1920s. Though the Republicans were now more closely identified with the interests of big business than any party in history, even the shock of the Depression, which totally discredited business dominance, brought no change. The AFL did not endorse Franklin D. Roosevelt, the Democratic candidate for President in 1932, and Lewis voted for Hoover.

This failure to back FDR, soon to become a hero of the common man, seems more surprising with hindsight than it did at the time. The Democrats had never been closely identified with labour. There was no sign that they were to become the champions of labour's rights, as happened in the 1930s. Indeed, with the party riven by internal faction fighting in the 1920s, and slumping disastrously at the polls in 1924, it had seemed that Southern racists and Northern crooks were struggling for control of a party that was terminally ill.

True, Al Smith's campaign for President in 1928 had revealed that with the right candidate the Democrats might become the party of emerging ethnic groups and the urban working class. What no one saw was how dramatically the Depression had changed things and how triumphantly Roosevelt, so different from Smith, was to emerge not just as the right candidate, but as both friend of labour and saviour of capitalism through the economic policies of J. M. Keynes.

FDR himself had given little indication of this during the campaign. He had accused Hoover of overspending, unbalancing the Budget, piling agency on agency, bureau on bureau. The Democrats promised the American people a 'New Deal' but at this stage nobody, least of all FDR himself, had any clear idea what this meant. Of course, his 'forgotten man' campaign speech had seemed sufficiently demagogic to mark the parting of the ways with old-style Democrats like Smith, willing to patronise labour but not support it. Meeting labour leaders, Roosevelt himself revealed none of the easy rapport he had with farmers. This weakness was not really repaired by anyone in his entourage. After his landslide win in 1932 the President's administration contained people like Frances Parkins and Harry Hopkins, whose experience as social workers among the poor made them sympathetic to labour's aspirations, but ambivalent at best to labour leaders like Hutcheson and Lewis whom they rightly saw primarily as power brokers.

Other Roosevelt advisers, like Donald Richberg and Leo Wolman, may have had great experience as labour lawyers, but events in the 1930s were to expose their paternalism. In fact, none of the President's advisers had grown up in the labour movement. So just as his economic policy emerged not from fixed principles but from inspired improvisations, so his policy towards labour was born of trial and error. The first step had been taken before Roosevelt was elected, with the Norris–La Guardia Act in March 1932. This gave full freedom of association, without interference by employers, outlawed 'yellow-dog' contracts, which forced workers to join unions, and prohibited Federal courts from issuing injunctions in labour disputes, as they had done regularly in the 1920s and earlier, except under carefully defined conditions. Sponsored by George Norris, champion of the old Progressives, and Fiorello La Guardia, hero of the new, it revealed how the 1930s were to become a watershed, and was overwhelmingly supported by both Congress and nation. But for all its importance in pointing the way to the labour policies of the New Deal, it did not meet the immediate problem of the nation's wage earners: chronic, growing, grinding unemployment.

IV

Once Roosevelt had won his landslide at the polls in November 1932, New Deal policy towards labour was based upon two premises: the need to create jobs, and the right for workers to organize as written into the Norris–La Guardia Act. A long step towards implementing this right was taken quickly with the celebrated Section 7(a) of the National Industrial Recovery Act. The NIRA, the Roosevelt administration's first experiment in overall economic control, was born of highly complex manoeuvring. In March 1933 Hugo Black and William P. Connery Jr introduced a bill in Congress to establish the thirty-hour week which the AFL had been demanding to spread work and relieve unemployment. Roosevelt was very sceptical of its value unless it included provision for maintaining wages for the hourly paid – always a problem when reformers reduced hours. So his Secretary of Labor Frances Perkins, the first woman to serve in Cabinet, suggested amendments to combine minimum wages with the reduction in hours.

This unprecedented idea of minimum wages naturally provoked a storm of opposition from business. Yet it was not supported too enthusiastically by labour, who feared minimum wages might easily become maximum ones. So both camps urged the administration to raise its sights and institute a far broader recovery programme. As scores of such plans began to appear, several independent groups of Presidential advisers began to try to work out specific measures. Little real progress was being made, however, and Roosevelt decided to intervene. Withdrawing administration support from the Black–Connery thirty-hour bill, in which his interest had been lukewarm or hostile, he called upon his advisers to work together until they could agree.

The result, incorporated into the National Industrial Recovery Act in June 1933, was to allow industry to write its own codes of fair competition, but at the same time to provide special safeguards for labour. Section 7(a) of the NIRA, drawing in part from provisions of the Railway Labor Act of 1926, stipulated that the new industrial codes should contain three important safeguards. First, employees should have the right to organize and bargain collectively through representatives of their own choosing, free from interference, restraint, or coercion on the part of employers. Second, no one seeking employment should be required either to join a company union or to refrain from joining any labour organization of his own choosing. Third, employers should comply with maximum hours, minimum pay and other conditions of employment approved by the President.

Thus ideas favourable to both management and labour, plus certain modified provisions of the Black–Connery bill, were brought together by the NIRA in a single all-embracing measure. To this overall plan was further added, under a separate title, a vast Public Works programme authorising appropriations of 3.3 billion dollars. Such Public Works were crucial, for the basic purpose of the NIRA was, in the President's words, 'to put people back to work'. Its agency, the National Recovery Administration, was both to insure reasonable profits for industry by preventing unfair competition and disastrous overproduction, and living wages for labour by spreading work through shorter hours. The NRA was also to be the basis for labour policy, a bold answer to the challenge of desperate times, 'the most important and far-reaching legislation ever enacted by the American Congress' in Roosevelt's words. Historians now believe that by trying to put a floor on wages and a ceiling on hours and profits, the NRA was trying to do the impossible in the wrong way. Its codes never worked and its Public Works provisions were enacted with painful slowness.

At the time, however, some critics of the NRA argued it aped Fascist ideas of the corporate state, and to many Fascism or Communism appeared to be the wave of the future. Others outside the labour movement were struggling for a solution to unemployment within the existing framework. One of these, the British economist J. M. Keynes, was to become the father of managed capitalism. He believed the crisis had been caused by under-consumption, not over-production; that ending under-consumption would end unemployment; but that for the cure to take permanently, due weight had to be given to the role of reflation, sustained public spending and above all raised aggregate demand to revive and control the economy.

In the real world, the function of strong labour unions, bidding up wages, was to prove crucial in sustaining demand. But for the moment, the theoretical basis for Keynes's idea had just been advanced by his student Richard Kahn in 1931.[5] Kahn's discovery of the 'multiplier', which confirmed what Keynes had guessed, was later spread as the key to prosperity by a generation of students, for whom the multiplier fulfilled 'one of life's dreams: getting something for nothing, or at least a great deal for very little'.[6] Tracing the primary increment of government expenditure through its successive stages, Kahn found that at each stage a portion of the income thus created was lost through various 'leakages': savings, expenditure on imports, relief payments and so on. The ratio of secondary to primary employment, stemming from public works, was determined by calculating the portion of income which was actually spent at the end of each successive stage on home consumption. Or as Keynes put it, 'The newly employed who supply the increased purchases of those employed on capital works will, in their turn, spend more, thus adding to the employment of others; and so on.'[7] In short, the logical theory of the multiplier simply stated the formal relationship between increments in net home investment and secondary, or induced, home consumption.

At this stage heretics proclaiming the prophet Keynes – William T. Foster, the economist, J. David Stern, the Philadelphia newspaper publisher, Gerard Swope, head of General Electric – were still voices crying in the wilderness. An unknown banker from Utah named Marriner Eccles, later a key figure in the Keynesian revolution, had jolted Senate Finance Committee hearings by his rigorous argument. If the Federal Budget was unbalanced for a while it would not matter; underconsumption, not overproduction, was the problem; wealth and income were not distributed widely enough; and too much had gone into capital goods. To restore prosperity, Eccles concluded, the Federal government must launch a vast public works programme, increase taxes and raise the income of the poor.[8]

The language might suggest Keynes; but Eccles, later to become head of the central bank or Federal Reserve Board, insisted he had never heard of the British economist when first advancing such ideas. More important, from the point of view of Keynesian notions winning acceptance, Eccles and the others at this stage lacked weight. Yet clearly there was a ferment of ideas at work. More authoritative advocates of high wage capitalism in the 1920s, such as Bernard Baruch and Henry Ford (and indeed Herbert Hoover himself), still existed. But in the depths of the Great Depression they did not see how high wages, or indeed any wages, could be paid. Labour leaders, naturally committed to higher pay, might have used Keynesianism to justify this aim. Yet they were equally baffled. Underconsumptionists like Foster, who argued that 'riotous saving' had caused the collapse, emphasised that 'the only sound way to stop the depression' was 'to increase total pay rolls'.[9]

Stronger labour unions would be best able to achieve this, and Foster's emphasis on 'sound' solutions was a warning against budgetary inflation. Against this view, Keynes saw the first step would have to be taken by the Federal Government. 'Can America spend its way to recovery?' he asked in an article written with Harold Laski. 'Why obviously!' was the reply. An economy produces in response to spending – it was absurd to suppose one can stimulate economic activity by declining to spend. When individuals failed to spend enough to maintain employment, then government must do it for them. 'It might be better if they did it for themselves', the article concluded, 'but that is no argument for not having it done at all.'[10] New Deal reflationists, like Frances Perkins or Rexford Tugwell, the leading left-winger in FDR's circle, agreed with Keynes and Laski on the overriding need for more public spending. Yet despite the NRA, Roosevelt himself was wholly innocent of such notions. Keynes, unsuccessful in his early efforts to influence the President, complained he had believed him more literate, economically speaking. For as far as FDR was concerned at this early stage of the New Deal, Micawber still applied: more spending than income, result misery. The Pittsburgh campaign speech in 1932 had committed him to cutting the cost of Federal government by a quarter. Yet by the end of the first Hundred Days, the most astonishing burst of legislation in American history, he had lost that decisive battle. Those advisers urging reflation had defeated those like Budget Director Lewis Douglas urging orthodox deflation.

Characteristically, FDR's choice came not out of any real conviction but from his chaos of improvisation. Reflation was the ultimate consequence of a whole series of decisions taken for other reasons during the hectic passage of 16 major laws in three months, of which the NRA had merely been one. The Thomas amendment to the Agricultural Adjustment Act, which conferred on the President powers of monetary expansion by issuing greenbacks, remonetizing silver and reducing the gold content of the dollar, created the opening. The proliferation of 'alphabet soup' Federal agencies like the AAA and NRA, 'pump-priming', recovery, relief and Public Works all accelerated the process, made easier by leaving the Gold Standard. 'Well, this is the end of Western civilisation', Lewis Douglas remarked of the last step.[11] In truth, it was the start of a generation in which controlled inflation became an acceptable answer to unemployment.

V

Conversion to the idea that high wages were good for everyone, workers and employers alike, was a crucial development in modern labour history. Of course the importance of wages from this point of view was no new idea. Labour had long maintained that only when workers were paid enough to buy the goods they made could the economic system function successfully. Assertion of this principle went back at least as far as the statement of the Mechanics' Union of Trade Associations on wages in 1827. But the argument had made slow headway, and in the 1930s was only gradually beginning to gain the acceptance which today is almost commonplace. Yet at what point did this acceptance occur? Frances Perkins told the President in March 1933 that 'We are beginning to appreciate today the close connection between the commerce of the nation and the number of persons employed . . . *The working classes are the great reservoir of purchasing power*'.[12] She urged 'complete unionization' to release this purchasing power.

A memorandum prepared by Leo Wolman, chairman of the NRA Labor Advisory Board, emphasised that the NRA should establish 'wages on high levels to develop and maintain wage-earner purchasing power comparable to our great mass production'.[13] Others like Gerard Swope, the enlightened head of the great General Electrical combine, argued that 'Redistribution of wealth and purchasing power' would right the economy, but only temporarily. Permanent prosperity would depend upon 'the volume of consumer demand or purchasing power'.[14] The Brookings Institution had come to much the same conclusion, while labour lobbyists urged that 'recovery depends upon the securing of mass purchasing power', adding, 'The sure and direct way of accomplishing this is the complete unionization of labour'.[15]

Once again, only labour leaders themselves could achieve this. Yet in the depths of the Depression they were in poor shape to do so. Only two important labour leaders – John L. Lewis of the coal-miners and Sidney Hillman of the clothing workers – challenged orthodox views. Lewis, a Republican in the 1920s, was a physically massive, psychologically puzzling leader: a powerful orator who had bulldozed the United Mineworkers together and then seen the UMW fall apart again in the 1920s. A conservative labour leader, and a largely discredited one too, Lewis was to become the dynamic inspiration of labour's great leap forward in the 1930s. What distinguished him from colleagues like Green and Hutcheson was his contempt for their limited ambitions, and the more important fact that he led an industrial and not a craft union. Though he had voted for Hoover in 1932, and so had no friends at FDR's court, Lewis believed the time had come to cast aside old concepts like 'laissez-faire', 'competition' and 'rugged individualism'. Balanced Budgets would not end poverty, and the planning he had long advocated for his own ailing industry should be extended to industry as a whole.[16]

Sidney Hillman, a man of quite different background and type, faced similar problems in the cut-throat garment trade and had reached similar conclusions. A Russian Jew jailed for his small part in the Revolution of 1905, he had fled to Chicago, quickly became a labour activist and established the Amalgamated Clothing Workers. He helped ACW members benefit from the wartime boom and defended their gains in the 1920s. Though primarily an intellectual, Hillman knew how to take care of himself and kept eclectic company: afternoons with Lepke Buchalter, of Murder Incorporated; evenings with Felix Frankfurter, of Harvard Law School.[17] At once practical and highly idealistic he was seen by some as the new embodiment of the new 'social engineering' concept of union leadership which was to dominate the future. Indeed, he came to occupy a unique position in the American labour movement within a decade. In 1933, his view of the present was clear. 'Cut-throat competition makes the unscrupulous employer the leader in each industry', Hillman observed, 'and the rest willingly or otherwise follow'.[18] The businessman who cut wages had the further satisfaction of knowing he was following the injunction of orthodox economics that the effort to maintain low wage rates increased employment.

'Really to control unemployment,' Hillman concluded, 'we must think and act in terms of economic planning;' and 'voluntary . . . planning is not enough.'[19] The NRA was trying to put a ceiling on hours and a floor on wages without really raising demand. Its Public Works provisions were being enacted sluggishly by the careful Interior Secretary, Harold Ickes. In agriculture the AAA, in historian Richard Hofstadter's mordant phrase, solved the paradox of hunger in the midst of plenty only by doing away with the plenty. Though Lewis was melodramatic and Hillman low-keyed, they had much in common. They were arguably the most influential labour leaders of the 20th century, crucial figures in shaping the modern movement. Both came from industries ruined by vicious competition. Both led industrial unions – the UMW and the ACW – often outside or at odds with the AFL. Both were masters of the mundane side of union bargaining yet retained a keen sense of labour's wider mission.

Each interpreted this in sharply different ways however. Lewis was fundamentally a great accumulator of union power which he used to secure Samuel Gompers's conventional aim: more. Hillman's ends were influenced by Socialist ideas and by the fact that, though a national figure for twenty years, he was younger than Lewis and, as an immigrant himself, appealed to a younger generation of new Americans. He told Lewis as they were setting up the CIO that:

> While in an immediate sense . . . industrial organization . . . concerns the workers in industry, in the last analysis it is an issue of national significance. Labor unorganized, or poorly and ineffectively organized . . . is a menace to the major national requirement of our time, that is, the need for the widespread of purchasing power among the large masses of people, so that they may purchase and consume the output of national industry.[20]

Such views meant that while in the short term Lewis was the more important of the two men, rising remarkably from utter defeat to galvanise the whole American labour movement into radical change, in the longer term Hillman was to exercise even greater influence. No one before or since has occupied quite the same position. He became, as the title of his papers at Cornell proclaims, 'Statesman of the new industrial order'.[21] Yet in 1933 he could be dismissed as an idealist unable to keep members in the ACW, and Lewis as the discredited leader of a bankrupt UMW.

VI

Encouraged by the new and more favourable legal and political climate of the New Deal, rank-and-file insurgents breathed life into moribund union locals in the clothing and coal industries. Norris–La Guardia had already outlawed the 'yellow-dog' contract and restricted injunctions against strikes. The NRA Codes had been planned more to regulate industry as a whole than give labour new powers. Yet Section 7(a) did reinforce the right to organise. This, plus the upturn in the economy which followed the Hundred Days, gave rise to an eruption of purely rank-and-file radicalism. The greatest gains were in the so-called industrial unions, especially those which had suffered most severely during the Depression.

Thus Lewis's United Mineworkers regained 300 000 members and signed agreements in the Alabama and Kentucky coalfields, Hillman's Amalgamated Clothing Workers recouped all earlier losses with 50 000 recruits, while David Dubinsky's International Ladies' Garment Workers doubled this figure. In addition to such activity in mining, the garment trades and textiles, other labour organisers enrolled members in hastily chartered AFL Federal Locals in the motor, electrical and rubber industries, created an independent grass-roots movement in the totally unorganized steel industry, captured company unions or joined unemployed protests for protection and relief. Finally, general strikes in Minneapolis, Toledo and San Francisco were a dramatic portent which showed that radicalism could break the mood of apathy and demoralisation typified by labour during the early New Deal.

Such militance went far beyond Administration policies. As we have seen, FDR was no instinctive friend of labour, while the great experience of advisers like Don Richberg and Leo Wolman as labour lawyers in the lean years of the 1920s was soon to become so irrelevant as to render them poor judges of union needs in the 1930s. So FDR warned Hugh Johnson, head of the NRA, of 'various misunderstandings and misinterpretations and the danger of further controversy and confusion' in the NRA Codes.

While there is nothing in the provision of Section 7(a) to interfere with the *bona fide* exercise of the right of the employer to select, retain and advance employees on the basis of individual merit, Section 7(a) does clearly prohibit the pretended exercise of this right by an employer as a device for compelling employees to refrain from exercising the rights of self-organization, or the designation of representatives and collective bargaining which are guaranteed to all employees in said Section 7(a).[22]

Like other Federal agencies during the first New Deal, the NRA was poorly planned and wretchedly administered. Labour was not alone in feeling badly let down by the way the NRA had worked out in practice, for the agency had virtually collapsed before it was declared unconstitutional by the Supreme Court in May 1935 – a generally unlamented victim of early New Deal enthusiasm. Yet for all its overall failure, the NRA's implications for labour had been decisive. Its guarantees of collective bargaining and Congressional control of wages and hours were, despite loopholes in enforcement which appeared in 1934, the most effective steps ever taken by the Federal government on the side of the working class in the field of industrial relations.

More decisive for the future, when the Supreme Court torpedoed the NRA, New Deal legislators picked up the broken pieces of Section 7(a) and reassembled them, far more carefully, in the Wagner Act of 1935 and later in the Fair Labor Standards Act of 1938. These two measures really transformed labour relations, revealing there would be no retreat under Roosevelt from safeguarding the interests of industrial wage workers. In the first half of the 1930s labour had largely been the passive receiver of economic calamity and reform. After 1935 all that was to change as labour erupted dramatically to become the instrument of change itself.

The Wagner Act, Social Security and Fair Labor Standards had not been envisaged when FDR entered office. They were to evolve gradually out of the needs of the times. A basic understanding and sympathy for the rights of labour was nevertheless inherent in the emerging philosophy of the New Deal by 1935. For the first time in American history, a national administration was to make the welfare of industrial workers a direct concern of government and act on the principle that only organized labour could deal on equal terms with organized capital. Hitherto, labour unions had been tolerated. Now they were to be encouraged, at a time when they were showing every sign of erupting like a force of nature.

The New Deal thus provided a momentous watershed in the history of the labour movement. Age-old traditions were smashed; new and dynamic forces were released. Never before had as much economic and political power seemed within the reach of organized labour. The struggles, hardships, and defeats of a century appeared to have culminated in the possibility of complete attainment of workers' historic objectives. Even more significant, acceptance of a reflationary solution to unemployment, and of the role of labour in raising aggregate demand, meant that the new economic ideas of Keynes were to act as catalyst in the process of change.

2.   New Deal Renaissance

I

The 1935 National Labor Relations Act, popularly named after Senator Robert F. Wagner who piloted it through Congress, is a major landmark in American labour history. Indeed, the Wagner Act is that point at which the modern history of American unions begins. Its sponsor was a lifelong urban liberal and reforming friend of labour. He had started in politics in 1910, when first elected to the New York State legislature at Albany on the Democratic ticket, along with young Franklin Roosevelt and Al Smith. The climate of the 1930s cried out for this kind of reform. Yet Wagner was only able to carry his bill through Congress because the New Deal had won overwhelming endorsement in the 1934 mid-term elections. These polls gave the Democrats a staggering majority of 45 in the Senate and 219 in the House.

More interestingly, in light of the emerging policies of reflation and rising demand, Wagner presented his bill in a wholly Keynesian context. The Supreme Court, he argued, apparently believed the fiction that labour and management were equals. Yet economic concentration had destroyed any balance in bargaining between employer and employee, and rendered the individual worker helpless in face of the vast corporations which controlled the economy. Moreover, anti-trust legislation, which had done nothing to prevent monopoly, was used by the courts with gusto against labour's feeble efforts to organize.

Finally, that same industrial concentration, which had destroyed the worker's bargaining power, left him with an inadequate share of the nation's wealth. Yet economic recovery and stability could only be achieved through wider distribution of that wealth. In the 1920s, when labour had been weak, the gains of productivity had gone into plant, profits and speculation rather than into boosting demand,

and the Depression had resulted. The time had come to change all that; but Section 7(a) had led to muddle, rancour and futility. The only way to secure 'that fair distribution of purchasing power upon which permanent prosperity must rest', Wagner concluded, was by strengthening collective bargaining and so raising those at the bottom.[1]

Removing such inequalities within the wage structure would benefit society as a whole by creating mass purchasing power to fill the troughs in the business cycle. This economic philosophy was combined in the bill with a constitutional foundation, vital because the Supreme Court was already striking down much New Deal legislation. Wagner's constitutional argument was that deterrents to mass purchasing power were detrimental to interstate commerce, and that strikes caused by bad labour law and discordant labour relations further obstructed it. The Act would remove disagreement over the right to associate as a prime cause of strikes and establish collective bargaining to eleminate other causes.[2]

Equally important, the Wagner Act would establish an effective enforcement agency, outside the Department of Labor, in the National Labor Relations Board.[3] The NLRB's new powers – to order elections to see who should represent workers, to define and prohibit unfair labour practices, such as employer-dominated company unions, unfair dismissal or refusal to bargain, and to firmly enforce its decisions – would have a dramatic impact on labour relations. They would reduce anti-union litigation substantially and transform the NLRB, whose three members were to be selected with union agreement, into a kind of 'Supreme Court' of Labour. Not surprisingly, employers fought the bill tooth and nail.

More surprising was the Administration's cool, if not hostile, reception of the proposals. Perkins described them as 'interesting'. Richberg, the most influential of Roosevelt's labour advisers, flatly opposed them which was at first enough to make the President oppose them too. The Department of Labor resented the NLRB's independence and encroachment on its territory. The AFL feared shopfloor elections would benefit industrial unions at the expense of craft ones. Farm workers wished the Act to be extended to cover them. Blacks believed closed shop unions which discriminated against them, as many did, could legally bar them from membership and so employment. Newspaper proprietors argued that unions in their industry might breach the First Amendment; and so on.[4]

Moreover, the President – never sure-footed on labour affairs – felt a continuing loyalty to the NRA, its administrator Hugh Johnson and Section 7(a) when Wagner first introduced his bill. The year before, FDR had claimed to have defined this clause when he settled the automobile strike. So he refused to take a stand. Then in May 1935 the Supreme court, in the 9–0 Schechter decision, tore the heart out of the first New Deal by striking down the whole of Title I of the NIRA, including Section 7(a). After fifteen months silence an angry Roosevelt finally endorsed the Wagner bill and signed it when it passed reasonably rapidly, without damaging amendment, on 5 July 1935.

II

The Wagner Act marked the apogee of New Deal reformism. It could not have passed at any other time. Fearful of the demagogic appeal of Huey Long's 'share the wealth' campaign, and backed by huge majorities in Congress, Roosevelt saw social security, public housing and wealth tax laws enacted in the legislative flurry of the second New Deal. The Wagner Act, was clearly the longest stride of all on the road to new power for labour within an increasingly Keynesian-style economy. Yet its supporters must have shivered when William Green of the AFL called it 'the Magna Carta of labor in the United States',[5] for his predecesor Samuel Gompers had said that of the labour provisions in the 1914 Clayton Act, later castrated by the courts. Such might have happened to the Wagner Act. Business hotly protested it was unconstitutional; lawyers of the American Liberty League agreed; while Southern Democrats only voted for it because they believed the Supreme Court would strike it down and save them the risk of opposing organized labour. The automobile and steel industries vowed they would ignore it.

Yet it was in steel and cars that the Wagner Act passed its first great test. For years Lewis, who had led a massive resurgence of his UMW membership from 150 000 in 1932 to more than 400 000 in 1935, had been urging Green to do something about organising steel. For years Green, who like Lewis had started work as a collier, had been promising millions of new members. But at the end of 1935 the nation's largest basic industry remained unorganized. Fears of craft union leaders like Hutcheson and Tobin, that the new law would stimulate industrial unions among ethnic groups Tobin dismissed as 'rubbish', reached a violent climax at the AFL's Atlantic City convention in October 1935, when Lewis floored Hutcheson in a fist fight. More than mere personal enmity was at work here. The AFL had been in existence for fifty years to protect craftsmen. It regarded semi-skilled and unskilled workers in mass-production as inferior, unorganisable and a danger because they could undercut wages and break strikes. Now Lewis, Hillman and the rest proposed to cut clean across AFL jurisdiction by launching the Committee of Industrial Organizations and organising all workers in each industry into one union. At a time of falling craft union membership, the CIO's proposed industrial unions were a further threat to AFL strength.

Moreover, industrial unions aimed at everyone – workers of recent ethnic origin, blacks, women. No one had really attempted this since William Sylvis and the short-lived National Labor Union in the 1860s. The Knights of Labor had spoken in the 1880s of forging 'a connecting link between all branches of honourable toil'. But their failure, and that of the IWW later, had demonstrated the dangers of industrial unionism. AFL hostility to the idea had shown itself earlier in the New Deal by its reaction to the upsurge of new industrial unions stimulated by the NRA and Section 7(a). The AFL leaders had shunted these new unions off into so-called Federal unions, directly affiliated to the AFL, until jurisdictional problems could be resolved. The growth in numbers of such Federal unions from 307 to 1798 between 1932 and 1934 showed the danger. Where craft unions had increased their membership by only 10 per cent, industrial unions had increased theirs by 130 per cent.

These Federal unions were where Lewis and Hillman planned to work. Blocked by the conservative leadership, industrial union activists like Lewis and Hillman moved immediately to have the CIO work with the AFL to reach the unorganized in steel, cars, chemicals, rubber, textiles, everywhere. Lewis, whose miners were economically closely linked to the steel industry, took the lead. In February 1936 he pledged 350 paid organizers, an annual budget of 500 000 dollars and his best lieutenant, Philip Murray, to establish the Steel Workers' Organizing Committee. SWOC'S organizing drive, launched in June 1936, marked the start of the CIO's offensive in mass production. The leader of SWOC was Philip Murray, who, like Hillman, was a member of the rising generation of younger labour leaders. A Scots immigrant of Irish Catholic stock, he kept a copy of Leo XIII's celebrated encyclical on the Condition of Labor on his desk, and sought to achieve the social reform objective it expressed – a kind of middle ground between Socialism and untramelled capitalism. Like Green, like Lewis, Murray had also started work in the mines. Unlike Green, he was imaginative and receptive to ideas. Unlike Lewis, who was imperious and moody, Murray was considerate and generous – everyone called him Phil. He was also a pious Catholic. This was no small point. Jews like Hillman may have been prominent in union leadership. But an increasing proportion of the American working class was Catholic – descendents of the great influx of Irish, Italian and Polish immigrants. Frances Perkins and others had long recognized Murray's outstanding abilities; but he had hitherto always worked in Lewis's giant shadow. Now at last he was free to play an independent and decisive role.

He began at the top with United States Steel, citadel of the open shop, where 220 000 unorganized workers produced more steel than Germany. Muray's strategy fell into three parts. First he planned to work with the ethnic groups who were so important in the steel workforce – Poles, Czechs, Slavs and blacks. Then he chose to exploit the Federal government, reviving the phrase 'The President Wants You To Join the Union', used so ambiguously but effectively by Lewis in NRA days, which had more force following the Wagner Act. Finally, and most successfully, Murray cleverly infiltrated and then captured the company unions hastily set up by US Steel in 1933 to make some pretence of complying with NRA Codes.[6]

While SWOC's campaign at US Steel was in progress throughout 1936, but before the CIO organizing drive had achieved clear results in mass-production industry, labour turned its attention to the political front, helping Roosevelt's triumphant re-election in November 1936. Lewis judged that 'labor has gained more under Roosevelt than under any President in history', and called for unequivocal support for the New Deal. Determined to secure effective enforcement of new labour laws, union leadership abandoned its old neutral approach in favour of the most active campaigning for FDR. By 1936 the New Deal had become a rallying point for all left-wing elements in the labour movement.

Liberals and the old Progressives went solidly for the New Deal. Socialist trades unionists believed the President's policies promised achievement of long-sought social reform. Lacking an effective party themselves, they deserted to the Democrats, or such staging posts as New York's American Labor Party. Communists, now that the Comintern had changed is 'line' and was backing anti-Fascist Popular Front movements, threw themselves behind the New Deal. Trotskyists forgot their hatred of Communists in common cause for FDR. For the great majority of the American labour union rank and file, less ideological and more pragmatic, Roosevelt's aristocratic manner, warm human sympathies and matchless popular appeal appeared to combine democratic capitalism with social justice in an irresistible blend.

Naturally enough, the CIO was far more aggressive in this burst of mid-1930s political activity than was the AFL. Its radical advocacy of industrial unionism carried over into political promotion of social reform. As a brand-new organization it was not bound by old shibboleths or obstinate conservatism like the AFL. Moreover, industrial unionists saw more clearly than craft ones that the Depression had created a vital need for greater control over the economy, and that all workers had become more dependent upon government. Accordingly, CIO leaders played a crucial part in launching Labor's Non-Partisan League in 1936 and supported the American Labor Party in New York. Their prime purpose was clearly partisan: the re-election of Roosevelt. No effort was spared to secure the backing of both AFL and CIO unions.

But while many State labour federations and individual unions supported Labor's Non-Partisan League, the AFL spurned it. Bill Hutcheson remained Republican, Dan Tobin led the Democratic Labor Committee, and though Bill Green backed Roosevelt personally, he attacked the League as a dual (and thus divisive) movement in politics just as he attacked the CIO as a dual union – one of labour's oldest fears. In contrast, the CIO threw itself wholeheartedly behind Labor's Non-Partisan League. Few unions were more politically aware than the Amalgamated Clothing Workers, and in 1936 the ACW leader, Sidney Hillman, anticipated his later role with the CIO's Political Action Committee in the 1940s. Money was available, and Lewis's United Mineworkers alone advanced 500 000 dollars to the League's political campaign fund.

Roosevelt responded by emphasising how much he had done for labour. 'Employment and weekly pay envelopes', he said in his 1936 Labor Day address, 'have increased steadily during the past three years, stimulated by the spending of the Federal government in useful ways. This increased buying power of wage earners and farmers has resulted in increased sales for merchants, more orders for factories and rising profits for investors'.[7] George L. Berry, print union leader and first president of Labor's Non-Partisan League, exchanged a series of letters with FDR throughout the summer and autumn of 1936 which took the same line on purchasing power.[8] The votes of labour – AFL as well as CIO – played a critical part in securing Roosevelt the greatest popular victory in history at the polls in 1936.

This political triumph, combined with the CIO campaign to use the Wagner Act to launch unions in major industries like steel, set the scene for the historic struggles of 1937 – struggles in which the President was a mere spectator. For Roosevelt's inauguration in January 1937, and the launching of his unsuccessful attempt to reform the Supreme Court, coincided not only with SWOC's continuing campaign in steel, but also with the most important strike of the decade, in which the United Autoworkers forced General Motors to recognize the UAW for bargaining purposes. The political crisis which occurred over the role of the Court was dramatic enough. Yet the UAW strike in Flint, Michigan, which began on 30 December 1936, was even more stirring. It was fought to establish the principle of the union shop at GM, and thence in the motor industry as a whole. As SWOC's legal counsel Lee Pressman put it, 'The success or failure of the Autoworkers' strike meant the success or failure of the budding CIO. The loss of the strike might have been the loss of the CIO'.[9] What was new about the strike – and what caught national and international headlines – was its new technique. Instead of marching out and staying out, the strikers stayed in and sat down, so that the dispute became known as the 'sit-down strike'. It was to be one of the most important events in the history of American labour.

III

The United Autoworkers had been established in the motor industry through a merger of the Federal unions originally set up in the early 1930s by the AFL, and its organizers were actively at work. Still, progress was slow. Growing unhappy with the AFL's weak support of the Federation, the new union thereupon broke away in 1936 under the rank and file leadership of young men like George Addes, Richard Frankensteen, Homer Martin and Walter Reuther – the last destined to be one of the major figures of his generation – and threw in its lot with the CIO. There were some scattered strikes during the summer of 1936, and by late autumn the UAW – now some 300 000 strong – was coming out into the open, prepared to demand recognition from the giants of the industry – General Motors, Chrysler and Ford. But these huge international companies, defying the provisions of the Wagner Act, were not yet willing to make any concessions on collective bargaining. William S. Knudsen, General Motors vice-president, merely suggested that if the workers had any grievances they should take them up with the local plant managers. Before national UAW or CIO leaders could respond, union militants in Flint, Michigan, the birthplace of GM, took matters into their own hands. This small militant minority, composed mostly of union radicals, closed down the Chevrolet No. 1 factory on 30 December 1936. Thus began the strike which, before it ended on 11 February 1937, paralyzed production throughout GM, affected 112 000 of the company's 150 000 workers, and transformed American labour history.

The first full-scale use of a new labour tactic, the sit-down strike, proved doubly effective in that such a strike could be broken only by the forcible removal of the workers from company premises. Excitement ran high. Management saw the sit-down as unlawful invasion of property rights and called for the immediate ejection of the strikers. Strikers countered that GM proposed to invade their legal rights, and the right of workers to jobs. The strike leader was Homer Martin, elected president of the UAW when it broke away from the AFL in 1936. Young, idealistic, a former Kansas City preacher, he made up in energy what he lacked in experience. Although Lewis was by then deeply involved in the steel organizing drive, he and his CIO associates gave Martin and the Flint strikers total support. 'You men are undoubtedly carrying on one of the most heroic battles that has ever been undertaken by strikers in an industrial dispute,' Lewis declared. 'The attention of the entire American public is focused upon you.'

Strikers were determined not to be dislodged from the occupied plants. The cutting off of all heat – even in the depths of a Michigan winter – made no difference. When police tried to rush the plant, they were met by a hail of missiles – coffee mugs, pop bottles, iron bolts, and heavy automobile door hinges. When the police – 'bulls' in Americal slang – then returned to the attack with tear-gas bombs, the strikers retaliated by turning streams of water on them from the plant fire hoses, until they were forced to retreat in what victorious workers promptly dubbed the 'Battle of the Running Bulls'. As the strike dragged on worker discipline was rigid. Moreover, women in Flint formed their own vital auxiliary, carrying food, warm clothing, news, encouragement and bedding into the strikers, and also picketing and propagandizing themselves. In face of a whole working-class community in revolt, GM demanded the State militia be mobilised to clear the plants. But the Democratic Governor Frank Murphy of Michigan, sympathetic to the strikers and fearful of bloodshed, refused. Finally, GM obtained a court order setting 3.00 p.m. on 3 February as the deadline for striker evacuation.

The strikers remained solid. 'We have decided to stay in the plant,' they replied. Realising they meant what they said, Governor Murphy coolly summoned a peace conference. CIO president John L. Lewis rushed to Detroit and began negotiations with GM's vice-president Knudsen. But 3 February arrived without any settlement. The sit-downers were barricaded in the factories. Outside the besieged plants thousands of sympathetic workers and members of women's emergency brigades, who had played a crucial role in feeding the strikers and in picketing the plant, milled about as loudspeaker trucks blared forth the slogan of 'Solidarity Forever'. The 3 o'clock deadline approached and passed with Murphy refusing to instruct the national guardsmen to enforce the court order. In spite of mounting pressure from management and others, he was unwilling to precipitate violence in Flint on an unpredictable scale.

Next day, as Roosevelt added his pressure for negotiations to that of Frank Murphy, the Lewis–Knudsen talks were resumed. For a full week, while the sit-downers grimly held the fort, the conference, attended by other representatives of management and strikers, continued until finally Governor Murphy was able to announce agreement. General Motors undertook to recognize the United Automobile Workers as the bargaining agent for its members, to drop injunction proceedings against the strikers, to take up such grievances as the production-line speed-up and other matters, and not to discriminate in any way against union members.

It was not a complete victory. The UAW did not achieve exclusive representation rights, although GM promised not to bargain with any other organizations of its employees during the term of the new agreement. Nor did the temporary settlement provide any form of union security. Yet it achieved a decisive labour objective: the fundamental right to organize and bargain collectively, in one of the largest multinational business enterprises in the world. It proved to be only the first step on the road to total unionization of the auto industry. More important, its repercussions rippled throughout the economy, and spread a wave of unionism and strikes across the nation.[10] Steel was the first industry to react to the news from Flint about the UAW, when the following month, to general incredulity, US Steel signed a similar agreement with SWOC. This contract went even further, granting a 10 per cent wage increase, an eight-hour day, a forty-hour week, and recognition of SWOC as the bargaining agent for its members – all this without even a strike. Over a hundred other independent steel companies followed suit, and by May 1937 SWOC claimed more than 300 000 members. These victories were decisive landmarks. The nation's two greatest open-shop bastions – GM and US Steel – had fallen. The whole pattern of labour relations in mass-production – essentially based on brutal paternalism – was unravelling. What the AFL had failed to accomplish in half a century, the CIO had achieved in the first three months of 1937. Having organized autos and steel, the CIO's future seemed unlimited.

The immediate consequences were dramatic: general assault on the mass-production industries revolutionized the labour scene. Organizing drives among rubber workers, radio and electrical workers, lumbermen, longshoremen and many others, served to build strong and powerful unions. The campaign of the new Textile Workers' Organizing Committee, under the skilful leadership of Sidney Hillman, was especially significant in reaching hitherto-unorganizable Southern mill towns. Numerical gains for the CIO by the end of 1937 were impressive enough: 600 000 mine workers, 400 000 automobile workers, 375 000 steel workers, 300 000 textile workers, 250 000 ladies' garment workers, 177 000 clothing workers, 100 000 agricultural and packing workers. More important, these campaigns had achieved a broader base for organized labour as a whole. The CIO had organized the unskilled workers into industrial unions and broken through the narrow exclusive craft unionism of the AFL. It had welcomed, as the Federation had never done, immigrants, blacks, and women without regard to race, gender or nationality. In light of all this, many were misled into thinking the CIO triumph complete.

Yet in steel, 1937 was the exception to the rule that where US Steel led the rest of the industry followed. The real trouble for SWOC came in the so-called Little Steel companies like Bethlehem, Republic or Youngstown Sheet and Tube, who fought a bitter and bloody rearguard action. The Memorial Day Massacre at Chicago in May 1937 saw ten strikers killed and victory for Republic Steel. As the Little Steel struggle dragged on to defeat it revealed sharply the limitations of presidential support. Senator Robert La Follette's Civil Liberties Committee Investigation showed clearly where blame should be put. Steel executives found it hard to explain to the Senate why they spied on their own workforce, hired goon squads to attack them, stored guns, grenades and explosives, and practised sabotage.[11] Yet the President's view – preoccupied as he was with his political battle over the Supreme Court – had been 'a plague on both your houses' and he took no part in these decisive events in cars, chemicals, rubber, steel and textiles.

Though Roosevelt had spoken movingly in his second inaugural of 'one-third of a nation, ill-housed, ill-clad, ill-nourished' he neglected their plight while pursuing his primary objective of reforming the Court. True, the Court had struck down the NRA and much of the first New Deal. Moreover, there was sound reason for fearing it might do the same to the Wagner Act and the second New Deal. In fact the Court upheld Wagner in the Jones and Laughlin case later in 1937 and left the other legislation alone. By the summer of 1937 the President had abandoned his bid to reform the Federal judiciary. The Court changed partly because it was scared by FDR's plan to 'pack' it, partly because it became more atuned to changing public opinion on social questions, partly because some judges – notably Owen Roberts – changed their views. Finally, retirement of older and more reactionary judges enabled the President by 1940 to appoint his own court, including Hugo Black, author of the Black–Connery Bill, Frank Murphy, friend of the UAW, and Felix Frankfurter, Keynesian recruiter of liberal lawyers to Federal agencies. Moreover, though the President had been cool towards organized labour, he was a political opportunist who knew where the votes were. Labour had become the capstone of the Democratic Party's new reform coalition.

The fruits of this new political coalition between unions and the Democrats were not slow in coming. In June 1938 the Fair Labor Standards Act established a minimum wage (25 cents an hour, to rise to 40 by 1945), a 44-hour week (to be reduced to 40 by 1941) and ended employment of children under 16. These standards were not high – indeed, their minimal nature, and the fact that they excluded most categories of workers, showed how far labour still had to travel. Yet the Act not only set the seal on the advances labour had made during the Depression, but became a base for future advance. So the Supreme Court decisions upholding Fair Labor Standards, Social Security, Public Housing and everything else revealed how completely the New Deal was transforming affairs.

IV

Politics continued to be important as war clouds darkened after 1937. The activities of Labor's Non-Partisan League did not end with the 1936 election. The League tried to capture control of the Democratic Party in Pennsylvania, played an active part in New Jersey politics and backed a campaign for a labour administration in Detroit. In New York, the American Labor Party was strongly supported in the garment workers' unions: Hillman's Amalgamated Clothing Workers and the International Ladies' Garment Workers, led by another East European Socialist, David Dubinsky. They helped win some 500 000 votes to re-elect the reforming Mayor Fiorello La Guardia in November 1937. The League had backed the President's unsuccessful bid to reform the Supreme Court and threw itself behind all candidates who supported the New Deal, irrespective of party.

Some believed Labor's Non-Partisan League might even provide the nucleus for the kind of farm–labour coalition dreamed of in the days of Andrew Jackson a century before, or the Populists in the 1890s. Others hoped it would revive the old idea of a British-style labour party. There was never any real chance of this, however. The AFL flatly refused to have anything to do with it, while the CIO, as distinct from its constituent unions, shrank from endorsing such independent political action.

The problems confronting those who tried to establish third parties, and the dismal fate of most previous attempts, further inhibited growth. Moreover, Roosevelt was the greatest vote-getter in history, and the vast majority of the working class seemed bound to him. Finally, when the President was not running in the mid-term elections in 1938, the political pendulum swung against him for the first time. Democrats suffered significant reverses, and a coalition of Republicans and Southern Democrats emerged which came to control Congress until the 1960s. It scarcely seemed the moment to set up a third party, and historians who decry this 'lost opportunity' misread the mood of the late 1930s.

Third party or not, conservative and anti-New Deal forces rallied to combat such radicalism. They singled out the CIO as an un-American follower of the Communist Party line. By 1938 conservative opposition to labour and the New Deal was much better organized than it had been during 1932, and the days of the American Liberty League. 'At no point', as the historian Arthur Schlesinger has tartly observed, 'did the American Liberty League construe "liberty" as meaning anything else but the folding stuff.'[12] By 1938 the National Association of Manufacturers and other employers' groups were attacking Labor's Non-Partisan League and the American Labor Party in New York under the slogan 'Join the CIO and Help Build a Soviet America'.

This crude kind of anti-Communism, though effective a decade later, had limited impact in 1938. The vast majority of the American working class were uninfluenced by Communist ideology, even in Communist-led unions. The leaders of the CIO – Lewis, Hillman, Murray – were strongly anti-Communist. Lewis, who had driven them out of the UMW in the 1920s, was to help drive them out of the CIO in the 1940s; Hillman did the same in the ACW; and Murray's Catholicism engendered hatred of Marxism. Communists did play a part organizing many CIO unions. They held important positions in Lewis's staff, where Lee Pressman was legal counsel, and on the CIO executive board. But their power was exaggerated, even in the 1930s, by both Communists themselves and the enemies of Communism and unionism.

The idea that Communist unions all acted in unison was false. In everyday matters they functioned much like other unions. Their image as a small, well-disciplined, Moscow-directed army slavishly following the party line was based almost entirely on foreign affairs which, at least until Pearl Harbor in 1941, had no influence on shop-floor issues. Nor did the Communist Party engineer the CIO break from the AFL; indeed, at first it opposed it. The CP leadership was suspicious of Lewis. As the CP's William Z. Foster explained, 'Lewis is still Lewis' – the brutal anti-Communist. The reason Lewis and other CIO leaders were prepared to use Communists after 1935 was simple: they were the best organizers in the CIO. Even their opponents said so. Charles Owen Rice, who made a career leading the Association of Catholic Trade Unionists' attack on the Communists, admitted he was 'impressed by them'. The most influential Communists in the early days of the CIO were Lee Pressman, Len De Caux and Harry Bridges. Yet Pressman always maintained that the CIO was run by Lewis, Murray and Hillman, and that the CP went along with them, rather than they with it. Pressman outlasted Lewis at the CIO but his role was mainly to smooth relations between Lewis, Murray and the Communists, not make policy. Len De Caux, English-born and Harrow-educated, had dropped out of Oxford University and come to America in the 1920s, joining the CP via the IWW. He edited the *CIO News* from its launch in 1937 to the end of the 1940s. Moreover he helped other left-wingers find jobs in the growing labour press. Harry Bridges, Australian-born of properous parents, was a dynamic and intelligent leader who absorbed the traditions of West Coast radicalism.

Yet despite such apparent influence, Communists were least successful in gaining power in SWOC, the union they fought hardest to control because of its central economic importance. The fact that SWOC had been organized from the top down enabled Lewis and Murray to exercise bureaucratic control. By contrast, the CP was much more successful in the UAW, organized from the bottom up and most open to democratic control. Left-wing rank-and-file organizers thus came to exercise more influence in the auto industry. Their leader, Wyndham Mortimer, one of the few activists over thirty-five years old, had to yield to Homer Martin as the UAW's first president, and settle for the post of his deputy. Apart from Martin, the CP also confronted some formidable left-wing opponents in the union, such as Richard Frankensteen and Walter Reuther, who had both been badly beaten up by company goons in the 1937 organizing struggles, and Richard Leonard, of the nonunion Ford Company.

Ethnic and religious cross-currents further stirred the turbulent waters of UAW politics. Homer Martin, a fundamentalist preacher, appealed to the Appalachian migrants prominent in the Detroit workforce, who sometimes joined the Ku Klux Klan and were deeply hostile to their Polish Catholic fellow workers. For their part, Poles, Germans and Irish workers were frequently followers of Father Charles Coughlin, the Catholic priest whose vastly popular radio talks combined anti-semitism, anti-Roosveltism and corporate authoritarianism. Finally, Homer Martin's Protestant supporters were in turn deeply suspicious of the more cosmopolitan, racially mixed and often secular background from which both Socialists, like Reuther, and the Communist-backed caucus, led by Wyndham Mortimer and George Addes (another Catholic), sprang. Old stock German and Irish Catholic skilled workers felt threatened by the rise of semi-skilled workers of more recent ethnic origin who were being led by the secular left. CIO efforts to integrate black workers exacerbated such tensions, while the Catholic Church, always sensitive to state intrusion into family life and parochial school education, opposed CIO-supported attempts like the Fair Labor Standards Act to end the abuse of child labour because it struck at family autonomy and would reduce family income. The birth of ACTU – the Association of Catholic Trade Unionists – revealed more tensions than mere latent anti-Communism.[13]

The most effective anti-Communist in the CIO, Sidney Hillman, was Jewish. Walter Reuther, destined to destroy the Communists ten years later, had a wide personal following and Socialist beliefs. CP influence in the budding CIO unions as a whole was strongest in the United Electrical Workers, and weakest in SWOC and the Textile Workers' Organising Committee, controlled by Hillman's ACW. The UE was the product of amalgamation between a number of independent unions in the radio and electrical appliance industry, and took on powerful anti-unions employers like General Electric, RCA and the Ford subsidiary Philco. As with the UAW in the motor industry, this gave Communist organizers the chance to grasp union leadership in a series of strikes. Communists also managed to establish a presence in the International Union of Mine, Mill and Smelter Workers, the International Woodworkers (who had been driven out of the AFL by Hutcheson), the small Fur and Leather Workers, the Southern Tenant Farmers' Union and Farm Equipment Workers.

Communist influence made itself felt in the retail and wholesale trades, in Henry Bridges's breakaway West Coast Longshoremen, in the East Coast merchant seamen and in a number of other unions, of which the Hollywood Screen Actors' and Screen Writers' guilds became notorious ten years later. Yet Communism in 1938, at the height of the Popular Front, had not taken on the diabolic qualities with which it was to become invested between 1948 and 1950, at the height of the Cold War. What people noted in the 1930s was Communist zeal and enterprise in recruiting union members and getting them to vote. Warned about their influence, Lewis dismissed the danger. 'Who gets the bird?' he asked in his famous distinction, 'The hunter or the dog?'[14]

V

Labour had made great strides in the 1930s towards new powers and a new economic role. Yet severe limitations remained. Quite apart from the divisions discussed above about Communism, race, religion and ethnicity, the AFL's expulsion of the CIO in 1937 came at the very time when unity was needed most. The decision to organize the CIO – now called the Congress (rather than Committee) of Industrial Organization – on a permanent basis, with John L. Lewis as first CIO president, deepened AFL fears that new industrial unions would poach their members. Yet such fears proved largely groundless. Great advances had been made since 1935, with the CIO making most of the running.[15] Yet the great strikes of 1936–37 had involved only a minority of the workers, and the CIO actually had dared not call for NRLB elections when it won its first contracts with GM and US Steel because it feared it would lose them.[16]

Moreover after 1938 the AFL, stimulated by the CIO challenge, expanded much faster, while the CIO stagnated and even declined. Efforts supported by Roosevelt to heal the rift in labour's ranks in 1938–39 and reunite AFL and CIO proved fruitless, while the CIO suffered set-backs. The Little Steel and 'captive mines' struggles continued well into the 1940s, while Ford did not recognize the UAW, the CIO's largest constituent union, until 1941. In other industries – farms, machinery, meatpacking, the docks, Southern textiles – the CIO maintained only a scattered presence as the decade ended. Finally, since many CIO members did not actually pay dues, it was difficult to judge stable membership. Yet clearly one reason CIO leaders opposed rapid return to unity with the AFL was fear that they would be a minority.

This persistent weakness in the ranks of organized labour was worsened by political and economic events after 1938. In the wider world, unions were becoming dependent upon a Keynesian approach to public spending. By 1937 New Deal reform legislation had run its course. Industrial production was above 1929 levels, business activity buoyant. Just as the first labour upsurges had occurred during the tentative economic recovery of 1933 and 1934, so permanent gains for labour coincided with the more substantial growth of 1937 when profits, employment, pay and hope all recovered. Had FDR chosen to spend at the start of his second term, Congress would have complied and met his commitment to the needs of 'one-third of a nation'. Instead, he chose to take on the Supreme Court, and then became increasingly preoccupied with foreign affairs as war loomed. Expanded labour unions were safely in the Democratic fold, and the President felt it was time to mend fences with those angered by his attack on the Court. The moment seemed to have come to start to redeem the Pittsburgh pledge, repeated many times since 1932, to reduce the cost of Federal government by one quarter. But when FDR cut Federal spending in 1937 and 1938 the result was a sharp rise in unemployment – and this time people called it 'the Roosevelt recession'.

Shorter but steeper than after 1929, this economic downturn hit the CIO hard. Production declined by 70 per cent in steel, 50 per cent in autos, 40 per cent in rubber, and 35 per cent in manufacturing. Unemployment rose to one in five, not far short of the 1933 level. Hundreds of thousands of newly-organized workers were laid off. Those who remained in work saw their union, its collective power gravely weakened, struggle to sustain hard-won seniority and grievance systems. Between 1939 and 1940 union organizing work ceased abruptly. SWOC dismissed some 250 field representatives, put the rest on short-time and concentrated on steel mills where union members already had bargaining rights. The UAW alone lost fifty international staff members and abandoned any effort to unionize Ford for the foreseeable future. Lewis characteristically took a hatchet to the problem. The CIO sacked sixty-three staff members in 1940 and withdrew organizers from its campaign to establish new unions in the aircraft, meatpacking, textile and farm equipment industries. Lewis might claim the CIO had four million members; but the actual dues-paying figure fell as low as 1.5 million in the late Depression era.

This sharp economic slump had a decisive influence. Labour became more amenable to management. 'Enlightened union leaders', Hillman wrote in the 1938 CIO Handbook, 'believe that the attitude of organized labour must be one of co-operation with the employer in their mutual interests – increased prosperity for all.'[17] Philip Murray supported this view, and reflected the new realism of SWOC following the Little Steel drubbing when he observed, 'The fight for unionization is over in the greater part of the steel industry and we want no lingering spirit of contentiousness to survive. We realise that mutual interests are best served by working with and not against each other.'[18] In short, the emphasis had switched from confrontation to consensus. Hillman summarised his position thus:

> Greater production, guided by efficient management, means lower costs per unit. Lower costs tend towards lower prices. This enables our people to buy and use more goods. This, in turn, makes possible putting our unemployed back to work. With little or no unemployment, the bargaining power of labor is increased, resulting in higher wages. Higher wages, coupled with lower prices, mean a high standard of living.[19]

Yet the emerging political and economic picture, though increasingly Keynesian in complexion, was still not complete by the end of 1940. As the events of that year made clear, it excluded the outstanding labour leader of the past decade – John L. Lewis. He had led the campaign to throw labour votes behind the President in 1936, only to see him abandon labour in 1937. At the height of the UAW's crucial conflict with General Motors, Lewis explained to reporters that when labour had worked hard for the President's re-election year 'the economic royalists represented by General Motors' had bent every effort to defeat him. 'The same economic royalists now have their fangs in labour,' said Lewis, who then expected every effort from the administration to defeat GM. Instead, as we have seen, Roosevelt had left all crucial moves to Governor Murphy, while during the Little Steel strikes he had remained neutral, if not hostile.

Some believed with Frances Perkins that thwarted political ambition explained why Lewis turned so bitterly against Roosevelt. But as Lewis's biographers explain, there was little or nothing in this. Since the 1920s, when Republicans rebuffed his ambition to serve as Secretary of Labor, Lewis had neither sought nor wanted public office. Like many employers, Lewis believed the New Deal had failed. High public spending, new industrial unions and political support for the Democrats had not ended the Depression. Unemployment never fell below 10 per cent throughout the 1930s. Moreover international events deepened Lewis's suspicions. A lifelong isolationist, Lewis opposed the President's foreign policy not only because he feared it would end in military involvement abroad, but because he believed another world war would lead to the kind of losses labour had suffered after 1918. Yet his was a minority view in the ranks of labour after 1939. Until December 1941, while both AFL and CIO opposed actual American entry into the war, they supported the President's policy of rearmament, not least because it was stimulating the economy and providing new jobs.[20]

Nevertheless, as Nazi Germany set out to conquer Europe, Lewis evolved an increasingly anti-Roosevelt policy. He now detested FDR personally, and warned the UMW in 1940 that should the Democratic Party 'be coerced or dragooned into re-nominating him, I am convinced ... his candidacy would result in ignominious defeat'. When Roosevelt broke all constitutional precedent, crossed the Rubicon and ran for a third term in November, Lewis declared that the New Deal had failed to bring economic recovery and had in fact prolonged the Depression. FDR's re-election, he argued, 'would be a national evil of the first magnitude. He no longer hears the cries of the people. I think that the election of Mr Wendell Willkie is imperative'.[21] Finally, Lewis laid his leadership of the CIO on the line. Since Roosevelt could not be re-elected without the sweeping support of labour, Lewis pledged that he would regard such re-election as a vote of no-confidence in him personally and resign as president of the CIO. When Roosevelt was returned in November 1940 Lewis resigned as promised. As head of the CIO in the 1930s, he had done more than anyone else to transform organized labour. After 1940, though he remained head of the mineworkers for two more decades, and a formidable figure in labour affairs, he was never to recapture his days of glory.

VI

The 1930s had been a turbulent decade. Yet with hindsight it can be argued that given the Great Depression there might easily have been more unrest, violence and demand for radical change. Instead, two brief upsurges of rank-and-file militancy, coinciding with upturns in the economy, created radical new unions, which were eventually to become part of a new consensus based on corporate liberalism and Keynesian economics. Why was this? Some of the answer, as Professor Dubofsky has argued, lies in the fact that for many workers capitalism never collapsed.[22] For those in work, always a majority at any one time, or in regular employment, always a substantial proportion of the workforce, real wages actually rose during the 1930s as prices fell. Faced with this, as we have seen, the revolutionary left made little headway. Communists were too divorced from the American working class, too committed to sterile ideology and democratic centralism, and too obviously intent upon exploiting working-class grievances for their own ideological ends to have any lasting impact. Trotskyists were too small a group and too independent.[23]

Historians who have followed Professor Brody's suggestion, of the need to examine rank-and-file attitudes more closely to explain this failure of radicalism, and indeed the whole direction of union growth in this period, have revealed the more complex picture of shop floor ethnic–culutral conflict outlined above. Yet much of the debate which has occurred among historians about these crucial years has concentrated on the failure of radicalism at a period of unparalleled crisis for capitalism.[24] Only by implication has this discussion touched on another central question. Unions clearly helped create modern 'corporate liberalism' which has shaped America in the last fifty years. Yet what part did they play in spreading the ideas of the economist J. M. Keynes which underpinned this system? The Keynesian revolution, it is widely believed, ended unemployment and substituted a generation in which government intervention, high public spending and rising aggregate combined to create new prosperity.

From this perspective, the debate among labour historians has focused less on what happened than what might have done. In 1933, after a decade of corporate hegemony, class collaboration and trade union retreat, the AFL had a falling membership of fewer than three million. By 1938, after a period of class conciousness, violent conflict and radicalism, union membership had more than doubled and was rising. Though the CIO had been expelled from the AFL, the open shop had been eroded and manufacturing industry substantially organized, while labour formed the core of the Democratic Party's new coalition of liberal and increasingly urban reform.

By 1940, then, it was clear that a real and decisive shift in economic and political power had occurred. Yet New Left historians have argued that more could have been done: that independent, class-conscious unions of the kind some CIO activists wanted might have appeared. Instead, after the initial eruption, American labour leaders rapidly restored their chronic conservatism. Soon employers could co-opt them into management, with the vital tasks of disciplining the workforce, so that they became, as Mark Hanna had hoped, 'labor lieutenants of the captains of industry'. In this revisionist account the great enemy is the union contract, ending independence and binding labour to the employer. Despite a certain plausibility, such criticism is seriously misplaced. Fundamentally, it misinterprets the mood of the time. For most workers in the 1930s, engaged in desperate battle with the largest and most ruthless corporations in the world, the contract was not a sell-out but the supreme prize.[25] Equally important, this whole debate neglects the fact that unions helped solve the riddle of unemployment and replaced privation with prosperity in the generation which followed the New Deal.

Here Keynes's ideas were crucial; yet we need to know more about rank-and-file understanding of them. Did workers accept Keynesianism because it fitted in with the system and provided a convenient rationalization for higher pay? For unions, and also for President Roosevelt and his aide Harry Hopkins, Keynesianism simply served as a convenient rationalization of what they were doing anyway. And as far as Keynes himself was concerned they were not doing enough. In 1940 FDR for the first time discussed his budget in Keynesian terms. But Keynes himself was unconvinced this was a genuine conversion. 'It seems politically impossible', he wrote in July 1940, 'for capitalistic democracy to organize expenditure on the scale necessary to make the grand experiment which would prove my case – except in war conditions.'[26]

The fall of France brought such conditions into being. Within four months Roosevelt had won re-election and, through lend–lease and generous aid to embattled Britain, placed America's economy on a war footing. Within 16 months the Japanese attack in Pearl Harbor completed the process. Public spending was now not simply acceptable but a patriotic imperative. This produced a quantum leap. Public spending in the next four years rocketed upwards. Tax receipts rose tenfold, though never keeping pace with the cost of war, as the national debt rose from 40.4 billion dollars in 1940 to 258.7 billion dollars in 1944. Between 1942 and 1945 the real value of the nation's output rose by 70 per cent, private production expanded by more than half, while the government's share of output more than trebled and its share of the total output rose from just under 10 per cent in 1939 to between a fifth and a quarter in 1944.[27]

Labour may have made great strides in the 1930s but as late as 1940 the Social Security Board reported that less than 8 per cent of all industrial wage earners made what later was called 'a family wage': enough to live without hardship. At the other end of the scale, one-third of all American workers earned less than 500 dollars a year.[28] Stronger unions could use chronic wartime scarcity of labour, limitless public spending and reflation to begin to change all that. In that sense, and in many others, the impact of the Second World War on American labour was to be as decisive as the impact of the New Deal.

3.   The Crucible of War

I

The Second World War, like the Great Depression, was a major crisis for American capitalism. Yet both events provided American labour with matchless opportunities. The war gave unions, faltering since 1938, a chance to build on the advances they had made during the New Deal. By the end of 1942 war had ended unemployment, which had never fallen below 10 per cent during the 1930s. War effectively removed all limits on public spending, thus enabling the Federal government to make the grand experiment J. M. Keynes had wanted to prove his case. Moreover the new labour unions, launched so rapidly and aggressively in the wake of the Wagner Act, were able to consolidate, increase their membership to around 15 million, and play a crucial role in shaping the war economy on Keynesian lines. The United States did not fully enter the war until the Japanese attack on Pearl Harbor on 7 December 1941. Yet the dramatic defeat of France within six weeks in June 1940 had already transformed the world strategic situation. It impelled the United States, whose people feared involvement in the war, to embark on a programme of defence, or rearmament. Moreover American support for Britain in the role of Arsenal of Democracy had a crucial effect from 1940 onwards. After 1941, the great American war machine devoured everything the American economy could produce. The chronic labour surplus of the 1930s was replaced by chronic labour shortage, especially of skilled workers, while war workers as a whole enjoyed steady jobs, security of employment, union membership, and rising real incomes.

Yet the war was full of dangers as well as opportunities. Global in scope, and demanding total committment of domestic production, the war permanently transformed the labour market. Moreover the war economy drew rising numbers of men and women from the secondary to the primary labour sector. Millions of able-bodied workers conscripted into the armed forces had to be replaced in the civilian labour force if they were to have the weapons to fight with, and these new workers came from two main sources: women and blacks. Women worked for wages as never before. Though housewives did return to paid employment during the war, the great majority were working-class women who worked because they had to. Millions of them deserted not the kitchen but the low-wage ghetto.

Now they took better-paid jobs in what had previously been all male preserves: steel mills, motor plants (now producing tanks and planes), shipbuilding, railways and engineering shops. They often found themselves in jobs which the conventional wisdom said they could not do because they lacked skill, strength or stamina. In fact women did these jobs well, and even out-performed men when they could use the kind of nimbleness or dexterity learned from traditional women's tasks. Women also had to be given emergency apprenticeship training, which made men fearful of consequent skill dilution. By the peak of the war women formed 36 per cent of the full-time labour force, so that many men believed they would be unable to reclaim their old jobs when hostilities ended.

Blacks provided the other great new source of wartime labour, meeting the same kind of prejudice based on fears of wage undercutting, skill dilution and loss of jobs. Black women benefitted even more dramatically than white women from this wartime opportunity, but blacks as a group left poorly paid domestic, menial or agricultural work for more skilled and better paid jobs in defence plants across the nation. This black migration developed a theme which had opened in the First World War. Then the Great Migration took about 500 000 Southern blacks to Northern cities between 1915 and 1918, opening a movement of population which continued between the wars so that by 1940 something like a quarter of American blacks lived in the urban North. Now the movement occurred on a much greater scale between 1941 and 1945. Not only did some three to five million blacks leave the South, but moved far more widely around the country, not just to the traditional North and Northeast, but to the Midwest and such States as California and Washington where the aircraft industry was located.

This readjustment of the workforce did not occur smoothly. Generally white women found access to better jobs easier than black men or women. Yet even here union men insisted that women could only replace them for the duration of the war. Blacks met much more resistance. Old-style, white-only AFL craft unions denied blacks membership and tried to keep them out of skilled work. Even in the more open CIO unions white workers threatened to strike if blacks received more skilled jobs. The kind of peacetime, ethnic and racial conflicts discussed in the last chapter in the UAW continued into war, and the situation was far worse in non-union factories. Employers were equally prejudiced, regarding blacks as fit simply for menial tasks. Only the threat of a black workers' march on Washington, co-ordinated by the black Sleeping Car Porters' leader, A. Philip Randolph, in June 1941, persuaded President Roosevelt to sign Executive Order 8802 and establish the Fair Employment Practices Commission.[1] Though of very limited immediate effect, this was a landmark in race relations. The demands of total war – especially one fought against the racist regime of Hitler's Germany – helped undermine, though by no means end, the racism of workers, unions and employers.

The war was also important because it rescued the CIO and mass-production unionism from the decline which had set in after the Roosevelt recession in 1937–38. By 1940 the CIO was in serious organizational trouble. Yet by the end of 1941 it had finally succeeded in organizing the last great bastion of anti-unionism in the car industry at the Ford Motor Company. Here last-ditch opposition to the UAW was abandoned overnight in favour of a policy which embraced the union shop. In addition, the CIO had organized Little Steel and the major meat-packing firms, while stabilising those weak affiliates which had earlier won recognition and contracts. CIO membership increased as war production intensified.

Ford had changed its mind largely because it feared refusal to recognize unions might lose it lucrative defence contracts, while cost-plus clauses in such contracts with the Federal government enabled employers simply to pass on wage increases to customers. Moreover manufacturers preferred not to endanger production and profits by antagonising their workers. Union organizers had rarely worked in such a favourable climate. Two other influences combined to make industrial relations relatively peaceful in wartime. The first was a strong sense of national unity. The second was the high level of government intervention in the economy. Yet neither really came about until after Pearl Harbor. It took the shock of Japan's devastating air attack to swing people fully behind the President and welcome his war economy.

Between September 1939 and December 1941 many had genuinely believed the European conflict was nothing to do with them, and had been ignorant of the threat posed by Japan in the Far East and Pacific. Even the sudden fall of France in June 1940 only galvanized those already committed to the Allied cause. Chapter 2 discussed the influence wider economic and political events had on American labour: the devastation of the Depression, the almost accidental acceptance of Keynesian ideas about demand management, union support for Roosevelt in 1936, the creation of Labor's Non-Partisan League, and the New York Labor Party, and the story of Roosevelt, Willkie, Lewis and the CIO presidency in 1940. Yet to understand what was really happening to American labour between 1939 and 1941 – between the defence period and war – close attention must now be paid to detailed CIO internal politics.

II

The fate of the Communists within the CIO as war began revealed complex forces at work, which later helped shape the long-term destiny of American labour. The UAW was the largest, most important, and hitherto most democratic of the CIO unions. Its presidential election in 1939 was to prove decisive. Since Homer Martin's election as UAW president in 1936, and through the turbulent years since, this former preacher had found himself leading an uneasy coalition. Communism – indeed politics alone – was not Martin's primary problem. As shown above, a good old-fashioned American mixture of ethnicity, race and religion shaped events. For a generation and more the booming auto industry had sucked workers in from everywhere: the Bible Belt, the Appalachians, the South and from Eastern and Southern Europe.

No doubt the end of unrestricted immigration in the 1920s had helped the American working class settle down, and make easier the CIO organizing drives of the 1930s. Yet Protestant nativists and Roman Catholics of more recent ethnic origin still viewed each other with deep, historic suspicion. Each group had been prey for many years to the rabble-rousing evangelism of leaders like Gerald L. K.

Smith on the one hand, and the radio demagogue Father Charles Coughlin on the other. The Association of Catholic Trade Unionists was still active on the shop floor; but in opposition to ACTU, so was the Black Legion, the Ku Klux Klan and in different style the Communists. Moreover, Catholic and Protestant alike were united in fearing competition from blacks, semi-skilled and unskilled workers, of labour dilution and de-skilling. Both religious groups opposed the kind of agnostic, secular ideas advanced by Marxists and others active in the CIO.[2] Finally, if they were apprentice-served craftsmen, they were especially hostile when such left-wing leadership aimed at making blacks, semi-skilled and unskilled workers more powerful within both industry and union.

Against this general background, Homer Martin had tried to reduce Communist influence in the UAW between 1936 and 1938. Paradoxically, the CP itself in this period had been so anxious to try to sustain Popular Front unity behind the New Deal at home and against Fascism abroad that it had done little to resist him. Union retreats during the Roosevelt recession, and simultaneous employers' offensives after 1937, put the skids under Martin. Then, when he tried to purge all opposition, the CP finally did what Socialists had done all along and opposed him. As a UAW delegate put it, 'If Martin had fought the manufacturers half as hard as he is fighting the "Moscow conspiracy" we would have had a great union and there would have been no wildcat strikes'.[3] Even so John L. Lewis, as president of the CIO, was largely responsible for driving Martin out in 1938. Thus expelled, Martin then joined renegade CP leader and inveterate plotter Jay Lovestone to found a rival auto-workers' union, the UAW-AFL. Lovestone's successor as CP leader, Earl Browder, opposed the UAW-AFL not as a dreaded 'dual union', but in terms of the Popular Front and New Deal coalition. Browder would do nothing to upset Governor Frank Murphy's Michigan re-election hopes, or antagonize the Socialists or Lewis himself. By 1939 it was clear the Communists would make no open bid for power in the UAW.

Yet with Martin and his followers gone, and charges mounting of his secret deals with auto bosses and Harry Bennett's notorious 'service department' at Ford,[4] Communists in the UAW-CIO now enjoyed broad support. Their candidate, Wyndham Mortimer, looked a good bet for the union presidency. But a non-Communist, George Addes, was an even better candidate. A generation younger than Mortimer, handsome, intelligent, persuasive, businesslike, Addes was a Catholic willing to go along with the Communists on all important issues – a trait he sustained through his remaining years in union office until 1947. Once the UAW Communists had united behind Addes, his only remaining rival seemed to be the emerging, ambitious social democrat, Walter Reuther. Later the hammer of the Communists, Reuther – who had spent two years working at Ford plants in the Soviet Union in the early 1930s – was still only president of the union's GM section and did not feel ready in 1939 to take on a man with Addes's appeal and experience. On the principle that if you can't beat him join him, Reuther offered to support Addes a few days before the convention at Cleveland in March.[5] 'Addes is our leader,' sang his supporters, 'we shall not be moved.'[6]

So the key figure in defeating the Communist coalition forming behind Addes in the UAW was not Reuther but Sidney Hillman, one of the founders of the CIO, but a man from outside the UAW. Soon to exercise unique power in both CIO and national politics, he had fought Communists within the ACW as fiercely as Lewis had in the UMW in the 1920s. A Jew who led a largely Jewish union, Hillman was deeply worried in the 1930s about the rise of Fascism in Europe, which Communists fought too. Like Lewis, he thought Communists were the best organizers the CIO had, and believed further that they could be controlled by men like Lewis and himself. But when they threatened to become the dominant force in a union, he was ready to step in and stop them. Arriving at the 1939 UAW convention with Philip Murray, another CIO outsider, he moved the meeting into closed session. 'Are we holding a convention for Hillman and Murray or anybody in the CIO?' an angry delegate asked. 'Who the hell is running this convention: the CIO or the rank and file of the United Autoworkers of America?'[7]

The answer to this question soon became clear. As Reuther put it, 'When the CIO steps in you can always be sure what the UAW will do. We have always been with the CIO and always will be until the day of our death.' Hillman and Murray, vice-presidents of the CIO, lobbied forcefully for the abolition of vice-presidencies in the UAW because they were centres of factionalism and Communist power. This was heartily endorsed by Maurice Travis, Richard Frankensteen and Wyndham Mortimer himself, though the latter pointed out amid laughter, 'As a matter of fact, the biggest crook in the union was not a vice-president'. Addes's support was melting. 'The

CIO is behind us, we shall not be moved,' delegates now sang.[8] Hillman and Murray then urged election of the ineffectual R. J. Thomas, who had only recently returned from the Martin/ Lovestone UAW-AFL, but was a close friend of Murray. Murray himself was under pressure from ACTU to do something to curb Communist influence, and when Addes's CP supporters bridled, Hillman played his trump card: Earl Browder, head of the CP, would also endorse R. J. Thomas.

Anxious to sustain the Popular Front at all costs, and fearful that if Addes won the anti-Communists would be herded into Martin's corral, Browder's endorsement was delivered in the name of UAW-CIO unity, and the overriding need to win back the 17 000 members Martin had taken with him out of the CIO. Mortimer and other Communists still resisted, so Browder arrived in person in Cleveland to enforce his will. While Addes declined the nomination to cries of 'We want Addes', a voice called 'We want Thomas', and another shouted amid laughter 'You are going to get him'. Addes's explanation that he had made his decision in 'the best interests of this Union, for the best interests of the Labor Movement as a whole, and particularly the CIO' was greeted with loud, prolonged applause. The CP and their allies switched to Thomas. Addes made do with the post of secretary-treasurer and afterwards his demoralised supporters roamed Cleveland singing, 'Addes is our leader, Thomas gets our votes'.[9]

This was a decisive election. Though the Addes-Thomas coalition included Communists, the high water mark of formal CP influence in the UAW and the CIO had passed, and despite later surges in the 1940s, the tide was to rush out at the end of the decade. In the view of the historian Steve Fraser, the CP and its CIO sympathisers had become a lightning rod for hatred which had little to do with their backing economic and civil rights for blacks or more use of government power to help the poor. 'Ironically, then,' Fraser notes, 'anti-communism as a mass movement was profoundly anti-capitalist insofar as it rebelled against the corporate, bureaucratic, centralizing and statist tendencies of the modern industrial order. With equal irony, "communism" in America only counted to the degree it articulated the central assumptions and aspirations of the CIO and the New Deal.'[10] Further, the whole episode was a reaction against the militancy released by the Flint sit-down in 1937. After that, shop stewards were prepared to act boldly and lead strikes if necessary, so that grievances were settled quickly and workers' powers expanded without regard to contracts. Not the UAW leadership, nor (more important) Lewis, Murray and Hillman at the CIO, nor GM management found this tolerable.[11] So union leadership and corporate management sought a new plan, based on union control of rank-and-file activism, which continued throughout the war and bore fruit afterwards.

On the UAW side, Thomas tried to avoid commitment to the leftist coalition, while Reuther built a powerful machine of his own after 1940 which eventually defeated both Thomas and the CP and its allies.[12] Reuther's eventual election to the UAW presidency in 1946 occurred because Thomas was unable to resist this prolonged assault on his position which Reuther was carefully organizing throughout the war. Moreover, Reuther's later victory proved crucial in turning the balance of power within the CIO as a whole against the Communists, so paving the way for the sweeping anti-Communist purge of the late 1940s. In this context, Browder's intervention in the March 1939 UAW election for Thomas against Addes was a self-inflicted wound which became mortal. His abrupt *volte-face* over the Nazi–Soviet pact on 23 August 1939 turned the knife. Overnight, CP support for the Popular Front and all attempts to check Fascism – which had justified the debacle at Cleveland in March – was completely abandoned. When war broke out in Europe a week later it was denounced as an imperialist conspiracy. Roosevelt's support for the Allies was the policy of 'war-mongering Wall Street'.

Browder believed that while this sudden U-turn behind Soviet foreign policy lost the CP middle-class, intellectual and Jewish support, it actually strengthened the party's base in the unions because it did not conflict with members' economic interests. Moreover it moved the party closer to the isolationist position of John L. Lewis. By 1940 Lewis's opposition to involvement in war had brought him into a strange alliance not only with the CP but with the America First Committee, which included some of the most reactionary corporate and other leaders in the United States. German invasion of the Soviet Union on 22 June 1941 forced the CP to do another overnight somersault and become the most vigorous supporters of the war. By the end of 1941, with the Soviet Union and the United States allies in conflict, all opposition, including that of Lewis, collapsed. Hitler's war, as it was known, was now clearly an

Allied crusade to save democracy from Fascism – for workers as much as bosses. Moreover, unlike between 1914 and 1918, the Federal government now showed itself much more willing to intervene regularly in labour relations, and to do so on the side of the workers. Indeed the unprecedented extent to which Washington boards and officials managed the national economy was nowhere more clear than in industrial affairs.

III

Thus while these crucial developments in UAW and CIO union politics were taking place, the war was transforming the wider role of organized labour within the economy. In May 1940, while France was falling, the President appointed a seven-man National Defense Commission with Sidney Hillman, the CIO garment workers' leader, in charge of employment.[13] Lewis was angered, for not only had he not been offered the post – which he would have refused – he had not even been consulted. Though a Socialist by conviction, Hillman looked less like a labour leader than a 'typical, successful businessman' with 'his trim appearance, graying hair and quiet, dignified manner'. In an article headed, 'Is Sidney Hillman CIO Machiavelli?' the New York *Daily Mirror* noticed 'the faintest hint of an accent creeping into his slow, precise English'.[14]

The press made much of the fact that Hillman and his boss on the commission, GM president William S. Knudsen, were both immigrants. Hillman's was clearly a key post. From the spring of 1940 until the spring of 1942 he headed the Labor Division of the National Defense Administration, first in the National Defense Advisory Commission, then in the Office of Production Management, and finally in the War Production Board. When he began government work, German armoured divisions were driving towards Paris, and after Dunkirk the British army was almost totally disarmed. If America was to act as the Arsenal of Democracy, then labour's co-operation was clearly crucial. And in Hillman's view what made this war different from any other was that it was the first that would be fought and won by the might of labour and industrial production.[15]

The *New York Times* compared Hillman to the British trade union leader Ernest Bevin, now Minister of Labour in Churchill's War

Cabinet. Of course Bevin exercised far more executive power than any American labour leader, but the comparison was a portent. In another prediction, the newspaper also referred to 'a young tool and die maker' named Walter Reuther of the UAW who, 'encouraged by the Labor Division of the defense organization, . . . worked out a plan to utilize the unutilized machine and man-power of the automobile industry for the mass production of airplanes'. The article added that Philip Murray, now president of the CIO, was preparing a similar plan for the steel industry, concluding, 'Direct responsibility for such plans by labor in equal partnership with industry . . . is a novel departure'.[16]

In fact, though, the Reuther plan for building 500 planes a day was pregnant with further significance. Exploiting the defence emergency, the plan linked unions to a form of industrial activism which combined vastly enhanced government power to regulate industrial relations, and re-order economic life, with a thrusting foreign policy. Time and again Reuther would use this strategic approach: an assault on management prerogatives in the name of social and economic efficiency; an appeal to public support in the wider liberal interest; a shift in power relations through tripartite government agency planning for whole sections of the economy. His remarkable rise to national prominence in the early 1940s occurred because he saw that in wartime the state would become the arena of conflict between the working class and its adversaries. The process had begun during the New Deal. But the transformation of the economy to a war footing in 1940 and 1941 meant that traditional collective bargaining issues – wages, union recognition and working conditions – had become thoroughly politicised. As auto executive George Romney explained early in the war, 'Walter Reuther is the most dangerous man in Detroit because no one is more skilful in bringing about a revolution without seeming to disturb the existing forms of society'.[17]

Philip Murray understood the resistance such imaginative think-ing met. 'Labor's chief difficulty today,' he said during the defence period, 'as in days gone by, lies in the unwillingness, the obvious unwillingness, of government and business to accept labor in good faith.'[18] Yet his own proposals were in a sense as radical as Reuther's. For they amounted to scrapping the existing structure of labour relations and replacing it by a system of industrial councils – an idea also favoured by John L. Lewis – in which unions played a full and equal part with management, stretching all the way to the White House.

The industrial council proposal was to remain current throughout the war and its immediate aftermath – part of the belief of leaders like Murray that they could use the war emergency to transform the industrial landscape. In fact, industrial councils indicated the route which American labour did not take. Reuther, for his part, was to become the most innovative and creative figures of his generation, suggesting radical ideas of his own and then shaping the course of events in the postwar period.

But for the moment nothing came of either the Murray or Reuther plans, revealing the advisory and non-executive role of American labour leaders in the wartime government. Yet as the military crisis deepened throughout 1941, and the United States gave generous backing to Britain through lend-lease and other policies, labour leaders like Hillman stimulated both production and propaganda. In an NBC radio broadcast to the nation on 3 June, for example, Hillman called for

a new spirit of national unity as bombs fall on London and Liverpool. . . . By peak production alone can we guarantee our own national safety and bring about the victory of Democracy. . . . We must put modern weapons into the hands of Democracy's front-line defenders – the Army, the Navy, the Air Force and the people of Britain.[19]

Within three weeks, when Hitler invaded the Soviet Union on 22 June 1941, the Russian people had joined the British in the front line. Within six months Pearl Harbor had completed the conversion to a war economy. On the home front, the CIO's struggle in the 'captive mines' – wholly owned by the steel companies – to establish the union shop continued throughout the year.

On this issue the miners' leader Lewis won a substantial victory, which partly offset his humiliating defeat over Roosevelt's decision to run for a third term. But news of the arbitration board's favourable decision on 7 December 1941 was swamped by events in the Pacific. Meanwhile, in the Little Steel dispute, the CIO had forced the smaller steel companies to recognize at last the steel workers' industrial union and accept other important principles, notably the 'checkoff' provision, whereby employers deducted union dues and fines from the pay packet before handing it over to the worker. SWOC became the United Steelworkers in 1942, and in return for complete co-operation in the war effort, the USW gained security and power over its members – at least during the term of the contract.[20]

Because labour leaders were well aware of the emerging Federal government role in the wartime economy, they insisted on their right to full representation on the Federal agencies created to deal with the crisis. Roosevelt partly recognized the justice of such demands. In first establishing the Office of Production Management in 1941, he appointed Hillman to serve as co-director. Labour representatives were also appointed to the subsequent War Production Board, the Office of Civilian Defense, the Office of Price Administration, the Office of Economic Stablization and the War Manpower Commission. However as time went by it became clear that something more was needed than cooption into the Federal bureaucracy to ensure labour's full support for the war effort after Pearl Harbor, and guard against the constant danger of strikes which might threaten war production.

The war economy bristled with other problems: the need to maximise production, minimise inter-union disputes and strikes, avoid bottlenecks, keep prices stable and to avoide profiteering were among the most important. Though Federal government control of the economy increased during the war, the paramount belief in free enterprise meant that such control was always limited. Moreover it was plain that none of the production problems could be solved without the full co-operation of labour. Such co-operation was not to be easily secured. Jurisdictional disputes between unions, like those between AFL and CIO welders in the Kaiser shipyards, had been a constant source of bad publicity and lost production in vital war industries since mid-1940. The Federal government investigation found against the CIO welders, after a long correspondence had taken place between Roosevelt, Hillman, union officials and the National Labor Relations Board.

IV

The NLRB had entered the war years in 1939 as the most important institution in the field of labour relations, interpreter of the Wagner

Act since its constitutionality had been upheld in 1937, and generally favourable to the CIO. Although the war presented peculiar difficulties – greatly increasing the number of representation and certification elections, for example – the questions the NLRB dealt with remained essentially the same, at least at first. However events were to undermine the authority of both the NLRB and the Wagner Act. Wartime disputes eventually expanded beyond the question of union contracts, bothersome though that was, or even pay and conditions, to include employers' 'free speech' and the right of foremen to organize – issues later crucial in the passage of anti-labour legislation stimulated by the unpopularity of many of labour's wartime attitudes and policies.

AFL criticism of the NLRB, which diminished when the pro-labour Harry A. Millis became chairman of the board in 1940, mounted again when its wartime decisions nullified contracts which involved too few workers. In the Kaiser dispute the NLRB examined three of the company's West Coast shipyards where the AFL had required union membership as a condition of employment. In one, only 66 employees worked in May 1941, while in the other two the figure was 191 and none at all in April 1942. Yet in the first yard 10 000 new workers were expected in six months, and all three yards eventually employed some 40 000. The AFL's stake in this was obvious: it was the old game of increasing membership and power, in which the CIO eagerly joined. But as the NLRB pointed out, union membership as a condition of employment was illegal under the Wagner Act unless the unions making the contract had been chosen by a majority of the workers as their bargaining agent.

William Green of the AFL called the NLRB decision in this case 'the outstanding Axis victory of the month' and eventually found a way round it with the notorious 'Frey rider', so named after its sponsor, AFL metal trades president John P. ('Colonel') Frey. The AFL, government officials and a Congressional committee vigorously lobbied by Green recommended continuance of the Kaiser contracts because they had created stable labour relations and increased war production. Yet the NLRB refused to reverse itself during hearings on the complaint.

Accordingly, the AFL sought and obtained from Congress an amendment to the NLRB's 1943–44 appropriations bill, drafted by Frey outside Congress, preventing the Board from invalidating contracts which had been in effect for three months or more. Seldom friendly to the NLRB, the House passed this by the overwhelming margin of 169 to 11, and the Senate by 40 to 25 in July 1943. Legal change thus came in through the backdoor of an appropriations bill. The AFL itself had forced an important breach in the wall the Wagner Act had built around labour's rights. Company unions were protected along with legitimate ones, while 'sweetheart' agreements – made with union leaders who lacked members in the plants concerned, as at Kaiser – were now enforced.

Moreover, the central Wagner Act provision that workers bargain through representatives of their own choosing was weakened. On 19 June 1943 the *New York Times* reported an NLRB protest that the Frey rider would 'immunize the most lucrative labor racket which has perverted the war production program'. The AFL's response was that the Frey rider would stop the CIO poaching AFL members with NLRB support. The NLRB lost 500 000 dollars of its appropriation, had to drop 56 similar cases covering company unions and faced other problems. Congress included the amendment, with minor variations, in subsequent appropriations for the NLRB. Thus the Frey rider served public notice that the NLRB enforced the law against politically powerful opponents at its peril, and that the AFL would continue to support racketeering in the interests of higher membership.

Though the Kaiser issue was the most important point in dispute between the AFL and the NLRB in the war years, the case of foremens' unions and employers' 'free speech' raised other significant issues. The bid to organize foremen, which began in wartime, was in part a result of the CIO drive for new members and in part a consequence of upheavals on the industrial shopfloor which the war itself brought about. This had important repercussions which will be discussed more fully below. For the moment it is enough to note that the attempt to unionize supervisory workers was strenuously resisted by employers, who regarded it as a wholly unaccepable attempt by unions to invade the prerogatives of management.

In a series of test cases, the NLRB had to decide whether foremen were employees within the meaning of the Wagner Act, but it changed its mind several times until the issue was finally resolved after the war. Difficult though this was, the foremen issue could at least be answered with a yes or no. The free speech issue, by contrast, was much harder to resolve, since it involved weighing the constitutional right of employers to speak out against unions, and in favour of the open shop or company unions, against the danger of threats, coercion or other unfair labour practices prohibited by the Wagner Act. As with the problem of foremen's unions, the free speech issue rumbled on for several years until it was given more precise legal definition in 1947.

The speed-up of production was another fertile source of industrial friction during the war. Union leaders argued that productivity had increased, because of worker patriotism, while pay had remained static. S. H. Dalrymple, president of the CIO's United Rubber Workers, told Philip Murray, president of the CIO, that in his industry, 'Productivity had practically doubled and in some cases trebled ... while hourly rates are practically the same'.[21] Throughout the war strikes, unfair labour policies and union excesses continued to preoccupy businessmen, politicians and public opinion, fearful that pay increases would lead to spiralling inflation.

Wartime strikes preoccupied President Roosevelt too, who set the chairman of the Federal Power Commission, Leland Olds, to investigate. Olds had experienced the problem during the 1914–18 war in both Europe and the United States. The 1917 munitions strike in Britain, Olds told FDR, had been led by spontaneous committees of shop stewards. When British strike-leaders had been arrested, others had sprung up in their place. A major cause of trouble had been that strikes had been legally prohibited; and since British labour in 1917 had been much further advanced than American labour in the 1940s, that experience 'may afford a basis for understanding the feelings underlying unrest in America today'. In Sweden, Olds added, steelmakers would not think of operating their mills without having all their employees organized in a union, and the managers of Sweden's steel industry believed labour's status as a full partner in industry must be fully accepted through recognition of the union shop. 'Labour is striving towards permanent economic democracy,' Olds concluded, 'not power as the reactionary press claims. America's future strength may depend on recognition of that fact.'[22]

Against this background Roosevelt told Hillman that the time had come for Congress to set up machinery for treating labour fairly and equally; that 17 million man-days lost in the United States through strikes in the first eight months of 1941 indicated 'the lack of co-operation in the past'; and that 'we can't get to first base ... without your help'.[23] Accordingly FDR summoned a conference of labour and business leaders just ten days after Pearl Harbor to plan new measures for industrial co-operation. After some weeks discussion, representatives agreed to a three-point programme for industrial peace: no strikes or lockouts for the duration of hostilities; peaceful settlement of all industrial disputes; and the creation of a tripartite board with labour, management and the public each represented by four members to be called the National War Labor Board.

Part of the problem facing the new Board was clearly the continuing schism between AFL and CIO, as revealed in the Kaiser disputes. Influenced by FDR, the CIO proposed discussions with the AFL to seek unity. The talks led to agreement to submit all jurisdictional disputes to arbitration, but to little else; and no further efforts to merge were made during the war years. Meanwhile, after December 1941, the President was determined to get a binding 'No Strike' pledge out of both federations now America was fully in the war. To this end, on 22 January 1942 he wrote identical letters to both Green of the AFL and Murray of the CIO arguing that labour's part in the war effort could only become fully effective if both joined the War Labor Board and consulted the White House periodically on all matters concerning labour's part in the war. So, despite Lewis's strenuous objections, the National War Labor Board was established on 27 January 1942. In return for the promise that it would have a voice in determining conditions and terms of employment required by wartime necessity, labour agreed in the national interest to surrender the right to strike, while the War Labor Board, now challenging the authority of a weakened NLRB, would handle all problems which could not otherwise be settled.

V

The immediate result of this agreement in January 1942 was a steep decline in work stoppages: whereas 23 million man-days had been lost in 1941, the total for 1942 fell to only 4.18 million. But as the pressure and tensions of war mounted, this record could not be sustained. Labour leaders argued that workers' interests were being ignored by the Federal government in the powers it now exercised over pay and prices. Green declared that labour had only given the No Strike pledge on the understanding that collective bargaining would be sustained, and that Washington was now following a course wholly inconsistent with its earlier promises. Lewis as usual was far more belligerent and soon defied all government authority to protect the interests of the UMW. Strikes increased markedly in 1943, when a total of 13.5 million man-days were lost, and though they dropped the next year rose again as the war drew to an end in 1945.

Nevertheless, labour on the whole continued to support the war effort, and most unions sought to restrain strikes. Man-days lost actually averaged only one-tenth of 1 per cent of total working time in industry, or no more than one day per worker during the war years. Many of the strikes were unauthorised walkouts or wildcats. Workers whose grievances were intensified by the strain of long hours, speed-ups, complicated bonus systems and other hardships resulting from dislocation and other adverse war conditions took matters into their own hands. They laid down tools or walked out, but having let off steam quickly went back to work. The few more threatening strikes were the exception rather than the rule.

The key to understanding labour's wartime history is the National War Labor Board. A first and vital problem it faced was the issue of union security. It met this problem by adopting the principle of maintenance of membership. Though the closed shop or union shop would not be enforced in contract negotiations – as the Kaiser case had revealed – employees who were members of a union on 1 May 1941, or those who subsequently joined unions, would be required to maintain membership for the life of the contract.[24] Should they fail to remain union members in good standing they would be subject to dismissal. Labour members of the Board accepted this solution without qualification; management representatives acquiesced very reluctantly. Once agreed, however, the principle of maintenance of membership was consistently upheld throughout the war. It ultimately applied to some 3 million workers, or about 20 per cent of those covered by collective bargaining agreements.

This guarantee of both union security and individual freedom of action made a major contribution to industrial peace and was largely responsible for the low level of strikes during 1942. However the War Labor Board soon found itself facing an even more troublesome problem than union security. Rising prices induced by wartime inflationary pressure led unions to demand wage increases at least in line with the rise of the cost of living. When strikes were threatened to enforce such claims, action was needed. The Board first adopted a union-by-union approach. But when the government, gravely concerned about a wage/price spiral, adopted an overall stabilization programme, a more consistent and comprehensive policy was clearly required. Some sort of formula was needed to hold wages in line, yet allow increases plainly justified by the rise in the cost of living endemic during war.

The War Labor Board worked out and applied such a formula, which became the most influential wartime precedent in wage bargaining. In July 1942 workers at the Little Steel companies demanded a wage increase of one dollar a day. Lengthy hearings decided that a rise was justified, but should be limited to an equivalent of the increased living costs between January 1941 – a time of relative price stability – and May 1942, when the government stabilization programme began. Bureau of Labor Statistics reports showed the cost-of-living index had risen some 15 points during this period, and recommended wage increases to be kept to this percentage over existing levels. Accordingly, the War Labor Board on 16 July 1942 awarded Little Steel workers 44 cents rather than the dollar a day they had originally demanded.

The Little Steel formula as it was known became the basic yardstick by which all wartime wage disputes were settled. It had been adopted, however, on the assumption that the new stabilization programme had ended what Board chairman William H. Davis called 'the tragic race between wages and prices', and a 15 per cent pay rise would be fair. This assumption soon proved false. Prices could not be held in line. The War Labor Board found itself trying to reconcile the Little Steel formula with price increases which progressively exceeded the figures on which it was based. By the end of 1942 Hillman had left government service to return to the Clothing Workers, and no labour leader of equal weight replaced him. What made it harder to secure labour's complete co-operation over the Little Steel formula and No Strike pledge was wartime profiteering. The President had anticipated this problem. As he told business leaders at a secret meeting at the end of 1941:

If we get like what happened in the [first] world war ... you almost inevitably get labor trouble. I can hold labor to the present level if I can say to them 'You [industry] won't profiteer, the cost of living hasn't gone up'. I think we can avoid the most dangerous spiral.[25]

Yet profiteering did occur. Lauchlin Currie, an influential Keynesian official at the Tresury, warned that the impact of war on profits had been spectacular, driving them to an all-time high in 1941 and likely to drive them even higher in 1942. Roosevelt was particularly incensed by the fact that some American firms appeared to be making profits from European subsidiaries now under German control, which were effectively part of the Nazi war effort.

His anger and astonishment were increased when American directors of such firms tried to pursuade the government to spare them from Allied bombing. At home, the cost of living had increased a further 7 per cent since December 1941, with the greatest increase – around 10 per cent – occurring in food prices, so hitting the poorest hardest.[26] Rising costs were initially controlled by the Office of Price Administration and by mid-1942 FDR's adviser Leon Henderson was able to report, 'For the first time since November 1940 the cost of living hasn't budged since last month. In fact ... it actually declined by one-tenth of 1 per cent'. Roosevelt commented, 'This is good news indeed', and in April 1943 issued his Hold-the-Line order on prices and wages.

But by then inflation had started again in earnest, and by June 1944 the CIO was arguing that the cost of living had actually risen 43 per cent during the war.[27] Not only did higher prices for food bear most heavily on those least able to pay, but workers directed to war industries frequently faced extra expenditure on keeping two homes, while working mothers had to pay for child care, laundry, meals out and so on. What compounded these problems was the way the October 1942 Economic Stablization Act was working out. It gave Congressional sanction to the government's programme and expanded the War Labor Board's authority beyond the original disputed Little Steel cases and others. Now the Board was obliged to restrict all pay rises to 15 per cent in straight hourly rates unless flagrantly sub-standard conditions existed. For the rest of the war the War Labor Board had two distinct functions: settlement of pay disputes and supervision of voluntary agreements. In both cases the Little Steel formula was now set in concrete as the official ceiling on all wage rises.

Organized labour felt cheated. They had given the No Strike pledge in 1942 on the understanding that they would have more say in determining pay and conditions. Now the Little Steel formula was being interpreted so narrowly it made nonsense of such promises. Employers sought to evade the formula by offering more, and more generous, fringe benefits – a development full of future influence. But in the short term, these circumstances encouraged the rising strike wave of 1943. Labour leaders for the most part tried to control the unrest. Walter Reuther told those who urged union representatives to resign from the War Labor Board that, on the contrary, they should demand greater representation in policy-making boards and the creation of an Economic High Command for the entire war economy. He further urged clarification of war aims and postwar planning. 'The Atlantic Charter must be supplemented by a Pacific Charter for the millions in China and India who long for freedom, security and independence, and in our country by a Mississippi Charter for disfranchised and disinherited white and colored people in our Southern States.'[28]

Such an idealistic world-view was not universal, and a quite different situation developed in the coal industry. The UMW had left the CIO in July 1942, but not re-joined the AFL, so was functioning as an independent union under the leadership of Lewis. He believed the War Labor Board had breached its contract with labour in establishing the Little Steel formula and had no intention of submitting the UMW to its authority.[29] Coal miners had suffered more than other groups of workers because faster war production had led to a much higher level of accidents and deaths. With miners growing more restive and rebellious in consequence, Lewis was fearful that he might lose control of them. Instead he led them in a series of strikes which bluntly defied the Federal government and provided the most dramatic chapter in labour's war at home.

Trouble began in April 1943 when the annual contract between coal operators and the UMW expired. The union demanded not just a raise of 2 dollars a day, but the new concept of portal-to-portal pay, covering the time it took miners to get from pithead to coalface, which could often be as long as an hour.[30] Lewis, as usual, was ready to compromise part of this original demand. Yet the War Labor Board, to which the dispute was referred, treated the UMW case with disdain. Lewis walked out of the hearings, attacked the Board as 'prejudiced and malignant', and announced that while he would not, of course, call a strike in wartime 'the miners were unwilling to trespass upon the property of the coal operators in the absence of a contract'.[31]

This somewhat jesuitical distinction was all the encouragement his members needed. As they began to quit even before the old contract expired, the nation found itself facing the gravest industrial crisis of the war. Fearful of the disastrous effects a coal stoppage would have on production, President Roosevelt gave orders that the coal mines be seized and on 2 May 1943 went on radio to ask the miners to go back to work. Blaming UMW officials for the breakdown in negotiations, FDR warned that every man who stopped mining coal was obstructing the war effort, gambling with the lives of the fighting forces and endangering the security of all the American people. While expressing sympathy for the miners, and promising that any new agreement would be retroactive, he insisted that they must return to work pending further negotiations. The miners returned to work, not because of the appeal of the President of the United States but on the orders of the president of their union. Minutes before the radio broadcast began, Lewis had announced a 15-day truce (later extended to 30 days) to seek a settlement with Secretary of the Interior Harold L. Ickes, who was now directing the mines. But Lewis made no promises about what might happen when the truce expired, nor concessions on his original demands.

Six hectic months followed, punctuated by renewed work stoppages and temporary truces. At one point, the government returned the mines to private operation, but contract negotiations made no progress, the miners struck again, and the government took control again. This time FDR ordered Ickes to reach a special wage agreement, to be approved by the War Labor Board, which would be limited to the period during which the government operated the coal mines. Throughout this period Lewis remained in control and intransigent. He insisted the war was no excuse for the operators to exploit the miners, whose struggle for higher wages was a matter of simple justice. Union president and members were in complete agreement. When Lewis ordered the miners back to work, they went. When he ordered them out, they quit. Whipped up by an anti-labour press, public opinion became increasingly angry and alarmed. Though critical of an apparently powerless President, the newspapers reserved their greatest vituperation for Lewis himself, calling him arrogant, unpatriotic, and heedless of national security in time of war. He treated all this with contempt, pointing out that mining communities had not only sent more than their share of men to war, but had also suffered deaths and casualties 'which exceeded all casualties in the military forces' up to 1943.[32] In return, they had been made to bear the brunt of the wage freeze.

Clearly, this crisis had to be resolved. After the government's second seizure of the mines a compromise was finally hammered out between Ickes and Lewis which met most of the union leader's original demands. In return for increased hours, and the inclusion for the first time of the principle of portal-to-portal pay, the miners settled for an increase of 1.50 dollars a day on prevailing rates. By such expedients the coal settlement conformed, nominally at least, to the Little Steel formula and the War Labor Board reluctantly approved it. Lewis had forced the government's hand. Other labour leaders were bitterly critical of Lewis: the CIO condemned him for undermining wartime agencies and jeopardizing the UMW in pursuit of his personal vendetta against FDR and the legacy of the New Deal.[33]

Walter Reuther agreed, replying to Earl Browder's charges that he was plotting with Lewis and Hitler to wreck the CIO and the country. The CP line of total support for the No Strike pledge was at the other extreme from Lewis, Reuther explained. It meant unconditional surrender by the labour movement to government. 'No responsible labor movement', Reuther concluded, 'can, during a period of war . . . strike against the government . . . without literally crucifying itself. But . . . that does not mean that I am prepared to surrender the American labor movement.'[34] Government should establish adequate machinery for solving labour's grievances and plan for a wide-ranging postwar Welfare State. The Communists remained keen supporters of the No Strike pledge right to the end of the war, and attacked the UAW referendum on the pledge as 'part of a conspiracy against the war effort, President Roosevelt and labor . . . by Reuther . . . the Trotskyites and other pro-Lewis forces'.[35]

Labour's critics could not charge the Communists with conspiring to undermine the war effort. Yet fearful that other union leaders might be tempted to follow Lewis's example, angered by his confrontational tactics, and alarmed by the threat of inflation from the coal settlement and other pay settlements in the spring of 1943, corporate and Congressional conservatives exploited public alarm to seek new legislation which would curb union power.

VI

Such pressure had been building up ever since early 1941. Strongly influenced by hostility towards the CIO during the Little Steel and 'captive mines' disputes, an anti-labour bill brought in by the conservative Democrat from Virginia, Congressman Howard W. Smith, had passed the House in July 1941 and then been delayed in the Senate. During the delay, Mary T. Norton, chairman of the House Committee on Labor, warned the President that 'the situation in the House has become acute and probably dangerous' and offered to advise him on how best to deal with the House on labour matters when Congress reconvened in November.[36] The bill which appeared before Congress listed such issues as the coercive power of one union to prevent an employer bargaining with another; graft and extortion; prevention of more efficient machinery, materials and methods of production; fixing prices; allocating customers; restructuring production; limiting the number of firms and otherwise restraining commercial competition. Calling strikes on government contract work without seeking government arbitration was another cause of complaint.[37]

Pearl Harbor had cut short this clamour for Open Shop and No Strike legislation. Pro-labour members of the administration argued that union solidarity in wartime would best be harnessed by giving the whole labour movement a more responsible role in defence planning along the lines of the industrial council proposals made by Philip Murray. Though the Senate voted the Smith anti-labour bill down, as FDR had hoped, Senate Labor Committee support for industrial councils had come to nothing too. Labour co-operation in wartime was vital; but the Little Steel formula seemed to have been breached, and the No Strike pledge to have failed, by the end of 1943. The coal strikes encouraged Congressman Smith to revive his 1941 proposals in partnership with Senator Tom Connally of Texas. Unrest in the mines and elsewhere clearly helped passage of the Smith–Connally Act in 1943.

This was one of a number of restrictive bills introduced that year into Congress, but the one which acquired the strongest support. Initially, it merely gave clear statutory power to the War Labor Board but then added a whole series of provisions which were clearly anti-labour. It empowered the President, whenever government mediation in a labour dispute failed, to seize any plant or industry where a halt in production threatened the war effort. It further enforced criminal penalties against anyone who instigated or promoted such a strike. However it did not place a ban on strikes where the government had not felt compelled to intervene. In contrast to the existing No Strike policy, and in anticipation of the Taft–Hartley Act of 1947, the Smith–Connally bill in such cases proposed a 30-day cooling-off period, during which the NLRB would hold a strike ballot among the workers concerned. For a government solemnly to conduct a strike vote while seeking to enforce a No Strike policy was quite illogical. The most important of its other provisions was the absolute ban on union contributions being used to help fund political campaigns.[38]

Hostility created by the coal strikes hastened passage of this bill by decisive majorities in both houses of Congress. Labour was incensed. The Smith–Connally Act ignored widespread observance of the No Strike pledge, by applying criminal law, yet at the same time undermined this by allowing strike ballots. Murray called it 'the most vicious and continuous attack on labour's rights in the history of the nation',[39] and Roosevelt promptly vetoed it, arguing that it ran wholly counter to the No Strike policy and would incite labour unrest rather than promote industrial harmony. In testimony to the temper of the times, Congress paid no attention to these arguments and overrode the President's veto to make the measure law on 25 June 1943. The *New York Times* described the War Labor Disputes Act, to give the measure its official title, as 'a hasty, ill-considered and confused measure'. Though never fully invoked, the act and its criminal provision remained on the statute book for the rest of the war. In fact it was counter-productive as far as strikes were concerned.

Though union leaders had bitterly denounced the Smith–Connally Act, they soon learned to take advantage of it. Workers often voted for strikes they had no intention of starting simply to pressure employers during bargaining. In the first three months of the new law, the NLRB held 53 strike votes, of which 47 resulted in a majority for striking, but of these only 15 led to strikes. Yet in the same period at least 500 strikes occurred. Only 34 of the 1919 strikes that took place during the last half of 1943 followed strike ballots. Even in 1945, when unions were more experienced at using ballots tactically, fewer than 5 per cent of stoppages had been authorised by votes. Yet at the same time, the NLRB's small staff had to neglect more important work to conduct them.[40] Strikes declined in 1944 but then increased to record levels in 1945 and 1946, despite the new law.

Moreover the most disturbing crisis occurred in an area which fell outside the Smith–Connally Act when a threatened railway stoppage imperilled the war effort much more seriously than even the coal strikes had done. When talks between railway unions and operators broke down in the autumn of 1943, FDR appointed an Emergency Board to settle the dispute under provisions of the Railway Labor Act of 1926. But when its award went far beyond the Little Steel formula the Office of Economic Stabilization refused to approve it and the railway unions – like the UMW, independent of both AFL and CIO – prepared to strike. Faced with a situation where 'American lives and victory are at stake' Roosevelt seized the railways and announced he would act as arbitrator in the conflict between the Emergency Board and the Office of Economic Stabilization. Before the strike actually began the President upheld the Emergency Board's award. Though this violated the Little Steel formula, FDR justified his decision on the grounds that the railwaymen's generous wage increase was in place of overtime and holiday pay to which they would otherwise have been entitled. The railway unions, which had refused Federal arbitration, now accepted it and withdrew their strike notices. On 18 January 1944 the government restored the railways to private hands where they remained peacefully for the remainder of the war.

Looking back on 1943, Len De Caux, editor of the *CIO News*, summarised the position of left-wingers like himself. He believed the CIO had 'held the fort' against 'a reactionary coalition [which had] seized control of Congress ... many of whose members had been elected by default' because millions of those sent away to the military or on war work had been unable to vote. He concluded:

This coalition has made war against the Roosevelt administration.... Many of the CIO's fights in 1943 revolved around stabilization of our war economy. It fought for extension of democratic rationing, for strict price control, for a victory tax program based on ability to pay, for real social security and for fair wage stabilization.... The CIO demanded equal job rights for Negroes and other minorities and an end to the polltax ... [it] consistently opposed inflexible policies that prevented the remedying of inequalities and the adjustment of wages to increased living costs. It fought long and hard for the rollback of prices to the 15 September 1942 wage-freeze level. . . . Even after passage of the vicious strike-provoking Smith–Connally Act, the CIO emphatically reaffirmed its No-Strike pledge. It has consistently hewed the line of setting victory first, opposing interruption of production for any cause, and mobilizing labour 100 per cent behind the war effort.[41]

Such also was the CP line, and De Caux added that 'along with the above struggles, the CIO in 1943 led the fight in labor's ranks against the disruptive and defeatist policies associated with John L. Lewis'.

Labor Action of Detroit expressed rank-and-file views. 'American labor is fed up with low wages, high prices, wage freezing, job freezing and the whole WLB set up. In Detroit, Pittsburgh, Akron, the coal fields, in big industries and in small industries workers are fighting mad . . . They are demanding WAGE INCREASES . . . AND . . . AN END TO THE NO-STRIKE PLEDGE. . .' The paper also published a list of top executive salaries, ranging down from the 275 000 dollars earned by Tom M. Grindler of Republic Steel in 1942.[42]

Labour unrest during hostilities was of course closely related to problems of union security, pay, conditions, complicated bonus systems, prices and inflation. Yet other underlying problems were equally important and part of the complex social upheaval which the war had brought about. Since Hitler based his appeal on doctrines of racial superiority, and Americans had long viewed the Japanese with suspicion, it became important throughout the war that the United States appear to treat blacks, Jewish and other ethnic groups fairly. No attempt was made to do this with 60 000 Japanese-Americans who, in response to paranoid public clamour after Pearl Harbor, were rounded up and interned in early 1942.

Yet similar threats confronted other minority groups, immigrants and refugees from Europe who had not had time to become American citizens yet worked in sensitive war production industries. Philip Murray sent a memo to the President on behalf of the CIO and his own steelworkers pointing out that such aliens were frequently strongly anti-Fascist and had come to the United States to escape poverty and exploitation. 'Many innocent people are being affected by evacuation,' the memo concluded, calling on FDR to 'provide decent living quarters and useful work for evacuated people in order that their continued support for the war effort be assured'.[43]

Much government effort was expended throughout the war on fair employment practices. Though the Commission dealing with this had only been set up in 1941 under the threat of the black march on Washington, material on the question in the Roosevelt papers is vast, and attention to racial discrimination heralded a decisive shift in race relations which was to last far into the postwar period. Black workers were becoming more mobile again as the war economy created new jobs. In Los Angeles, a major aircraft manufacturing city, public hearings where black, Jewish, Japanese, Mexican and Latin-American groups were all represented discussed ways of tackling racial prejudice.[44] Meanwhile FDR's so-called 'black-cabinet', comprising Ralph Bunche, Robert Weaver and others, grew more influential.

The problem of racial prejudice for unions was revealed starkly during the United Autoworkers' wartime organizing drives at Ford, the last major motor manufacturer to be unionized. Blacks had long regarded Henry Ford as 'the great white father of Dearborn', because he had employed them in large numbers and given them a chance. But under the pressure of union membership drives in 1941 and 1942, Ford's paternalism cracked, revealing the same kind of prejudice he felt towards Jews. By 1942 in Detroit, a city vital both to the aircraft industry and the whole war effort, the UAW had replaced Ford in the eyes of blacks as the provider of better opportunities. Yet the union was not always a reliable friend to black workers. Seniority rules, necessary in union eyes to preserve job security, often gave white workers better claim to the semi-skilled and unskilled jobs they already had. Moreover the UAW leadership was far ahead of its own rank and file in racial attitudes. The Ku Klux Klan infiltrated many UAW Locals, especially at the Packard plant, where nearly half the delegation to the UAW's 1941 convention were Klansmen.

The union's leadership was in a bind. In battling to end discrimination and advance black interests, the UAW constantly risked arousing fears and prejudices in recently-won white members or union officers. But if it soft pedalled on this, it encouraged black contempt and hostility. Though in the long run the UAW played a notable part in accelerating integration and civil rights in the postwar years, in the short run such episodes as the Sojourner Truth Housing Project disorders in 1942 and the full-scale race riot in Detroit in 1943 showed that an important function of unions – even left-wing unions like the UAW – was to reinforce structural weakness within the black community.[45] Just as more than forty years earlier the eminent black scholar and political activist W. E. B. Du Bois had argued that political machines made it impossible for blacks to develop fully independent and effective institutions of their own, so now white-led unions tended to act in the same way, excluding blacks or placing low ceilings on their possible advancement both at work and in unions.[46] Nevertheless, the number of black union members rose significantly from 150 000 in 1935 to 1.25 million by the end of the war.[47]

VII

The dilemma of race was part of a far wider pattern of demographic change within which the whole course of wartime labour relations must be viewed. Older workers, radicalized and unionized by the great CIO upsurge of the 1930s, were by the 1940s being drafted into the military or promoted to foremen and other supervisory grades to replace those that had. Their places on the shopfloor were being filled not only by blacks but by others – women, teenagers, rural Okies and Arkies and mountain people from the Great Smokies – mostly from low-wage, non-union or agricultural jobs. For them, wartime wages were far higher than anything they had ever earned, sometimes by as much as 150 per cent, making unions seem irrelevent. Yet for those still in low-wage industries – textiles, retail and aircraft, for example – labour's initial acceptance of the Little Steel formula kept their pay rises below those in higher-wage work, which seemed no reason to support a union. So veteran industrial unionists saw wartime newcomers – Okies, blacks, women – as disruptive elements now reaping rewards for which others had sacrificed.

Moreover, while widespread promotion to supervisory grades may have improved pay and conditions for millions of workers, it brought new problems too. Inexperienced foremen had to grapple with conflicts and resentment stemming from the demographic upheaval just discussed, while dealing with the chaos of piece-rates and bonuses created by government contracts in the war economy. War production undermined factory discipline and quality standards while stimulating shopfloor militancy, especially when the Little Steel formula became more constricting and discredited. Thus the old foreman system collapsed forever and the new one proved unable to cope.[48]

The problem was exacerbated for management by the union movement which swept through the foremen's ranks after 1941. For although management defeated wartime efforts to organize foremen, the decisive battle on this issue came after the war. Both the calibre and status of foremen had fallen sharply as a result of the wartime draft. As one big employer put it, 'We recognized that in some of our shops the union committee man exercises greater authority than the foreman'; or another in cars, more explicitly: 'If any manager in this industry tells you he has control of his plant he is a ... liar'.[49] Labour unions had been sucked in to fill this vacuum. Management accepted that disciplining the workforce had become, in part at least, a union task. This was a development of major long-term significance for American labour. Increasingly in future its role would be not to lead, but to contain, shopfloor militancy. Despite the rising strike rate through much of the war, unions did manage to contain rank-and-file activism stimulated by all these pressures.

Such control was made easier by the rising real incomes many workers enjoyed despite inflation. The nation's wage bill more than doubled between 1940 and 1944, while average earnings in manufacturing industry rose by 65 per cent. Allowing for inflation, real income went up at least 26 per cent in steel, 36 per cent in coal, 20 per cent in cars and 27 per cent in all manufacturing. True, much of this rising real income came from overtime, which was really a disguised cut in the workers' standard of living. The work week expanded from 40.6 hours in 1941 to 54.2 hours in 1944. So despite these wage advances, many made by poorer-paid workers, the war did not provide labour as a whole with an inordinate increase in living standards. On the other side, corporate profits, after tax, rose from 6.7 billion dollars in 1940 to 10.8 billion dollars in 1945. Agricultural income also rose substantially, partly because of government policy, partly because the world was short of food.

Yet wages alone were regarded as inflationary. The salary of the executive, the dividends of the stock holder and the profits of the farmer, were seen as necessary incentives and the proper reward for competent performances, initiative and willingness to take risks. The outcry from supporters of the Little Steel formula, the labour historian Joel Seidman concludes, 'against the President's proposal to limit individual income after taxes to 25 000 dollars a year suggests that many of those who examined the problems of consumer purchasing power suffered from a pronounced class astigmatism'.[50] Yet most workers prized their new prosperity and job security, and feared it would end with the war. In fact the wartime union drives not only made labour stronger but also helped raise aggregate demand, so stimulating the conversion to the kind of Keynesian economic management which was to be the hallmark of the postwar period.

While economic policy was being transformed, the 1944 Democratic Party nominating convention highlighted the growing political importance of the CIO in the wake of the Smith–Connally Act. The CIO Political Action Committee, a reincarnation of Labor's Non-Partisan League, revealed that far from evolving into the labour party some of its founders had hoped for in the 1930s, the Non-Partisan League had become a mere appendage of the Democratic machine. The PAC favoured retaining the pro-labour incumbent Henry Wallace in the vice-presidential spot, while the AFL backed the more conservative Missouri Senator, Harry S. Truman. Before Truman's selection FDR was said to have warned advisers to 'clear everything with Sidney'. In fact, Roosevelt and his aides cleverly managed the convention and got everything they wanted.

So on election day, when the President won a fourth term, the London *Times* commented 'Crude attempts to invoke the "communist" bogey – whether in the form of alleged subservience to Marshall Stalin abroad or to Mr Hillman's Political Action Committee at home – seem to have conspicuously missed fire.'[51] Later Roosevelt thanked Hillman and the PAC, adding, 'I was glad to learn that the CIO . . . authorised the continuation of the PAC. I can think of nothing more important in the years to come than the continuing political education . . . of the people'.[52] FDR had cause to be thankful: CIO support provided the winning margin in his closest election. In fact, with Roosevelt's death and the rapid onset of the Cold War after 1945, what *The Times* had called 'crude attempts to invoke the "communist" bogey' became much more successful and destroyed organizations like the PAC. The crucial point about the Wallace affair was that it revealed labour's subordinate role in the consensus which was emerging to rule postwar America. Conservative Democrats were more attracted to Henry Luce's 'American Century' than Henry Wallace's 'Century of the Common Man'. Hillman, who died in 1946, spent his last two years trapped between the centuries.[53]

With victory over Germany in sight, FDR had campaigned for re-election in 1944 on a platform which included a strong bid for labour support in the postwar years. His Economic Bill of Rights, proposed in a Chicago campaign speech, was a piece of propaganda couched in Keynesian terms which envisaged huge government investment in industry. Yet such planning was not Socialist–indeed, as the President was at pains to point out, its whole purpose was to head-off any possible Socialist challenge. 'All the measures proposed in this program', he said at Soldier Field on 28 October 1944, 'are . . . designed to make American capitalism and private enterprise work in the same great manner in peace as in war.' War in fact had revealed how to make capitalism successful in the second half of the century.

> Greater output is not the only benefit from this plant expansion. In fact, our benefits also include the wages paid to the labor employed in building these plants, in constructing the machinery to be used in these plants and in operating the plants after they are erected. These payments as wages all contribute to the nation's buying power so that as a nation we will have the money to buy the goods produced by these expanded plants. . . . Why, just the job of *building* these plants and the machinery for them would give America five million more jobs a year than we had in this work before the war. And this does not include the workers who would be needed to operate these plants after they are built.[54]

When Roosevelt spoke these prophetic words no one could confidently anticipate the future. For though the Economic Bill of Rights was by no means fulfilled, the speech did anticipate the trend of postwar economic thinking which developed on Keynesian lines. Labour leaders and employers feared that when the war ended chronic mass unemployment, which had characterized the prewar period, would rapidly return. Acceptance of the idea that the Federal government should regulate and control the economy ensured the opposite outcome.

So the wartime partnership which had grown up, however haphazardly and uneasily, between labour, management and government had important consequences for peace. The role of the War Labor Board was instructive here. Though increasingly criticised by both labour and management, and apparently undermined in the coal and railway disputes later in the war, the Board had done a remarkable and unprecedented job. It had imposed settlements in 17 650 cases of industrial dispute involving more than 12 million workers, and in 95 per cent of these cases averted any further threat to production. It had also approved 415 000 voluntary wage agreements covering some 20 million workers.[55]

This was a gigantic and time-consuming task without parallel in labour history. Despite this, the Board had shaped wartime industrial policy quite differently from the hopes Lewis and Murray had entertained with their industrial council plans. Businessmen and bureaucrats had come to dominate government bodies, with labour leaders playing only a limited role. After Hillman's departure in 1942 no one of similar stature and independence of thought was appointed to government work, and by the end of 1946 Hillman was dead, aged only 59. Moreover as the war went on the Federal government had increasingly restricted collective bargaining and the National War Labor Board had evolved from an agency designed to adjust differences between labour and management into an institution to check wage inflation through wage controls.

Yet the manner in which the Board had found its way round the increasingly rigid Little Steel formula was also significant for the future, though in a different way. Fringe benefits, which boosted workers take-home pay without violating strict limitations on hourly rates, were to become increasingly popular in the 1950s. They provided holidays with pay, allowances for travel time and lunch breaks, shift differentials, incentive and bonus payments, premium rates and the like. Insurance, hospital benefits and other welfare provisions also became topics for collective bargaining. Partly as a result, total union membership rose between 1940 and 1945 from just under 9 to almost 15 million, or from 27 per cent to 36 per cent of the non-agricultural workforce. The CIO had doubled its membership. Labour may have been co-opted into capitalism and given the job of disciplining the workforce; but by bidding up wages, and thus aggregate demand, it had helped solve the riddle of unemployment. Finally, it had built the stable membership in manufacturing industry which would make it a force to be reckoned with in the economic, political and social history of the postwar world.

4. Reconversion and Reaction

I

During the Second World War propaganda played an important part in justifying United States involvement and clarifying her war aims. Utopian notions were current about the kind of world which would emerge once the enemy had been defeated. Yet just as the Cold War crudely was to destroy this optimistic climate of opinion in foreign affairs, so labour relations proved more troubled in the period of economic reconversion after 1945. This came as no surprise to more thoughtful observers. Unlike Britain, where the Beveridge Report, the Butler Education Act, and the whole commitment to full employment and the Welfare State had played a central part in raising wartime morale, American objectives had been much more limited.

Such brilliant pieces of propaganda as Frank Capra's film *Why We Fight* had concentrated on the aggressive policies of Germany and Japan, which had brought on the war, and the need for the United States to act as the champion of liberal democracy. It said nothing about social objectives. Government attempts to limit profits had been less successful than their attempts to limit pay increases. The No Strike pledge, Little Steel formula and wartime inflation had combined to build up a demand for wage increases which was bound to burst when war ended. Meantime, no real progress had been made in ending racial discrimination: the armed forces were still segregated. Despite Roosevelt's optimistic Economic Bill of Rights speech, employers and labour leaders alike believed that once the war had ended the most likely consequence was an immediate return to prewar depression and unemployment. Then in April 1945, on the brink of victory over Germany, Roosevelt died, leaving the whole reform consensus which had emerged since 1935 leaderless. In this situation, management and unions strove to secure what advantages they could from the extraordinary conditions of full employment and economic boom.

This meant that the origins of the postwar strike wave could be seen while the war itself was still in progress. At its peak in 1944 the war effort had absorbed more than half the national output of goods and services, while nearly half the workforce had either been engaged in war production or in the armed services. When these 12 million men and women were demobilised could work be found for them? What could be done for the men, and more importantly the women – now more than a third of the labour force – who had replaced drafted men in factories and mills they had left behind while they went to fight? What of the sheer physical task of retooling plants geared up for war production, such as car factories which now made planes? What about investment, marketing, profits and wages?

More important, in the short term, the Little Steel formula, designed to check wartime inflation, had not in fact controlled profits or prices, but merely kept wages back. This inevitably stimulated union militance while building a pent-up demand for pay increases which was bound to burst soon. As the war drew to a close labour was in no mood to extend the No Strike pledge nor accept a further wage freeze. Labour leaders wanted no more truck with a War Labor Board synonymous both with the hated Little Steel formula and with aggravating delays in pay settlements. They were bent on ending Federal control over wages as soon as possible. Restoring free collective bargaining while shortages of labour were still acute would likely give them a crucial edge in negotiations with employers. These considerations were what shaped the reconversion period.

II

So despite all the talk in 1945 about a planned reconversion to peace, unions soon started to protest. They felt Congress was neglecting civilian workers, in sharp contrast to its generous treatment of servicemen and war contractors. With fighting still raging in both Europe and Asia in the early spring of 1945 such grumbling remained a minor theme. But with FDR's death in April, and German surrender in May, it suddenly became more dominant. Closure of the huge bomber plant at Willow Run, Michigan, later that month meant the loss of 20 000 jobs and threatened a further 100 000 in supply plants. According to their local unions, only 41 per cent of the men and a mere 3 per cent of the women found other jobs in Detroit, and those that did were obliged to accept pay cuts of 25 per cent.[1] As these figures showed, reconversion was particularly hard on women workers, displaced from jobs they had taken during the war by returning servicemen. The same kind of insecurity hit black workers, millions of whom had filled gaps left by white men drafted into the armed forces. Walter Reuther of the UAW wrote to H. W. Anderson, vice-president of GM, urging that the no discrimination order No. 98–6, issued by the President to cover war incentives, be incorporated into future GM contracts; but Anderson thought not.[2] Both women and blacks, lacking seniority or the kind of skills and status which came from having served proper apprenticeships in engineering or other industrial trades, found it hard to find new work once displaced, and almost impossible to earn the kind of money they had made during the war.

Not surprisingly, the number of days lost through strikes, which had declined after the peak year of 1943 when the coal mines were in turmoil, began to increase in the spring of 1945. The sheer number of strikes may not have risen much, but more workers were involved and the stirkes lasted longer. What further worsened the situation was ironically what everyone had been working for: the rapid collapse of Japan. The devastating use of atomic bombs on Hiroshima and Nagasaki in August 1945 took labour negotiators, like everyone else, completely by surprise. No one had expected the interval between victory in Europe and Asia to be so short. Estimates of two more years fighting had been common. Now it was suddenly over in three months. With war news gone, the press began paying more attention to strikes, giving them front-page coverage. Nevertheless the number of man-days lost to strikes, though increasing, still averaged well below two million a month until V–J Day, 10 August 1945.

After that, however, the strike-rate rocketed to 4.3 million in September and double this in October. In percentage terms, working time lost, which stood at one-tenth of 1 per cent early in the year, rose to one-quarter of 1 per cent in the summer and to well over 1 per cent in the autumn of 1945. In 1943, chiefly because of coal strikes, the number of man-days lost had been 13.5 million. In the last four months of 1945 alone this figure was 28.4 million. Clearly this was a serious situation. Yet the CIO tried to put a good face on it. 'Strikes are crowding all other news off the front pages,' it argued. 'Yet ... the loss in work-time from unemployment dwarfs that caused by strikes. .... Man days lost because of strikes, and lockouts [is] about one-thirtieth of the loss due to unemployment.' Moreover, the CIO concluded, strikes which ended in pay increases raised purchasing power thus increasing the general good, while unemployment was a total loss.[3]

This mounting labour unrest took place against a background in which war-control machinery was being quickly dismantled. Labour had wanted the War Labor Board wound up, and wartime controls ended, so that wage rates could be permitted to rise. They felt they had borne the brunt of the wage freeze which stemmed from the Little Steel formula. Moreover, they placed their argument in a wider economic context. The problem was the old one of sustaining aggregate demand. In a clear statement of view about the objectives of reconversion policy, the CIO pointed to the dangers inherent in the sudden dislocation of millions of soldiers and workers, and the withdrawal of consumer demand when the Federal government stopped buying half the 200 billion dollars' worth of goods American workers produced. The loss of extraordinary earnings from overtime rates and wartime bonuses, which accounted for an additional 15–20 billion dollars a year, would be a further blow, which became a major cause of postwar strikes. Wartime savings would help only for a short time, and only if spent. If 60 million people were to be kept working, the CIO concluded, this great hole in purchasing power would have to be filled.[4]

The AFL likewise urged upward revision of wage rates to provide sufficient purchasing power for wage earners to match the nation's productive capacity. The weakening of Federal control over wages was based on a government belief that the inflationary dangers of wartime wage increases would end with the war. Labour fully endorsed that view. It argued not simply that employers could afford increases in wages without increasing prices, but also that it was imperative they do so in order to sustain purchasing power. This in turn was the only way to avoid business collapse and the return to large-scale unemployment. The AFL believed hourly rates could rise 20 to 30 per cent without increasing prices, while the CIO argued that even greater pay increases were possible. 'Manufacturing industry', Philip Murray explained, 'can pay an increase of 31 per cent in basic wage and salary rates, and still earn a 100 per cent more – twice as much takehome profits after taxes than in the prewar years of 1936–39'.[5] Such views, naturally enough, were strenuously resisted by employers. Yet these union arguments about the imperative need to raise demand to avoid a postwar recession soon received authoritative support. On 16 August 1945 Roosevelt's successor, Harry S. Truman, announced a wage policy by which pay increases which did not result in price increases would be free from government control. Truman was in complete contrast to FDR: a fiesty, no-nonsense little Midwesterner from Missouri. But he had inherited the Keynesian/labour coalition from Roosevelt and was to leave his mark on events in the next few years. Truman established a Wage Stabilization Board to function during the transition from a controlled to a free market economy. Yet popular support for economic controls was rapidly diminishing, so the Wage Stabilization Board remained weak and was soon largely discredited among both management and labour leaders.

More important, the Office of War Mobilization and Reconversion estimated in October 1945 that industry could afford to raise wages 24 per cent without raising prices and still earn profits at prewar levels. A few days later President Truman told the nation by radio of the paramount importance of higher wages. 'Unless checked', Truman concluded, 'the . . . wage bill will shrink by over 20 billion dollars. This is not going to do anybody any good. . . . Wage increases are therefore imperative – to cushion the shock to our workers, to sustain adequate purchasing power and to raise the national income. Fortunately', he concluded, 'there is room in the existing price structure for business as a whole to grant increases in rates.'[6]

This background of government wage/price policy is essential to understanding the issues raised by postwar strikes, and the Federal government response to them. The War Labor Board, now in process of being dismantled, was in no position to decide wage rise cases where management insisted on price rises. Employers working on wartime cost-plus contracts had become used to passing pay rises on to customers. The problem was further exacerbated by the loss of lucrative overtime for most workers, and the ample wartime profits most employers had made. Unions naturally sought higher basic pay rates to sustain their members' takehome money. Moreover they wished to justify their demands by showing that higher pay could be sustained by their employers without increasing prices. Employers, in turn, typically replied that their profit position was beside the point, and that there could be no substantial pay increases without corresponding price rises. Throughout the autumn of 1945 labour presented its case within a Keynesian strategic context: purchasing power had to be maintained to sustain rising sales, bigger profits, full employment and general postwar prosperity.

On this analysis, not only could employers afford to raise wages substantially without increasing prices, but also this was essential to avoid business collapse and large-scale unemployment. Though the industrial scene appeared to be moving rapidly towards major confrontation, great expectations were raised by the President's national Labor-Management Conference, which met in November 1945. It was modelled on the conference Woodrow Wilson had held in similar circumstances in 1919.

Representatives of labour and management duly met and conferred, but were unable to make any progress towards formulating the 'broad and permanent foundations for industrial peace and progress' which Truman had set as their target. They did accept the validity of collective bargaining, a significant advance on what labour and management had been able to do in 1919. Moreover they denounced discrimination on grounds of race, colour, creed and gender. But they could not agree on any steps which might break the deadlock in current negotiations. This failure stimulated the rising tide of strikes throughout America; and even as they adjourned this tide came to full flood.

Machinists and shipyard workers in San Francisco went on strike; building service operators and longeshoremen in New York broke off talks; truck drivers in the Midwest quit; while elsewhere oil refinery workers, lumberjacks and glass workers walked out. Union security and takehome pay equivalent to wartime wages were the strikers' demands. By the end of 1945 these strikes assumed even more serious proportions as the major CIO unions launched an all-out attack in mass-production industries. Some 200 000 car workers had struck against General Motors while the Labor-Management Conference was still in session. Two months later 300 000 meatpackers and 180 000 electrical workers quit their jobs. Finally, with even more devastating effect on the economy as a whole, 750 000 steel workers struck. As 1946 began 2 million industrial workers were simultaneously on strike. The number of man days lost in January alone was nearly 20 million and in February 23 million – more than in the years 1943 and 1944 combined.

III

The most significant of all these immediate postwar strikes was that called by the UAW at General Motors. This dispute had been in the making for months. Three days after V-J Day Walter Reuther, who headed the UAW union at GM, asked the corporation for a 30 per cent hourly pay rise. This would maintain purchasing power, but should be done without raising prices: it was familiar CIO policy. But what made the GM strike new was that Reuther challenged the company to open its books to inspection if it denied its ability to meet union demands. He insisted they should not make excess profits at the expense of workers and consumers, and opening the books would demonstrate the link between wages, prices and profits.[7] Reuther went so far as to suggest that GM could probably reduce car prices and still make a profit. The audacity he had shown with his wartime plan to build 500 planes a day was revealed again, this time in terms of the emerging Keynesian consensus that a substantial boost in mass purchasing power was needed to sustain prosperity and full employment.

In reply GM refused to discuss its ability to pay or open its books. The relationship between wages, prices and profits, the company said, was nothing to do with the union. It fell wholly within the prerogatives of management, on which the survival of the whole private enterprise system depended. So far as pay was concerned, GM offered a 10 per cent cost-of-living adjustment, which the UAW refused to consider. The dispute, in short, was vastly more intractable than a mere collective-bargaining dispute or even an issue of principle such as union security. It was an ideological battle in which the union saw itself crusading for social progress, while GM believed it was defending the right of management to manage. So the strike soon became a grim war of attrition. Yet its conduct contrasted vividly with the sit-downs company plants had endured nine years earlier in the decisive events of 1937. Still less was this strike, or any others of the postwar period, fought as the great strikes after the First World War had been. Management made no effort, as it had done in 1919–20, to operate struck plants, bring in blacklegs, scabs and strikebreakers, or to smash the unions. It showed what significant changes had taken place in labour relations during the Second World War.

Nevertheless the strike appeared set for a long haul, accompanied by disputes in other vital sectors of the economy, notably the threatened strike by the United Steelworkers. President Truman was facing nothing less than the complete collapse of his postwar labour policy. Though still wishing to keep government interference to a minimum, he realised he had to act. So on 3 December 1945 he sent a special message to Congress urging a cooling-off period and the creation of fact-finding boards for the GM and steel disputes. Meantime he urged car strikers to return to work and steelmen to stay at their jobs pending these enquiries.

Labour did not comply, but the President nevertheless appointed the boards for the car and steel industries later in December; other boards soon followed, notably in the International Harvester and meatpacking disputes. Reuther reiterated to the car board that ability to pay was the crucial point: if the firm's books revealed it could not do so without raising prices, the UAW would forego the pay increase it sought. GM negotiators argued that the board was not competent to judge ability to pay, because future profits depended upon so many variables, and they walked out. Still, on 10 January 1946 the board recommended an hourly increase of 19.5 cents, 6 cents above the company's offer and more than half the union demand. The board asserted that such an increase was possible without increased prices, conceding Walter Reuther's point. GM promptly rejected this proposal.

So the strike dragged on through February into March. Then events elsewhere, notably in the steel strike which had begun in January, influenced the pattern of negotiations between GM and the UAW. The steel strike was in some ways more serious. It involved far more workers (more than 500 000), was in a basic, nationwide industry, and had led to thousands of lay-offs in other sectors when steel supplies stopped. Yet a simpler issue of pay was at stake, not steel's ability to pay without raising prices or opening its books. The crucial issue indeed was merely the *size* of price increase the government would permit. The board estimated that there had been a 31 per cent increase in the cost of living since 1941, and proposed wage and price increases to compensate for this. When US Steel was allowed a 5 dollar a ton increase, it settled for the 18.5 cents an hour pay rise Truman had suggested. The rest of the steel industry followed suit and the strike ended.

Meanwhile GM had raised its offer to the UAW to 18.5 cents, only one cent below that recommended by the board. Over that one cent GM let the strike drag on for another month, taking losses of 89 million dollars and, more important, losing ground to its competitors in postwar markets, to preserve what it considered management prerogatives.[8] At first, the UAW refused to concede. Then other unions at the plants, notably the Communist-led United Electrical Workers, accepted. So the UAW reluctantly agreed – angry at the way UE had pulled the rug from under them. On 13 March 1946, after 113 days, the GM strike finally ended.[9]

The GM and steel disputes were landmarks in the reconversion scene. The pay rises hammered out in these key strikes set a pattern widely copied throughout industry. From steel the terms of settlement spread not just to the car industry, but to electrical machinery, meatpacking and oil-refining. Yet the GM strike in particular was a turning point for what it failed to achieve. Walter Reuther's views on the long-range aims of labour had made no headway. His objectives had reached far beyond the pay packet. He was convinced that social controls had to be established over big business if workers' interests were to be fully protected and full employment assured. Like Hillman, Reuther believed that unions, on behalf of the workers in industry, and the government, on behalf of the public, should help determine major industrial policies. When Hillman died in July 1946, Reuther was to inherit his mantle as labour's most creative leader. But for the moment General Motors had successfully resisted Reuther's challenge. They had not had to open their books. They had stood out for an extra month rather than pay one penny to settle the strike. They had defended not merely their profit position but the authority of management.

While the struggles with GM, in steel and at other major manufacturing companies turned primarily on wages, with prices as a related issue, at Ford a new and different kind of issue caused conflict. Like GM and Chrysler, Ford had been asked by the UAW in autumn 1945 for a 30 per cent pay rise. It refused to consider this, however, unless the contract was modified to give Ford's management security against the union comparable to the security currently enjoyed by the union against the company. Ford had been the last of the big motor corporations to recognize the UAW in 1941, but it now termed its 5-year relationship an 'unhappy experiment'. It asked the unions to pay 5 dollars a day for each worker who took part in an unauthorized work stoppage, tighten discipline and increase production in other ways. The UAW made counterproposals, and in mid-December Ford offered a 15 cent an hour raise conditional upon increased production and company security guarantees. The offer was rejected, but amicable negotiations continued until agreement was reached some weeks later on an 18 cent rise combined with disciplinary measures for workers who failed to produce enough or took part in unauthorized strikes. Chrysler negotiated a similar settlement about the same time.[10]

All this was part of the employers' counter-attack, which gave the Ford and Chrysler security issues their true significance. Unions were being made responsible for controlling the workforce, and the next essential step for management was to secure their foremen from the possibility of being unionized. Foremen's unions, as we have seen, made much progress during the war, while foremen's authority on the shop floor had been undercut. As a foremen's handbook pointed out, collective bargaining was bound to clip 'the wings of many foremen. . . . The union contract sets forth certain rules . . . [on] many subjects which you and I once considered to be the sole concern of management.' A foreman's study in 1946 reported 'deep anxiety in American industry about the future status of its foremen' while the *Washington Post* on 10 January 1946 stated that 'The question of how far employees should have voice in dictating to management is at present one of the hottest issues before the country'. The national Labour-Management Conference had considered it 'fundamental that there be no unionization of any part of management', while a motor industry director concluded, 'If any manager in this industry tells you he has control of his plant he is a damn liar'.[11]

Important in terms of management's right to manage in the motor industry, the strikes of 1946 revealed the future in other industries too. In postwar industrial relations, pay was beginning to take precedence over industrial democracy or other related issues. The history of both GE and Westinghouse is instructive here. Among craft workers, who formed the vanguard in organizing drives, money itself had not been a major issue in the 1930s. Electrical workers had been mainly concerned with job security, the speed-up, work rules and of course union recognition and security. By the mid-1940s, as the voice of production workers became more audible, priorities had shifted. The demand for shorter hours died with the Great Depression. Workers now favoured overtime rates because they boosted takehome pay, not because overtime limited the hours they had to put in at the plant. When cutbacks in shift times threatened in 1945, and later in 1948, they resisted work-sharing and insisted instead on lay-offs on a strict basis of seniority.[12]

IV

By mid-March 1946 the postwar strike wave, the most disruptive in history, had greatly subsided. But the end had not come yet. The coal industry had been ominously quiet. Mine operators were prepared to follow the pattern established in the steel settlement and grant an 18.5 cent increase. But the United Mine Workers leader John L. Lewis rarely followed the example of others, and he demanded a royalty on each ton of coal to finance a welfare fund. The owners baulked; and on 1 April 1946 some 400 000 UMW members struck in Pennsylvania and West Virginia, in Alabama and Kentucky, and in Illinois and Iowa. The coal dispute continued intermittently throughout the year. Electrical power reductions led to nationwide 'brownouts' – which revealed the importance of coal to the whole nation – until the government took control of the mines under the Smith–Connally Act. Secretary of the Interior Julius A. Krug administered the mines, much as his predecessor Harold Ickes had done during wartime disputes, and called a two-week truce in May. Colliers returned to the pits and on 29 May Krug and Lewis reached an agreement highly favourable to the miners. This established medical and hospital funds, Federal mine safety codes, an 18.5 per cent pay rise, higher vacation pay and, last but not least, unions for foremen. The government further agreed to return the mines to private hands as soon as production returned to normal levels; but the Alabama and Kentucky owners, highly critical of such generous terms, refused to accept them.

Stalemate continued until October 1946 when Lewis accused the government of violating the welfare fund and vacation pay provisions of his agreement with Krug. The government applied for a court injunction restraining further strike activity; Judge T. Alan Goldsborough issued one on 18 November; and two days later the UMW struck again. On 3 December Judge Goldsborough found Lewis and the whole union guilty of civil and criminal contempt, fining Lewis 10 000 dollars and the UMW 3.5 million dollars – by far the largest financial penalty ever imposed on an American union. Lewis promptly appealed, but ordered the UMW back to work.

In March 1947 the Supreme Court, in a 5–4 decision, upheld Judge Goldsborough on the grounds that, despite the Norris–La Guardia Act of 1932, which had ended the use of injunction, the government could obtain one if a strike threatened national welfare and security. The Court reduced the UMW fine to 700 000 dollars and the strike ended. Lewis appeared to have suffered a sharp reverse. Yet the UMW's power was intact. When the mines were restored to private hands on expiration of the Smith–Connally Act in June 1947, Lewis won a new contract. This confirmed all the old gains, raised wages from 11.85 dollars for nine hours to 13.05 for eight, and increased royalty payments for miners' welfare and retirement funds from five to ten cents a ton.

In a reprise of what had happened in 1943, a further strike was narrowly averted on the railways in May 1946. The elaborate machinery of the Railway Labor Act failed to settle wage negotiations, and the government once more turned to a special emergency board. This finally worked out a settlement acceptable to the employers and most unions – but not to the 300 000 strong Railroad Trainmen and Locomotive Engineers, one of the railway brotherhoods independent of both AFL and CIO. With a strike threatening which would entail almost complete shut-down of the nation's commerce, President Truman promptly seized the railways. When the trainmen and engineers began to quit work on 23 May, Truman went on radio the following day to deliver an ultimatum: unless the strikers returned by 4.00 p.m. on 25 May, the government would put troops in to run the railways. With frantic negotiations still in progress behind the scenes, Truman appeared before a joint session of Congress to demand sweeping emergency powers to break the strike.

Not only would he apply for an injunction, rendering strikers liable to fine and prison, but he would deprive them of their seniority rights and draft them into the Army. At a vital point in this dramatic speech, a clerk handed Truman a message that the strike had just been called off. This was all stage-managed: Truman had known this before he began. But he insisted on completing his speech, demanding Congress pass a bill which would apply to all vital industries. Labour leaders were horrified, and not just them: Senator Robert A. Taft, no friend of labour, and later a sponsor of the landmark anti-union Taft–Hartley Act, voted against the bill as a violation of civil liberty. Though the House passed it 306 to 13, the Senate let the bill die quietly in committee when the storm had subsided.

The coal and rail disputes further underlined the extent to which President Truman's labour policy was in ruins. Once seen by unions as their champion in the fight for higher wages, he was now denounced as 'the number one strikebreaker of the American bankers and railroads'.[13] Despite this, 1946 had set new records for strikes. The 116 million man-days lost was three times higher than the previous record set in 1945, so that the two years together represented a record total of time lost. The number of workers involved in these strikes in 1946 also set a new record of 4.6 million, a figure only approached once before, in 1919. The 4985 strikes that occurred – in the oil, lumber, shipbuilding, automobile, steel, electrical, manufacturing, coal mining, telephone, railway and other industries – also surpassed, though narrowly, the earlier record number and hit all sections of the economy.[14] Taken together, the last years of war and the period of reconversion – 1943 until 1947 – had seen a clear increase in labour unrest, however measured.

Nor was it apparent by 1947 that this epidemic was over. Rapid price rises were more than cancelling-out the wage increases unions had won. In one month from mid-June to mid-July 1946 the cost of living rose by 6 per cent, the largest monthly rise since records began in 1913, with food prices alone rising by 13.8 per cent. Between June and December 1946 consumer prices shot up by 15 per cent, food by almost 28 per cent. Unions favoured reimposition of price controls and the continuation of the Office of Price Administration for another year. Philip Murray still retained lingering hopes that his wartime industrial-council plans might be accepted, which doubtless accounted in part for his reluctance to see the lifting of the No Strike pledge and economic controls after the war.[15] But the Office of Price Administration, on which the influential Keynesian economist

J. K. Galbraith had served, had seen its powers severely curbed by the postwar Congress. Profits on the other hand were the highest in history; after tax one-third higher than they had been in the best of the prewar years. Manufacturers and farmers were benefiting from the very price rises which impoverished industrial wage workers. In such circumstances an irresistible demand was building up for a second round of wage increases by the end of 1946. The whole idea of 'wage rounds' was new; but it was soon to become an intrinsic part of postwar pay bargaining – another sense in which the postwar years set important precedents in industrial relations.

Yet the course of events in 1947 was rather different from the previous year. Having tested out each other's mettle in 1946, both labour and employers in the CIO sector of industry wished to reach pay settlements without more damaging strikes. Though Walther Reuther had been criticized by some for challenging GM the previous year to open its books instead of sticking simply to the issue of pay, his dynamic leadership of the strike had helped him defeat R. J. Thomas and so win the presidency of the UAW two weeks after the GM strike ended: an event discussed fully in the next chapter. In 1947 the CIO followed the UAW's example by engaging an independent economist, Richard R. Nathan, to prepare an analysis for them as they entered the next pay round. The Nathan report concluded that corporate profits after tax in 1947 would support a 21 per cent pay rise in manufacturing industry and a 25 per cent increase in total corporate business without an increase in productivity or expansion of volume, and without reducing after-tax profits below the 1936–39 level.[16]

Nathan prepared similar economic briefs in 1947 for both the United Steelworkers and UAW which proposed a 23.5 cents an hour rise. Nathan's work sparked off vigorous debate about the proper levels of prices, pay and profits, and the part played by pay and profits in a capitalist economy. Spokesmen for industry, along with other economists, pointed out that Nathan had selected depressed base years for his comparison of corporate profits. Yet 1936–39 were the years that had been commonly used in all postwar comparisons. A wage/price spiral clearly existed, but in its final report the government's Wage Stabilization Board came down clearly on the side of labour in this controversy. 'Contrary to popular theory,' it concluded, 'that the rise in prices was caused by the pressure of wage increases, our experience leads us to believe that the causal connections were more nearly the reverse.'[17]

Labour embarked on the second round of pay talks with an effective campaign that placed its demands within a Keynesian context of serving the public good. 'There is no question of the ability of our great corporations to pay', wrote Philip Murray, 'and to re-fill the reservoir of our purchasing power.' Without this, he concluded, there was grave danger of economic depression.[18] On the same day President Truman endorsed Murray's view, when he warned Congress in his State of the Union message of the risk of a 'marked decline in real purchasing power of great numbers of consumers resulting from the large price increases in the second half of last year'.[19] In lengthy testimony to the Senate Labor Committee in February 1947, Murray blamed government agencies, including the War Labor Board, for failing to secure 'an orderly transition' from war to peace. 'With the government having capitulated on price and profit regulation, only labor – with its demand for wage increases – stands as a major force actively striving for a proper distribution of purchasing power.'[20]

Against this background the first major break in the 1947 wage negotiations came on 16 April without a strike: GM agreed with the United Electrical and Radio workers on a pay increase of 15 cents an hour, of which 3.5 cents was for paid holidays and other benefits. For the second time during the reconversion period the UE had helped set the pattern by accepting a figure lower than the UAW had demanded – an interesting example of how Communist-led unions were often more conciliatory than a non-Communist one. On 20 April the United Steelworkers agreed to accept a wage increase from US Steel of 12.5 cents an hour, with an added 2.5 cents to reduce wage differentials. Four days later GM and the UAW settled for a direct wage increase on the same basis as UE. Chrysler fell into line two days later, as did Bethlehem, Republic and other Little Steel companies the following week. As in 1946, but this time without strikes, a new pattern had been set which was widely copied through industry. Ironically, in view of the Red Scare brewing in the nation as a whole, this conciliatory mood had been set by a Communist union.

V

Labour had revealed new powers and conducted huge strikes

without encountering the violent employer counter-attacks of 1919 and 1937. Nevertheless, the assault by business on price control during reconversion between 1945 and 1947 had been wholly successful. Moreover, the 1946 Employment Act had not guaranteed liberal Keynesian intervention by the Federal government to support capital formation and effective demand at or near full employment levels. The promise held out by Roosevelt's Economic Bill of Rights speech had not been fulfilled. On the political front, labour was losing even more important ground: attempts to revive the New Deal in Congress in 1944–45 had failed miserably. The limited success of the CIO Political Action Committees in defeating conservatives in 1944 had not been repeated in 1946, when the staunchly reactionary 80th Congress had been elected. With Republicans in control at a time of mounting labour unrest, anti-labour legislation was to be its first order of business.

Worse, since 1938, when it had actually opposed the Fair Labor Standards Act, AFL leaders themselves had actually helped draft several of the restrictive clauses now to be incorporated into effective anti-labour legislation.[21] For just as employers' callous and brutal treatment of their workers had rallied public sentiment behind the principles of the 1935 Wagner Act, so in 1947 perceived union indifference to public reaction helped create a climate of opinion which made the severely restrictive Taft–Hartley Act possible. Wartime strikes, undemocratic union practices, mounting anti-Communist hysteria, racial discrimination, the taint of racketeering, jurisdictional strikes and other abuses, culminating in the postwar strike wave, all caused mounting criticism of unions. The problem was compounded by the unions themselves. Had they shown any willingness to reform, or even confront perceived problems, restrictive law might have been avoided or softened.

But unions offered no proposals of their own and simply resisted all proposals made by others. Such short-sightedness was heavily punished with the Taft–Hartley Act. This measure opened a new chapter in American labour law. Its roots were to be found largely in the industrial relations conflicts and controversial practices of unions during the war and reconversion periods. Its passage marks the point of transition between reconversion to the postwar era, and the end of a 12-year period when the Wagner Act had prevailed.

Powerful anti-union forces building up since the late 1930s had resulted in the wartime Smith–Connally Act. Employers and manufacturers carried on a vigorous popular campaign against unions as a monopoly, citing industry-wide bargaining, the closed shop and secondary boycott as evidence of monopoly power. They proposed that secret ballots be held before strikes; that strikes be limited to wages, hours and conditions; that mass picketing be outlawed; and that employers not be required to bargain with foremen. The large number of such measures introduced in wartime became a flood once hostilities ended. The one which attracted most attention was the Ball–Burton–Hatch bill in June 1945. This complex measure, drafted by a group headed by Don Richberg (FDR's now discredited labour adviser) was designed to head-off more punitive measures. Based on the 1926 Railway Labor Act which Richberg had helped draft, it provided for cooling-off periods, adjustment procedures, voluntary arbitration and fact-finding boards. Strikes which endangered the public could be settled by compulsory arbitration, and unions – as well as employers – could be found guilty of unfair labour practices. Other provisions underlined how far Richberg had moved from his previous pro-labour stance. Union security was to be restricted, union interference with management rights outlawed, Federal jurisdiction over labour disputes reduced, and wide areas under the authority of the NLRB since 1935 to be returned to the authority of the States. Labour attacked such proposals, while Congress waited for the outcome of Truman's Labour–Management Conference.

When the conference collapsed Congress decided to act, and it had plenty to bite on: on the first day of the new session, 17 labour bills were introduced in the House, with the Senate not far behind. Within two weeks, more than a hundred such measures had been proposed in Congress. From all this activity a bill backed by Congressman Francis Case of South Dakota emerged, clearly revealing the temper of Congress. Passed by the House during the great wave of strikes in early 1946, it had languished when the disputes were settled. But then the dispute in coal and on the railways later that year pursuaded the Senate to pass it too.

The Case bill set up a Federal Mediation Board, prescribed a 60–day cooling-off period before any strike could be called, and stripped workers of their Wagner Act rights if they quit during the cooling-off period. It also banned secondary boycotts and jurisdictional strikes, while authorizing injunctions to stop obstructive or violent picketing. It so restricted labour's historic right to strike that President

Truman promptly vetoed it, arguing that it dealt with symptoms, not causes. Anti-labour forces in the House were only five votes short of the number needed to override this veto, and the mid-term elections of November 1946 greatly strengthened their hand. Republicans interpreted their landslide victory at the polls as a mandate to take even more drastic action against labour. More than 30 States had passed laws restricting labour's rights on the closed shop, the union check-off, the right to strike, unfair labour practices, political activity, financial affairs and elections, secondary boycotts, picketing and much else. Such local initiatives went hand-in-hand with the legislative drive in Washington which culminated in the Taft–Hartley Act.

Congressman Fred A. Hartley of New Jersey and Senator Robert A. Taft of Ohio introduced their bills separately in the House and Senate in April 1947. They had a stormy passage, for it was clear that not just labour but the whole New Deal approach to social legislation was under threat. The more severe provisions incorporated in the House were somewhat liberalized by the Senate. For example, it defeated – but only by the margin of a single vote – the proposal to restrict industry-wide bargaining which Taft had supported. Yet in its final form it very clearly reflected the strong conservative reaction against organized labour. On 20 June Truman vetoed it, as he had the Case bill, declaring that it would encourage rather than discourage strikes and 'make the government an unwanted participant at every bargaining table'.[22]

This time conservatives in both parties had the votes to defeat Truman, and they argued that he had completely misrepresented the Taft–Hartley Act's provisions. The House at once overrode the veto by 331 votes to 83, and three days later the Senate followed suit by 68 to 25. In both cases large numbers of Democrats joined Republicans in making the Taft–Hartley Act the law of the land. This Dixiecrat/Republican conservative coalition, which was largely to control Congress in the postwar period, had started to emerge as far back as the mid-term elections of 1938, but was now assuming the dominance it would enjoy in the 1950s and 1960s.

The Taft–Hartley Act was a long and complicated measure. Its declared purpose was to restore that equality of bargaining power between employers and workers which conservatives contended that the 1935 Wagner Act had destroyed. The rights guaranteed labour under Wagner were now matched by specific safeguards for the rights of management. Employers were given full freedom, short of threats or inducements, to express their views on union organization. Their right to 'free speech' had emerged as an issue in wartime, along with the foremen's unions and the damaging 'Frey rider' to NLRB appropriations in 1943. Employers were also authorized to call for elections to establish bargaining units. At the same time unfair labour practices were extended to include coercion, secondary boycotts, juridictional strikes or refusal to bargain collectively. Taft–Hartley also included a provision which weakened union security: in many ways this was the heart of the legislation. It expressly banned the closed shop, required highly complicated voting procedures to establish the union shop and – most significantly – left the door open to even more severe anti-union legislation by the States. Section 14(b) – a sort of mirror image of the celebrated section 7(a) of the NRA codes which had protected unions – permitted the States to bypass Federal law by the simple expedient of themselves banning the union shop. These so-called 'right-to-work' laws actually hampered further union growth more than anything in Taft–Hartley itself.

Other restrictions included 60 days notice to end or modify a contract, the outlawing of political funds, and making unions suable in Federal court for breach of contract. In a measure which revealed the tidal wave of anti-Communism now mounting in the nation, union officers were required to sign affidavits affirming that they were not members of the Communist Party or any organization supporting it. In Title II the Act broke new ground with an elaborate formula for dealing with strikes which created a national emergency. The President could apply for what was in effect an 80-day injunction against any strike found to imperil the nation's health or safety. Should negotiations held within that 80-day cooling off period fail, the President was to make appropriate recommendations to Congress. Significant administrative changes included an enlarged NLRB which had already become markedly more hostile to labour, and a new Federal Mediation Service.

Enlargement of the National Labor Relations Board, and appointment of a new general counsel, touched a raw nerve in union circles. Labour had been losing confidence in recent NLRB decisions, and was outraged when a former Board member, Gerard D. Reilly, whose rulings labour had bitterly opposed, became consultant to the Senate committee considering Taft–Hartley. The Act finally dealt with a problem which had been working its way through successive NLRB decisions right up to the Supreme Court for many years, and settled it authoritatively in a way which inflicted a decisive reverse against labour. Rapid growth of unions in mass-production industry since the 1930s, and the drafting of experienced men to the armed forces in wartime, had created a major crisis among foremen and supervisory workers, discussed in the previous chapter. The issue of the right of foremen to join unions was now brought to a conclusion.

Craft unions had long included foremen, but they had been excluded from mass-production industries until the Second World War. The rapid growth of powerful unions then made foremen dissatisfied, as they saw men under them win pay rises, grievance procedures and other benefits they themselves were denied. The wartime promotion of inexperienced foremen, struggling to enforce complicated wartime bonus payments, exacerbated the situation. Matters reached a head after June 1941, when the Ford Motor Company, having changed its mind overnight about recognising the UAW–CIO, signed an agreement with the union giving production workers substantial wage increases. Angered by their failure to receive corresponding rises to maintain their differential, Ford foremen launched the Foremen's Association of America in September 1941, which spread rapidly through the motor industry in Detroit and reached peak membership of 32 000 in the spring of 1945.

Yet it was the coal fields, where foremen were also organized, that presented the NLRB with its first test case early in the war as to whether or not foremen were 'employees' within the meaning of the Wagner Act. The majority, made up of NLRB chairman Harry A. Millis and the doyen of industrial relations William M. Leiserson, held that a foreman was in a dual position. Though an employer to the men under him, he was an employee of the firm, and this latter role entitled him to the benefits of the Wagner Act. Gerard Reilly dissented on grounds that the ruling would promote industrial strife. Stimulated by this favourable decision, the foremen's union grew rapidly, and in February 1943 won a consent election among Packard Motor Company supervisors. In March it signed an agreement with Ford covering six classifications from shop foremen to general foremen. Meanwhile, management spokesmen in the coal, motor and other industries protested that unionization of foremen would undermine discipline, reduce production, and compromise management's right to manage. GM president Charles E. Wilson lobbied Congress, while Representative Howard W. Smith of Virginia introduced a bill to forbid employers from dealing with unions which admitted foremen to membership.

While this was going on, the UMW demanded that its next contract should cover 50 000 supervisors in the coal industry. Then on 11 May 1943, in the Maryland Drydock case, the NLRB reversed its earlier decision in the coal case, holding now that units of supervisory workers were not appropriate under the Wagner Act and would impede collective bargaining and managerial efficiency. John M. Houston, a new member of the board appointed in Leiserson's place, had joined Reilly to form the majority against chairman Harry Millis's vigorous dissent. He believed earlier delay over dealing with the Kaiser union-recognition case had led to the disastrous Frey rider in 1943, while Board members' actions sometimes encouraged suspicion that their decisions were in part politically motivated. The Maryland Drydock case, for example, had been decided in haste to preempt action by the House Military Affairs Committee, which was then considering a bill to exclude foremen from bargaining rights. More significant (in view of the Frey rider cut in NLRB appropriations), the Board was shortly to appear before the Appropriations Committee to discuss its financial allowance.[23]

But the foremen's movement continued to grow, and in early 1945 the NLRB heard another case, this time involving the Foremen's Association at the Packard Motor Car Company. Because of the importance of the issue, and its widespread impact, the Board invited management in other industries to submit briefs, which they did. This time Houston joined Millis to hold that foremen were entitled to self-organization, while Reilly dissented. After so many changes of mind, this decision was appealed and while it moved through the courts other unions, notably the UMW in the Krug–Lewis agreement of May 1946, won the right to organize foremen. On 10 March 1947 the Supreme Court, in a 5–4 decision, upheld the NLRB decision in favour of foremen's unions in the Packard Case as being within the terms of the Wagner Act. Coming at the moment it did, this narrow Supreme Court decision made certain that the Taft–Hartley Act would put the matter beyond further dispute and outlaw foremen's unions, which it duly did.

VI

With hindsight, ultimate defeat by employers and Congress of foremen's unions, the NLRB and even the Supreme Court was a major turning point. Failure to win the right to organize foremen, like Reuther's failure to get GM to open their accounts, was a clear indication of the limits of union power. Indeed in some ways it represented a high point above which unions have never since been able to climb. Labour could be forgiven if it did not see this so clearly in 1947. For despite the Taft–Hartley Act, the failure to unionize foremen and other problems, the situation still looked promising. Workers and the labour movement had found the aftermath of the Second World War fundamentally different from the First. Not only did economic expansion, inflation and relatively full employment between 1945 and 1947 compare with economic contraction, deflation and unemployment between 1919 and 1921; more important, the emergence of stable unions and peaceful collective bargaining in mass-production industries had by 1947 become essential to the well-being of the economy. Organized labour may not have hit all the targets some of its leaders had aimed at in wartime. But it had certainly not shrunk back to its prewar state, as John L. Lewis had feared it would in 1940. The reconversion period between 1945 and 1947, characterized by business prosperity, full-employment and rapidly rising prices, proved a favourable climate for continued union growth. The AFL had some 7 million members, the CIO 6 million and almost 2 million – railway brotherhoods, coal miners – were unaffiliated. This meant that some 15 million workers were covered by union contracts in 1947, compared with 10.3 million in 1941.

Union power reached beyond union membership: wages and conditions for many unorganized workers were strongly influenced by the terms won by organized sectors of their industries. The great schism between AFL and CIO still remained a problem. Once again in 1946, as in the war years, the two bodies met to try to arrange a merger, but again without success. The problem was urgent because of pending Taft–Hartley anti-labour legislation. The CIO took the initiative after the mid-term elections, and when Taft–Hartley was actually being debated talks took place, at which the CIO suggested steps towards unity. In January 1946 the UMW, which had broken with the CIO in October 1942, had rejoined the AFL after nearly a decade's absence. Their 600 000 members were a major gain for the AFL, of which Lewis immediately became vice-president, and the AFL used this as an example of how unity might be achieved.

But the CIO feared the independent jurisdiction of its industrial unions would not be sufficiently protected within a merged labour organization, and criticized racketeering in some AFL construction, longshore and transport unions. For his part, the conservative William Green of the AFL rebuffed the CIO charges about gangsters and argued that Communists in the CIO were the real stumbling block. Though all this played its part, it was old rivalries among AFL and CIO leaders – between Lewis, Green and Murray, or Dubinsky and Hillman – which did more than anything to prevent a merger. Hillman's death in 1946 robbed the CIO of its subtlest operator and extinguished all hope of merger not only that year but also for another decade.

Despite their failure to re-unite, both the major labour organizations had long agreed on one thing: the key to postwar union growth was to unionize the South. 'Operation Dixie' had originally been conceived by the CIO in the 1930s as its next step after organizing Northern industry. This first attempt to organize in the South had revealed the limitations of labour's influence. The Textile Workers Organizing Committee had been set up under Hillman's leadership in 1937 and aimed at the Southern textile industry. TWOC's mass membership, FDR's purge of conservative Southern Democrats and the impact of the Fair Labor Standards Act would combine, liberals hoped, to make the Democratic Party a permanent force for economic and social reform. Unionizing the South's key industry would break the power of the planter and merchant–manufacturer oligarchy. The result was quite different. Although TWOC began well, it was struck down by the Roosevelt recession, which made textile workers fearful for their jobs. Then the Fair Labor Standards Act met tenacious Congressional opposition, backed by the AFL, in 1938 and drove a wedge between the CIO and the farm lobby. Finally, it was watered down out of concern for farmers, who feared its effects on agricultural wages, so that only one-fifth of the workforce fell within its provision, and just 325 000 workers gained its initial 25 cents-an-hour minimum wage. By 1940, textile organizing in the South had been abandoned.[24]

After the war the South seemed ready. Unionization there still lagged far behind other sections, but the war had greatly accelerated industrialization. A large slice of the rural population, particularly blacks, had moved to the cities, attracted by far higher wages in wartime industry. The great prize in Operation Dixie was textiles, now largely shifted to the South from New England, and the leading manufacturing industry in the area. Yet many non-union workers could be found in other industries: lumber, furniture, chemicals, food-processing, garment-manufacturing, the service trades and elsewhere. Their lower levels of pay were a constant threat to the higher rates built up so painfully by unions. Yet the initial failure to organize the textile industry in the 1930s had been followed by successes elsewhere during the war. In steel, for example, unions had secured a breakthrough, particularly in the Alabama mills at Birmingham. In the South's other great basic industry, coal mining, the UMW, under threat of a national strike in 1941, had forced government defence contractors to accept a union shop and the abolition of Southern wage differentials.

Resistance to Operation Dixie, which was fiercely intense, came from Southern Dixiecrats, large cotton landlords and capitalists. Yet it was no worse than national employer opposition unions had successfully overcome in the 1930s. There were several reasons why the outcome was different after 1945. First, as we have seen, the climate of national opinion was far less favourably disposed towards unions than in the New Deal. Second, the continuing struggle between AFL and CIO undoubtedly took a heavy toll in the South. More important, the comparative isolation of many Southern industrial towns made the embattled anti-unionism of local employers and officials harder to defeat. But the main reasons for the postwar failure to organize the South was that unions themselves were ambivalent about it, while the conservative 80th Congress had closed down the Fair Employment Practices Commission in June 1944. 'Organizing efforts', in Joel Seidman's terse phrase, 'were complicated by the race problem'.[25]

During the wartime upheaval the CIO, for all its rhetoric, had been reluctant to confront the problems presented by black workers fully. The situation remained the same postwar. However anti-discriminatory the views of union leaders such as Reuther, the white working class themselves were often deeply prejudiced, especially those who had recently come from the South in search of work. Racist demagogues like Father Coughlin and Gerald L. K. Smith had had a large following among Flint carworkers at the height of the 1930s sit-down strikes. During the war the Ku Klux Klan dominated many UAW Locals at the Packard Plant, and the union was on the horns of a dilemma as the 1943 race riots in Detroit had shown. If the leadership moved on integrating blacks into unions they risked losing rank-and-file white support only recently recruited. But if they failed to act, they would not enrol black members and would block off a whole area of future growth. Even the Communists, who always placed high priority on organizing blacks, and had won great prestige for defence of the Scottsboro boys and the Alabama Sharecroppers Association in the early 1930s, wound up such work later in the decade. The Communist-led New York City transit workers similarly were reluctant to attack discrimination in the 1940s for fear of losing their white majority power base.

The second reason why the labour leadership soft-pedalled Operation Dixie was fear of weakening the Roosevelt coalition. The rebirth of the Democratic Party during the New Deal had coincided, and in a sense depended upon, the rebirth of American labour. Yet the New Deal coalition had not depended solely on the labour movement, but on Northern liberals, Western farmers and sympathetic capitalists.

The labour movement may have been the great beneficiary of the New Deal. But the South had provided the party's bed-rock foundations since Reconstruction and did so right through the 1950s. With Roosevelt dead, Republicans back in power in Congress, Taft–Hartley on the statute book and a Presidential election looming in 1948 which the Republicans were expected to win, now was not the time to rock the boat.

In 1948 some Southern Democrats led a Dixiecrat breakaway when the party adopted a strong civil rights platform; part of the left supported Henry Wallace and rapprochement with the Soviet Union. Truman's re-election in November was crucial if Taft–Hartley was to be repealed, and the overriding importance of this issue in 1948 is shown in the next chapter. Yet, equality for blacks was essential for future growth. Fear of the impact this might have, both on labour's rank and file and on Southern Dixiecrats, inhibited labour leaders from backing it fully. In that sense, short-term considerations blinded labour to its long-term interests.[26]

Yet it could be argued that Operation Dixie was not a failure. The AFL boasted 425 000 new members, the CIO 280 000 as a result of

Southern organizing drives by 1947. Though the South remained the bastion of non-unionism in manufacturing, union membership in other industries still increased proportionally more in the South than any other region over the next generation, despite the influence of race and 'right-to-work' laws. Few blacks showed in this growth though, and in 1947 black workers' wartime gains had been, as women's had, last. Unable to rely on strong union support, and lacking both seniority and skills, blacks had been the first to be laid off, along with women workers, during reconversion. Black workers' problems were exacerbated by the fact that they had found themselves concentrated in wartime industries which found it most difficult to reconvert to a peacetime economy: tanks, munitions, small arms and explosives.

Added to Taft–Hartley, the problem of Operation Dixie, ambivalence about race and the vulnerability of blacks came mounting attacks on Communists within the labour movement. So by the late 1940s the period of rapid growth and dramatic confrontation was over. This was less to do with Taft–Hartley than with the changed public mood which had made that Act possible. Since the 1930s industrial relations had been shaped by the combination of two forces: thoughtful, effective labour leadership responding to insurgent rank-and-file pressure. Those days were done. Management had regained the initiative, and its first task was to persuade labour leaders of the dangers posed by their own insurgent members. Moreover, starting with the contract the UAW signed with GM in 1948, automotive firms and their unions began pioneering a new relationship which set the pattern in other industries in the 1950s. Keynesian ideas were winning wider acceptance. Worker productivity would finance wage increases, cost-of-living adjustments, extensions of the fringe benefits begun in wartime, even a form of guaranteed income. In return unions agreed to long-term contracts. Management could then plan more effectively, leaving unions to discipline the workforce and stop wildcat strikes.[27] 'Companies and unions revealed', David Brody has written, 'the common intent of their encompassing contractual relationship – the containment of spontaneous and independent shopfloor activity'.[28] In this situation, the loss of blacks and female unions members could be forgotten. But before this corporate liberalism, as historians call it, could really be made to function, Communist influence would have to be removed from American unions lest it challenge this emerging consensus capitalism.

5. Purging the Communists

I

In the late 1940s industrial peace had been traded for rising standards of living. Wages had replaced other demands, such as social reform, industrial democracy or co-partnership as the chief postwar goal of the labour movement, and union leaders had actually enforced the deal. In return for higher real wages, management was left with a free hand in controlling the labour process. Consensus capitalism had come of age. Yet the main obstacle in the path of this kind of corporate liberalism in postwar America, many labour and management executives believed, was the continuing presence within the labour movement of Communists.

The Communist Party itself had always been small in the United States, and its political importance minimal. Still it influenced, and even led, some unions in the CIO, and the position of these Communists and left-wing unionists had been enhanced by Popular Front attitudes in the 1930s, and wartime alliance with the Soviet Union. So the defeat of Communist unionists in the CIO between 1945 and 1950 was a decisive event. The United States alone among Western industrial nations had no credible Communist or Socialist party or overt left-wing influence on labour unions. The defeat of the Communists reinforced this trend, and enabled American labour leaders with social-democratic beliefs to distance themselves from the Communist left to play an energetic and effective part in supporting American Cold War policy. By 1948 both AFL and CIO were backing the anti-Communist labour movements of Western Europe and Latin America.

Rank-and-file Communists had offered a style of class-conscious union leadership which would have challenged the emerging liberal consensus, and moreover gave top priority to organizing black workers. Communism was, of course, a revolutionary creed, and fear of subversion had deep roots in American history. Specific fear of Communism went back to the time when Marx sent the First International to New York in 1872, to the Red Scare after 1917 and to the Red-baiting and probing of the Dies Committee in Congress in the 1930s. Yet the CIO had managed to maintain a mutually beneficial relationship with Communists and the fellow-travelling left since 1935. The CP had provided some of the CIO's most effective organizers: a small but dedicated cadre of local activists. Later they had formed part of the anti-Fascist, social reformist Popular Front as war clouds loomed after 1937 and, following the embarrassing interlude of the Nazi–Soviet pact between 1939 and 1941, benefited from the pro-Soviet atmosphere of the war. With the onset of the Cold War after 1945 the mood changed rapidly and completely.

Yet even without the Cold War, the problems Communists encountered in the American labour movement were deeply rooted and largely of their own making. In the 1920s the party had made virtually no headway because American conditions, and working-class attitudes in particular, failed to conform with the Moscow line. This strategy changed in 1935, so that with passage of the Wagner Act and the upsurge of unions which followed, Communists found themselves for the first time working with the grain of history rather than against it. Even so they had made bitter sectarian enemies on the left among Trotskyites, Socialists and others who had challenged their tactics and objectives. Real trouble started in 1939. In March, for tactical reasons related to the anti-Fascist Popular Front, the CP backed a weak man to lead the UAW. The intervention of the party leader Earl Browder at the UAW convention in March 1939 has been discussed above in chapter 3. By siding with such senior CIO anti-Communists as Hillman, Lewis and Murray in support of the pliable R. J. Thomas as president, Browder had compromised the party. His tactics may have been determined by a desire to keep the anti-Fascist Popular Front in being; but within six months the Hitler-Stalin pact, which precipitated war in Europe, had torpedoed the Popular Front and placed the CP in the untenable position not simply of opposing the war but actually supporting Hitler. In June 1941, when Germany invaded the Soviet Union, the American CP was able to join the anti-Fascist front again, and by the end of the year United States participation in what was now a world war partially restored the old Popular Front. Such cynical changes in party line, dictated by the Comintern to support Soviet diplomatic objectives, damaged the party's standing in the United States. More important, slavish support for American government attempts to restrict pay and stop strikes during the war isolated the Communists from anti-Communist union militants and working-class activists in general.

Harvey Levenstein's account of these events concludes, 'It is stupefying to think that something as important as the political structure of the postwar American labour movement may have been decided by a puffed-up Communist bureaucrat rushing to Cleveland on an overnight train.'[1] Of course, the wartime and postwar political history of American labour is much more complex than that. What can be said is that during the war and after some CIO union coalitions were prepared to accept Communist support, while others vigorously repelled it. Throughout hostilities President Roosevelt kept close contact with both pro- and anti-Communist factions, using his wife Eleanor in her usual role as go-between with the left, despite the fact that the CP's abrupt change of line in August 1939 had ruined her own Popular Front activities. In 1944, for example, FDR took a close personal interest in the CIO's successful efforts to help unseat the Red-baiting Congressman Martin Dies, who had been endorsed by William Green of the AFL, in the Texas Democratic party primary.[2]

In fact, by 1944 American Communists had gone much further down the path of a united front against Fascism than any other group. Browder looked forward to a period when a liberal, progressive, Popular Front, which had begun in the 1930s and been enhanced by the wartime alliance with Soviet Russia, would shape the postwar world. The war, in his view, had rendered a large part of the business community more progressive, and Communists must support progressive capitalists against the reactionary ones. To emphasise that this was no short-term, tactical alliance, Browder presided over the dissolution of the Communist Party of the United States – which claimed 80 000 members – in May 1944 and its reconstitution as the Communist Political Association.[3] The incredulity this creation of the CPA caused, and the changing mood of both American Communists and the American working class as the war drew to an end, escaped Browder. In March 1945 the most sincere supporter of Browder's revisionist line, the UAW's Roy Hudson, attacked the Reuther–Hillman–Dubinsky groups who wished to abandon the No Strike pledge as soon as the war ended. Strikes, Hudson argued, could not provide the 60 million jobs needed in the postwar period to protect the wage gains of the war years. Only support for Roosevelt's programme could do that.

But when Roosevelt died in April 1945 the programme and the times changed rapidly. FDR's replacement by the untried Harry S. Truman, combined with growing impatience with labour during the postwar strike wave, helped Republicans win control of Congress in 1946 partially on the promise of passing tough anti-labour laws. Yet bad news for labour on the political front was balanced by good news on the economic front. The depression that had been so widely expected to follow the war had not occurred. Workers and returning servicemen who were buying new cars, or making the first payment on new homes, with their wartime savings soon reacted angrily to postwar prices and inflation. President Truman's reaction to the subsequent postwar strike wave – threats followed by cave-ins, hasty advances and retreats on price control, the replacement of FDR's liberal advisers with his own conservative ones – alarmed the CIO and unionists of all economic and political beliefs in 1945–46. In this emerging situation, Browder's talk of Communists embracing international financiers like J. P. Morgan looked ridiculous and in May 1945 Jacques Duclos, head of the French CP, published a devastating attack on Browder's revisionism.[4] Duclos had the backing of Stalin and soon leading American Communists were falling over each other to dissociate themselves from the American's brand of class collaboration. Browder was replaced by the ressurected William Z. Foster, the CPA wound up and the CPUSA reconstituted.

II

Ironically, as so often happens in cases like this, change of leadership did not lead in the short run to any real change of line. The CP continued to search for bourgeois–liberal allies, and court anyone who supported unity of the Big Three – the United State, Britain and the Soviet Union – into the postwar period. But the initiative within the labour movement no longer lay with the Communists but with their foes – in particular with Walther Reuther and the UAW.

In his factional battles within the UAW, Reuther had learned that the best way to defeat the Communists was to avoid ideology and concentrate on pay and conditions. The coalition which supported him was very diverse, ranging from social democrats, lapsed socialists like himself who now called themselves labour liberals, to Catholics from the Association of Catholic Trade Unionists group, who were by the mid-1940s essentially conservative business unionists in the Gompers tradition.

ACTU had been formed in the mid-1930s as the response of liberal Catholic churchmen to the rise of industrial unionism. It sought to steer the CIO away from Socialism, Communism and other forms of secularism towards goals more compatible with those of the Church. Often charged with being the Catholic equivalent of the Communist Party, ACTU resembled the CP in that it was small and usually consisted of two or more bitterly warring factions. Like the Communists too, ACTU often exercised an influence greater than its small membership would suggest, especially on a Catholic labour leader like Murray. By the early 1940s it was playing a major part in the factional quarrels dividing the UAW–CIO by lining up support for the anti-Communists coalescing behind Reuther. But the only important issue which united ACTU with all the other factions was anti-Communism.

The opposing UAW coalition, in which Communists and their supporters played a major role, was equally diverse. It included New Deal anti-Communists like the ambitious former college football star Richard Frankensteen, who had made deals with the left during the war years to further their own careers; followers of Richard Leonard, head of the UAW's Ford department, who had recently quit the Reuther camp; and UAW president R. J. Thomas, close personal friend of CIO president Philip Murray. George Addes himself, the most substantial figure in this caucus, believed in the kind of Popular Front social unionism the CIO had supported since 1935 and was still willing to rely upon Communist backing. Though a large majority of blacks supported the Addes–Thomas–Leonard Communist-backed caucus, it included anti-Negro forces too. For just as anti-Communism was the only idea unifying Reuther's group, so fear and hatred of 'Walter Ruthless' united the faction in which Communists placed their hopes after 1946.[5]

This emergence of Communist and anti-Communist coalitions within the UAW and the CIO by 1946 forms the background not only to the postwar strike wave, but to the labour movement's response to the new pattern of foreign policy too. For the Cold War dominated all events, domestic and foreign, between 1945 and 1950, and indeed for a generation. Some sections of the American labour movement and the left had hoped to sustain the United States wartime alliance with the Soviet Union into the postwar period. But this had started to sour even before hostilities ended. Conflict began as the Red Army overran Poland, failed to honour promises made at the Yalta Conference to hold free elections, and tightened its grip in other East European countries. In 1946 Churchill's landmark 'Iron Curtain' speech at Fulton, Missouri, set the mood for the postwar scene. The West was suspicious of Soviet intentions towards oil-rich Iran, while the following year the President announced the Truman Doctrine of providing military and economic aid to Greece and Turkey to resist Soviet pressure in the Balkans and the Eastern Mediterranean, and to all countries everywhere facing the threat of Communist invasion or subversion. In 1948 the Communist *coup d'état* in Czechoslovakia, and the Berlin blockade and Allied air lift, stimulated the United States to set up the North Atlantic Treaty Organization for the defence of Western Europe and embark on massive rearmament. By 1950, with the outbreak of the Korean War, the Cold War had become hot and brought China and the United States into open and bloody conflict.

As this global confrontation between the United States and world Communism became the central issue of postwar American life, the labour movement could not escape its ramifications. Just as the American Socialist Party in 1917 had relied heavily on foreign-language federations, and the Communist Party in the 1920s had had a disproportionately high membership of Central and East European origin, so the left in the CIO in the 1940s was over-represented by 'old language' activists from Armenia, Romania, Hungary and Yugoslavia, second-generation immigrants radicalized by depression and war.[6]

Yet a significant section of the non-political majority of the American working class could trace their ancestry back to Central and Eastern Europe, which had now fallen under Soviet domination. So organized labour took an active, enthusiastic part in the politics of the Cold War and the domestic Red Scare. In fact, few Americans were more militantly anti-Communist than labour leaders. Both the AFL and the CIO fully endorsed Cold War foreign policy. They supported the Truman Doctrine, approved the Marshall Plan to revive the war-shattered economies of Western Europe, backed American leadership of NATO and defended intervention on behalf of the United Nations in Korea. They were also happy to accept funds from the CIA to combat left-wing influences in the labour movements of West Germany, France, Greece, Italy, Latin America and elsewhere. In 1948 they withdrew delegates from the World Federation of Trade Unions, which they believed had fallen under Communist domination, and set up a new, anti-Communist International Confederation of Free Trade Unions. At home, the CIO disqualified Communists from holding office and expelled unions which it claimed followed the Soviet line. Labour leaders were thus in the vanguard of those who repeatedly stressed the danger of the Red menace, and consistently called for common action to defeat it. Moreover, as the most effective anti-Communist Walter Reuther pointed out, all this served labour's own self-interest, for defence and foreign aid programmes not only provided help for other countries but also created extra jobs for American workers.

As American–Soviet relations deteriorated rapidly, the anti-Communist crusade mounted at home until it reached its climax during the dominance of Senator Joe McCarthy between 1950 and 1954. Yet impact of anti-Communism on American labour unions had occurred before McCarthy appeared. Employer fears about Communist influence surged after the war, stimulated largely by the great wave of strikes in late 1945 and 1946 in which, ironically, Communists played a moderating part. Closely linked with anti-unionism in general, these fears gained new momentum with the sweeping Republican gains in the mid-term Congressional elections of November 1946. Though the influence Communists exercised in some CIO unions was used to justify the employers' offensive, its real aim was to crush the kind of militant unionism Reuther had led in 1946–47 rather than to crush Communism.

Yet despite all this, as far as the CIO was concerned no really unbridgeable problems appeared before 1947–48. Despite the Stalinist purges in the 1930s, the overnight *volte-face* of the 1939 Nazi–Soviet pact, and even the CP's vigorous support of the No Strike pledge after 1942 and Browder's antics in 1945, Communist union activities had not really been discredited. CP members had served loyally and effectively in CIO national offices. Affiliated unions led by Communists, such as United Electrical, Fur and Leather Workers or the Transport Workers, bargained with employers and aided their members no differently from other unions. Indeed, Communists had supported American capitalism more strenuously than anyone else after 1941. Considering the size of the postwar strike wave it is surprising how little part the Communists played in it. What destroyed Communist influence on the American labour movement was not so much outside attacks as pressure from within which fractured the party's brittle structure. And what came to separate the left from other sections of the CIO was not really ideology, nor even bread-and-butter questions, vital though these were at times, but ultimately foreign policy and left-wing tactics in the 1948 Presidential election – issues unconnected with the economic problems of labour unions.

III

The greatest single factor was, of course, the onset of the Cold War. This provided the historical context in which the events between 1945 and 1950 must be seen, and made the kind of Red-baiting long endemic in the United States more widespread. The Communist-backed left, by and large, opposed the Truman Doctrine, the Marshall Plan and the establishment of NATO. Such opposition to the very cornerstones of United States foreign policy was important in labour union politics because it was a threat to the kind of relationship CIO leaders like Hillman and Murray had patiently built with the Democratic Party coalition during the war. True, this coalition had not seemed quite so invincible since the mid-term election in 1938, when Roosevelt's attempt to 'pack' the Supreme Court and other issues had led to a conservative revival and the start of the Dixiecrat/Republican bloc which tended to control Congress until the 1960s. Republican victories in the mid-term elections of 1942 meant that, despite the war, FDR had looked vulnerable in 1944 and had failed to carry the Democrats with him in State and Congressional elections. Only two parts of the party's New Deal machine were still in good working order in 1944: the solid South and the CIO. Indeed, the CIO's Political Action Committee had arguably been decisive in securing Roosevelt's re-election.

FDR's death in April 1945 had left the New Deal reform coalition leaderless, and when the Republicans recaptured Congress in 1946 they had hastened to reverse the Wagner Act with Taft–Hartley the following year. As the 1948 Presidential election approached, therefore, labour had learned the painful lesson that union gains brought about by broader political participation in the life of the nation could be lost through loss of power in Washington and subsequent passage of hostile industrial legislation. To have any hope of repealing Taft–Hartley, labour must subordinate everything to making sure that Harry Truman was re-elected, along with Democratic Senators and Congressmen who would fight hard for repeal. With the danger of Dixiecrat Democrats bolting the party ticket, and left-wing Democrats supporting the Progressive candidate Henry Wallace, any significant split in labour's ranks would destroy Truman. With hindsight, too, it can be seen that the 1948 election began a generation when Democrats would usually control both the White House and Congress, while labour unions prospered as part of this governing coalition.

Communist opposition to American foreign policy and support for Henry Wallace would threaten to turn the CIO into the kind of political movement which, strong enough to spread unease in Washington and the nation, would for that very reason be weak enough to invite Republican retaliation. The Communists and their allies were further challenging both working-class patriotism and the loyalties of leaders like Murray, which had been enhanced by war. Finally, American labour unionists were used to dissenting, often quite strongly, from Government policy, but only in domestic affairs. Because they had been enthusiastic supporters of New Deal domestic reform, now increasingly under challenge from the Republican Congress, they felt they had to bend over backwards to demonstrate their patriotism in foreign affairs by vigorous attacks on Communists, both abroad and at home.

The most effective anti-Communist in the postwar years was Walter Reuther, yet as a young man in the depths of the Depression he and his brother Victor had visited the Soviet Union and worked as skilled toolmakers at Ford's Gorky plant for 18 months. Walter was then enthusiastic about the Soviet experiment, and returned to Detroit in 1934 determined to organize the American industrial working class so that they might exercise the power he believed workers had in Russia. A key rank-and-file UAW organizer between

1935 and 1940, he had been investigated by the Military Intelligence early in the war when Frances Perkins considered him for a Government job in the defence economy. Intelligence told Perkins that in 1934 Walter had urged American workers to 'Carry on the fight for a Soviet America' when in fact Victor had merely urged that they fight for the right to organize.[7] Clearly by 1940 Reuther had lost many of his illusions about the Soviet Union and was already intent on resisting the American CP as 'misleaders of labour'.

Reuther was to become master of both the UAW and CIO in the postwar period. Yet the General Motors strike he led in 1945–46 seemed, on the surface, to damage his earlier reputation as a union leader whose policies brought dividends on the shop floor and in the pay packet. But he cleverly turned this against the Communists. For the Communist-led United Electrical Workers, representing 30 000 GM workers, which had struck alongside the UAW then, had also scuppered the strike by settling for 18.5 cents. Just as during the war the Communists had supported piece work, pay restraint, a 'draft labor' bill and the No Strike pledge, so this UE 'stab in the back' was used by Reuther as further evidence that Communist-dominated unions could not bring bread-and-butter gains to their members. So successful was Reuther's charge that the left coalition avoided a floor fight on the issue at the March 1946 UAW convention. And when Reuther ran against the Communist-backed incumbent R. J. Thomas for president of the UAW he squeezed by with a majority of barely 100 votes in more than 8000 cast, overturning the Communist-backed Addes–Thomas coalition which had led the union for seven years.

Presidency of the UAW gave Reuther a secure base from which to launch further advances. Yet for the moment his power was severely limited. Though Thomas had lost, his Communist-supported coalition still had a majority on the union's executive board. In private Reuther admitted that little, save personal ambition, divided the two groups, while at his first executive board meeting he emphasised that there was no basic disagreement and called for an end to factional strife.[8] Yet both sides were implacable in the 18 months which separated the UAW's 1946 and 1947 conventions. Addes and Reuther detested each other personally, while in the CIO as a whole, Communist efforts to lead the coalition which had formed behind George Addes of the UAW alienated their allies and paved the way for Reuther's group to take power. Moreover, some of Reuther's supporters used Red-baiting to break support for Addes.

In the midst of all this, CIO president Philip Murray faced many problems. His personal friendship for Thomas was balanced by his growing contempt for the Communists, while as a Catholic he was a prime target for ACTU's anti-Communism, as was Addes too. Yet Murray's overriding objective was to maintain the integrity and unity of the CIO, and his principal fear was that in defeat a frustrated Reuther might take his UAW faction out of the CIO into the AFL, as Homer Martin had done in 1938, and that in victory he might take the whole union with him. The social-democratic David Dubinsky, who had just done the same with the ILGWU, was covertly subsidising Reuther's campaign, and Murray suspected that the maverick John L. Lewis, now back in the AFL and still seeking a return to the power he had enjoyed in the 1930s, might be doing the same.

Two issues exacerbated relations between the factions: the 1946–47 Allis–Chalmers strike and the proposed UAW merger with the Farm Equipment Workers Union. The large Communist-led Local 248 of the UAW at Allis–Chalmers' Milwaukee plant had fought for a union shop since 1937. The War Labor Board had granted maintenance of membership, but at the end of the war management broke the agreement. The 11-months' strike which ensued became a battle for survival. Refusing bargaining or arbitration, the company waited for a rival union to contest Local 248's right to represent Allis–Chalmers workers and encouraged a back-to-work movement. When a rival group called a certification election, Local 248 was forced to conduct an exhausting election campaign in the middle of a life-or-death strike and also face attacks from the Hearst press, FBI harassment and probing by Congressional Red-baiters. Finally, anti-Communists in the Wisconsin CIO, many of them Reuther supporters, refused to back the strike.[9]

Reuther himself hated the Local's Communist leadership, but could not condone the employer's refusal to bargain. He tried not to divide the UAW executive, asked Addes and then Thomas to work out a settlement, and then finally took on the job himself with Murray's personal representative John Brophy. Discussions gradually widened from company refusal to bargain to include wages and other issues. The UAW policy committee, still dominated at this stage by Reuther's opponents, denounced Reuther for going behind the Local's back. Reuther was thus forced to take the leaders of the caucus he had beaten in March – Thomas, Addes, Richard Leonard – together with the president of Local 248 to the next meeting with management. This proved fruitless because, so Thomas argued, Reuther was forced to renege on the secret deal he had planned to impose. When Local 248 won the certification election by only 31 votes in over 8000 cast, the company still refused to negotiate and in March 1947, amidst a massive return to work, Reuther and Brophy managed to persuade the company to take the strikers back with no reprisals.

This was an almost complete debacle. The strikers had won no concessions, yet Reuther believed he had salvaged all he could from the situation by saving the strikers' jobs and managed to turn the whole Allis–Chalmers episode into a personal victory, as he had with the GM strike the previous year.[10] This time the 'stab-in-the-back' charges were made by the left against Reuther, rather than by him, and were combined with accusations that he had conducted 'back door negotiations'.

But none of this could be made to stick. Reuther could not be saddled with all the blame for the failure of his Wisconsin supporters to back the strike initially. Anyway, his intervention in December had made them co-operate. As for 'back-door negotiations', they occurred in January when the Allis–Chalmers company was in an impregnable position and could not be forced to talk with the Local's leadership. By March 1947 even Addes had come to see that something had to be done to get round this obstacle, and had agreed to consider putting Local 248 under CIO administration to negotiate a new contract. Later the UAW did this, expelled the Communist leaders and brought Local 248 into the Reuther camp – but only later after Reuther had won total control of the UAW at the November 1947 convention.

So the Allis–Chalmers dispute enabled Reuther to neutralize an important focus of rank-and-file Communist power in the UAW and emerge unscathed. His defeat of the attempt to merge the left-wing Farm Equipment Workers and Metal Workers Union with the UAW was even more significant. In 1941 FE had rejected Philip Murray's proposed merger with the UAW, but during the war the UAW organized several farm equipment manufacturing plants instead of the relatively weak FE. When a number of jurisdictional disputes broke out between two unions a CIO executive board committee, consisting of three anti-Communists, again proposed a merger, which the FE again rejected. But Reuther's wafer-thin victory at the UAW convention in 1946 had transformed the FE's attitude. The reason was simple: the addition of the FE's 80 000 members would tip the UAW convention balance to the left in 1947, adding about 500 delegate votes. So the FE's left-wing leadership proposed a merger which would maximize their political advantage: FE would merge with the UAW but retain its own identity, becoming in effect an 'FE Division' of the UAW.[11]

Though this plan was devised to destroy Reuther's chances of gaining control of the union in 1947, he once again used his opponent's strength cleverly against them. He had the merger proposal submitted to the UAW membership in a referendum, and then campaigned vigorously against it. Though the political motives behind the merger were plain enough, Reuther did not attack them for fear of Communist cries of 'Red-baiting'. Plenty of other UAW members were happy to use 'Red scare' tactics. Instead he argued that the merger would open the door to that dreaded Trojan horse: craft unionism in the UAW.[12] If farm equipment workers were granted craft autonomy it would be impossible to resist similar demands from machinists and other skilled workers in the UAW. This would be a small step from separate bargaining for skilled and unskilled workers, with consequent loss of bargaining power for the unskilled, who were the bulk of the union's total membership.

So the UAW rejected the merger proposal, with only 7 per cent of the membership voting, and Reuther went on to sweep all before him in the months leading up to the convention. Now that FE delegates could not come galloping up like the Fifth Cavalry to save them, the Communist-backed left gave up all hope of heading Reuther off and his delegates swept Local after Local, even capturing some CP strongholds. At the UAW convention itself in November 1947 the Addes–Thomas coalition, which had lasted for eight years and linked the era of the Popular Front to that of the Cold War, did not even run a candidate against him. The UAW executive board was transformed. Where the Communist-supported coalition had held a majority, Reuther supporters now had 18 of the regionally elected seats out of 22.[13]

The significance of this win was not that it prevented a Communist takeover of the UAW and CIO. This was never a possibility.

Communists never comprised a majority in the Addes–Thomas caucus and could not therefore have shunted Reuther aside. But neither could Addes have used non-Communist allies to defeat Reuther and, within two or three years, ejected the Communists himself. The Reutherites were just too powerful for this to have happened, but their power was not based on any sense of popular outrage aginst the CP. The derisory turnout in the crucial FE referendum showed that, even when passions ran high, the political affiliations of their leaders were only important to the membership if they perceived that 'outside' loyalties cut across shop-floor interests. Traditionally, as Professor Levenstein has argued, 'union members were as willing to accept Communist leadership as they were to take conservative, liberal or corrupt leadership, provided it paid off at contract time'.

Moreover another tradition of the American labour movement – that factional conflict was about the spoils of union office – was born out by the events of 1946–47. Hundreds of local UAW bureaucrats had emerged from the war with comfortable jobs which they wanted to keep. The fact that Reuther seemed destined to win in the Cold War climate of 1946–48 was really what drove both office-holders and office-seekers to flock to his side. Both pro- and anti-Reuther caucuses were fundamentally patronage machines in the American tradition, built around national officers and regional directors, and dispersing (or withholding) services and favours in return for votes. Nor could the rout of UAW Communists be blamed on wartime dilution of militant, class-conscious unionism. The drafting of many prewar militants into the armed forces, and the influx of new workers from the South and Appalachia, had led to significant changes in the composition of the workforce, and to conflicts outlined above. Prewar militants who had been drafted did not all return to industry. In the crucial Detroit area at least, WASPs from Appalachia could be just as class-conscious, pro-union and radical as the rank and file of the 1930s had been. Black workers, heavily concentrated at Ford and radicalized by the strike over recognition and the race riots of 1942–43, provided disproportionate support for the Communists. Yet in the last analysis, workers in the middle, preoccupied with pay and conditions, swung behind Reuther because he looked a winner and had cleverly stolen the militant bargaining image the Communists had abandoned for the duration of the war between 1941 and 1945.[14]

IV

Reuther's victory in the UAW in 1946–47 was an event of central significance. Effective, militant, bureaucratic, anti-Communist leadership now quickly came to control the emerging corporate liberalism which was to characterize American labour in the 1950s. Reuther's victory was important because it swung the UAW decisively into the anti-Communist camp at a time when anti-Communism was the most important domestic issue. Of the three largest CIO unions the Communist-led UE, with 650 000 members, was now clearly out-gunned by the anti-Communist UAW and Philip Murray's own United Steelworkers, each with around a million. Defeat of the Communists in the CIO as a whole might now involve expulsion rather than schism. As president of the CIO, Murray had not backed the anti-Communists in the UAW partly out of friendship for Thomas and dislike of Reuther. But Reuther's victory in 1947, and other events, now drove him into the confrontation with the Communists in the whole of the CIO which he had anticipated and feared. Hitherto Murray's erratic course had been dictated by his pursuit of two apparently irreconcilable goals: to preserve and enhance CIO unity, and to reduce and eventually expel Communist influence. When both Communist and anti-Communist factions within the CIO had been shaping up for a conflict in 1947, Murray had been caught in the middle. Reuther's initial UAW victory had encouraged rumours that CIO anti-Communists planned that he replace Murray as president. Instead, they tabled a motion at the federation's 1947 convention calling on all CIO unions to 'vigorously resist all anti-democratic and totalitarian philosophies or forces' such as Communism and Fascism.[15]

The Communists, for their part, came to the CIO convention determined to forstall this, and though they could now no longer count on so much UAW delegate support they could still expect the backing of unions representing 20 or 30 per cent of the CIO membership. Murray avoided open conflict by threatening to resign, and so shatter CIO unity. The two sides then agreed to the appointment of a committee. This drew up a compromise resolution which urged delegates to 'resent and reject efforts of the Communist Party or other political parties and their adherents to interfere in the affairs of the CIO'.[16] Though this represented a major setback for the left, their representatives on the committee were persuaded by Murray to accept it.

Ben Gold of the Fur Workers, Michael Quill of the New York Transport Workers, and Abraham Flaxner of the United Public Workers did so because in a period of growing public hatred of Communists it was about the best they could expect. At least the resolution did not sanction purges. Moreover, they could argue that it preserved CIO unity, and even that it was in the oldest traditions of American labour, by proclaiming that the CIO was not the creature of *any* political party, including the Democrats, although the thrust of the resolution was clearly against the named party. After the executive voted unanimously to accept this resolution, Gold and Flaxner thanked Murray effusively, while Quill added, 'I found out for the first time that no matter what side of the fence we are on, we are all CIO members'.[17]

The Communists pressured their supporters into voting for it, but outside the convention the Communist Party had trouble with members who, in historian Harvey Levenstein's phrase, were 'unable to leave bad enough alone'.[18] Worse followed as anti-Communist CIO delegates returned to their unions demanding they vigorously endorse the 'resent and reject' policy. In most cases they went much further towards a 'resist and fight' approach.[19] Yet Communists remained strong in the CIO councils of New York, Detroit and Los Angeles. In Northern California and Washington CIO councils were dominated by supporters of the Australian-born Communist longshormen's leader Harry Bridges, whom the Federal government was making strenuous, but unsuccessful, efforts to deport.

The anti-Communists, with John Brophy in the lead, now restricted these CIO councils in a number of ways. For example, they forbade the Los Angeles CIO council from contributing money to the National Negro Congress, which they claimed was a Communist-front organization, and expanded on this approach by circulating a list of 36 approved organizations, none of which were front organizations but some of which were anti-Communist.

Meantime, other CIO councils, following the lead of James Carey's opposition faction in the UE, passed resolutions barring Communists from office. Passage of the Taft–Hartley Act in June 1947 had made this problem more pressing by requiring all union office-holders to sign affidavits affirming they were not members of the CP, with stiff prison sentences for perjurers. Any union whose officers refused to sign affidavits would lose certification rights, be open to raiding by rival unions and find that employers could legally refuse to bargain with it. The entire CIO, along with the AFL, was united in its complete opposition to Taft–Hartley as a whole, mainly because of its other anti-labour provisions. Reuther and most of the CIO liberals agreed that whatever the merits of its anti-Communist clauses, the Act as a whole had to go, while Murray, whose philosphical objections to Communism were stronger than Reuther's, had much more serious civil libertarian qualms than the UAW president about affidavits and feared they would encourage witch-hunters to ride roughshod over the whole union movement.[20] As a Catholic, Murray could see that such tactics might at some future time be used against Catholic unions too.

In April 1947, Murray had vigorously protested against President Truman's executive order calling for loyalty checks on all government employees and firing those that belonged to 'subversive' organizations. This deprived thousands of due process and, moreover, meant that the Federal government had assumed power to declare any labour, consumer, religious or educational organization 'subversive' without explanation. In that sense Truman's loyalty programme marked the onset of McCarthyism. Much as Murray might resist, and prevent his own United Steelworkers complying with the law until mid-1949, most other anti-Communist labour leaders fell in and signed affidavits.

By August 1948 81 000 union officers had done so, including officers of 89 of the AFL's 102 unions and 30 of the CIO's 45.[21] Yet the real damage Taft–Hartley did the Communists came not from the affidavits, nor its other provisions, but from the central position the Act now came to occupy in labour affairs. With repeal the most important item on labour's agenda, Truman's veto of the bill, and his vocal opposition to the Act, reversed labour's previous dislike of him. His re-election in 1948 became the only hope of repeal. No Republican candidate for President would back repeal and a third party was not only hopeless but ran the risk, by dividing the Democratic vote, of throwing the election to the Republicans, especially as Southern Democrats were about to bolt their party.

Yet this was just what the Communists now asked labour to do by backing Henry Wallace's Progressive campaign for President in 1948. Moreover the question of Wallace's candidacy was decisive because it alone brought together the major domestic issue of Taft–Hartley and the increasingly important one of foreign policy. Once again the CP had failed to keep pace with the changing attitudes of American workers and most of their leaders. Wallace, Secretary of Agriculture during the New Deal and FDR's running mate in 1940, had been dumped in favour of Truman in 1944. He was campaigning now as inheritor of Roosevelt's wartime policy of liberalism at home and *rapprochement* with Russia. Initially many CIO labour liberals had shared the left's concern over Truman's tough line towards the Soviet Union, his support for right-wing regimes in Greece and Italy, endorsement of European imperialism in Africa and Asia, and the bankrupt policy in China. The Truman Doctrine in the spring of 1947, which justified economic and military aid to Greece and Turkey by America's duty to support free governments everywhere against internal or external threat, was clearly the opening shot in a new kind of world-wide offensive against Communism.

The left, both Communist, Communist-backed and anti-Communist, was thus wary of the next major initiative, the Marshall Plan, announced in June 1947, by which the United States embarked on a massive programme of economic aid to rebuild the war-torn nations of Europe. This aid was initially aimed at both Eastern and Western Europe. But it was clear that acceptance would involve the kind of coordination with, and thus subordination to, Western capitalism that the Soviet Union and her client states in Eastern Europe could never accept. Yet at the same time the Marshall Plan struck a chord of compassion and generosity which raised the hope that a cold and hungry Western Europe would not be driven into Stalin's hands by internal discontent, and that Western capitalism, with the United States at its head, would recover from world war in better shape than it had done after 1918.

In such circumstances, the determined campaign by American Communists urging the CIO to resist the Marshall Plan had no real chance of success, but the danger of a serious CIO split on foreign policy was clearly there. The struggle reached its climax in October 1947 when George Marshall himself addressed the CIO convention, the first Secretary of State to do so. He warned that the world faced a clear choice between freedom and dictatorship; that the labour movement would be the first victim of such dictatorship; and that

American unions must support aid to Europe to secure liberty, peace and security for both Europe and the United States.[22]

Reuther, believed by opponents at least to have an eye on the 1948 Democratic vice-presidential nomination, backed Marshall with a ringing attack on 'totalitarianism' and a defence of American foreign policy. Those who had denounced Roosevelt and others as war-mongers for opposing Hitler in 1940 were now calling Truman the same.[23] But in urging unions 'to back the country's defense and foreign aid program' Reuther was appealing to self-interest too, noting that in providing help for other people the American government was creating extra jobs for American workers.[24] As with the 'resent and reject' resolution at the 1947 CIO convention, Murray avoided a floor fight by shuffling the whole subject into committee and then backing a resolution which supported the general principle of aid to Europe without backing the Marshall Plan specifically. The Communists supported this by emphasising those parts of the resolution more favourable to their position. But what really drove them into a corner, and ultimate destruction, was once again a change in the Moscow line. Stalin's wartime gesture of disbanding the Comintern in deference to Western susceptibilities had been reversed by the founding in September 1947 of the Cominform, which launched an all-out offensive against the Truman Doctrine and the Marshall Plan which was conducted with strict Soviet control of national CPs.

Disaster followed for the American party. Hitherto it had merely backed Wallace as a contender for the Democratic nomination in 1948, not as a third-party candidate. Now it was committed to supporting Wallace in all circumstances, despite the fact that as incumbent Truman would clearly win the nomination, and irrespective of the overriding importance a united labour movement, both AFL and CIO, was now giving to repeal of Taft–Hartley by backing Truman. Party boss William Z. Foster ordered Michael Quill of the transport workers to 'go down the line' with Wallace 'even if it meant splitting every CIO union' and to start a third labour faction if that happened.[25] For Quill this meant choosing between his union and his party, and he left the party. As in 1940, in the political crunch most Communist labour unionists put self-preservation above the party line, this time because the damage caused by Taft–Hartley had changed the nature of the political game. The only major Communist-backed union to endorse Wallace was the Mine, Mill and Smelter Workers. Even the UE, whose leaders had played an active role in Wallace's campaign, did not endorse him but left it to their Locals to decide.

None of this saved them. Events enfeebled Wallace's challenge while still leaving the Communists once more open to the charge that when unity was needed most they had split the labour movement. Murray was again caught between sentiment and expediency. He actually despised Truman and liked Wallace personally; but he knew Truman's election in November 1948 was essential. 'Henry Wallace is not exactly the saviour of the working class in America or the world,' he pointed out. His record as Agriculture Secretary and Vice-President had been unremarkable. 'Then about six months before the Democratic convention he began talking of the Century of the Common Man.'[26] The passion this political struggle had released was revealed in 1948 when a hired gunman tried to murder Walter Reuther and put him in hospital for six months.

For Reuther, Murray and the other CIO leaders, Communist tactics of supporting Wallace in 1948 were a betrayal. By endangering Truman's re-election, they threatened labour's vital interests, especially repeal of the Taft–Hartley Act. It was ironic that Taft–Hartley required American union leaders to file affidavits affirming they were not members of the CP or any organization supporting it. For the CIO, in the vanguard of opposition to the 'slave-labour' act, now moved on its own initiative vigorously to expel such leaders and unions it deemed Communist. Murray fired the editor of the *CIO News*, Len De Caux, and the CIO's legal counsel, Lee Pressman, for their Communist sympathies and support for Wallace. Harry Bridges was sacked as California regional director, and his jurisdiction sliced into northern and southern California districts on grounds of administrative efficiency. Worse was to follow. At its annual convention in Cleveland in 1949 the CIO revised its constitution to make Communists ineligible for executive office and provide for expulsion by a two-third vote of 'any union whose policies are consistently directed towards the achievement of the program or purposes of the Communist Party'.[27]

The following year, after a long struggle, the CIO finally expelled the United Electrical Workers, by far the largest of the Communist-led unions. This proved to be the first step in a concerted drive so that by 1950 ten others had been purged. The expelled unions were the Farm Equipment Workers, American Communications Association, Food and Tobacco Workers, Fur and Leather Workers, Mine,

Mill and Smelter Workers, United Office and Professional Workers, United Public Workers, International Longshoremen's and Warehousemen's Union, Marine Cooks and Stewards, and the International Fishermen's Union. The United Furniture Workers had been listed too, but then restored to the CIO when the union voted its Communist leadership out of office. Apart from UE, and to a lesser extent Mine, Mill, most of these expelled unions were individually small and relatively unimportant. Yet together they comprised almost a fifth of total CIO membership. Though Taft–Hartley had outlawed Communist-led unions, the CIO leadership threw them out not to comply with the law, which they hated, but out of resentment against the left's tactics in support of Wallace in 1948 and under compulsion of the anti-Communist mood of the time.

Anti-Communists of course accused the CP of exploiting the working class, which in some ways was true. By 1949 it was easy to portray American Communists as at best dupes, at worst stooges, of Soviet foreign policy objectives. Red-baiting played a part too. Yet by and large Communists in the CIO had pursued union policies similar to those followed by most of the federation's non-Communists. They had been effective and loyal in office, and indistinguishable from other unions in the way they bargained with employers and looked after the interests of their members. Nor had they all slavishly followed the party line: some of the most completely Communist unions, such as the Fur Workers, rarely did so. Separation had come over non-union issues and the special political circumstances of 1948. Yet even here, had they limited their opposition to the Truman Doctrine and the Marshall Plan merely to rhetoric, they might have escaped. It was backing Wallace which scuppered them and led the CIO to expulsion.

This was a decisive moment in American labour history. Communists had never been numerous or even especially influential. But they had been the best cohort of organizers the CIO ever had. In purging them the CIO not only lost some of its most militant, experienced and effective grass-roots leadership, but more important turned its back forever on the concepts such leadership embraced, which had played such an important part in launching the CIO a decade earlier. For example Communists were the only group to take the problem of organizing black workers seriously. Combined with the failure of Operation Dixie to organize the South, and the collapse of the foremen's unions, it set a limit on further union expansion. Moreover, it ushered in an era when not only Communists, but Trotskyites, Socialists, Fabians and left-wing New Dealers of all kinds would fall under deep suspicion as subversives.

V

Foreign affairs proved decisive in other aspects of labour history in the postwar period. Forging the Grand Strategy in wartime, FDR had encouraged 'representatives of all sections of the American working population ... to visit Great Britain and the Soviet Union' and had urged his wartime labour adviser, Sidney Hillman, to give this top priority. Hillman, a key figure in the creation of wartime union-management-government partnership and convinced anti-Communist, died prematurely soon after. But Murray, Reuther and the other CIO leaders who had worked with Hillman had joined the British and Soviet labour movements in January 1945 to form the World Federation of Trade Unions in London. The AFL had refused, on the grounds that Soviet trade unions were not really unions – a view which had gained much wider currency by 1948. The CIO had joined in because it seemed to support FDR's foreign policy, but by 1948 this too was in tatters. In fact, since 1944 the AFL had been mounting a vigorous anti-Communist crusade among unionists abroad, well financed because it was backed in large part by the Federal government through the Central Intelligence Agency. The campaign was led by Jay Lovestone, leader of the CP in the 1920s, now a vigorous anti-Communist, whose close aide was Irving Brown, formerly of the UAW.[28]

General Secretary of the American Communist Party in the 1920s, Lovestone had been purged when the line changed in 1928 and replaced by William Z. Foster, who in turn was ousted by Earl Browder when the line changed again in 1934. Still a Marxist, Lovestone had nevertheless fought the Communists in the UAW, along with Brown, by backing Homer Martin's faction in 1939. When Martin was defeated, Lovestone threw in his lot with David Dubinsky of the ILGWU in drumming up labour support for intervention against the Axis Powers in 1940. Dubinsky made Lovestone head of the ILGWU international department, and William Green took him over to head the AFL's European work in 1944. Lovestone's task, aided by Brown, was to free European unionism, emerging from the war, from Communist influence.

In France they found that the General Confederation of Labour (CGT) was controlled by Communists, despite the fact that the mass of CGT members were non-Communist. This was partly because the CP was organized and effective, but also because the Communist role in the Resistance during the Nazi occupation, at least after June 1941, had greatly enhanced the party's prestige. Moreover, many anti-Communists had been deeply compromised during the wartime puppet Vichy regime. This was even more marked, Brown and Lovestone found, with unions in Italy. The Communists sought to rebuild the prewar Popular Front to defend French interests and control European labour through their leading position in the WFTU. Brown strove to build up the Force Ouvrière (FO) in opposition to the Communists, but faced the dilemma of how to split the CGT without being blamed for it.[29]

At the CGT convention in 1946 the French CP tightened its grip. But as part of the De Gaulle postwar coalition government of reconstruction, the CP pursued a conservative policy. In a manner reminiscent of American Communist support for the No Strike pledge, the French CP supported postwar piecework and speed-up in production. Bad conditions and a rising cost of living gave Brown a chance to organize rank-and-file unrest against them. By playing the capitalist game, the French Communists had given Brown an excuse to try and split them. Between 1947 and 1950 widespread strikes took place for wage increases, with the Communists (now out of government) using them for political purposes.

Brown asked the AFL to put pressure on the State Department to keep US Ambassador Jefferson Caffrey in France because he 'has been a bulwark for the right side in this struggle', by which Brown meant the FO.[30] Brown had also forged links with the French socialists and asked the AFL for substantial financial aid. At a meeting in New York with William Green, Matthew Woll, David Dubinsky, Jay Lovestone and the future AFL leader George Meany, Brown reported that the AFL had 'penetrated every country in Europe' and was a 'world force in conflict with a world organization in every field affecting international labour'. The FO in France tried to break the Communist-led strikes and Brown hoped they would form the core of a rival trade union movement. But in 1949, when

CGT membership had fallen from six million to three, the FO still had only 800 000 members.

All this was achieved with close liaison between the AFL and the State Department and the financial support of the CIA, which was paying two million dollars a year for such work. Not only was the CIA giving money to Irving Brown, but it also paid 50 000 dollars in 50-dollar bills to Walter Reuther to help him build anti-Communist unions in Germany.[31] Moreover O. A. Knight, chairman of the CIO hearing which recommended the expulsion of Harry Bridges's ILWU, was later revealed to have been a major channel of CIA funds to the CIO.[32] Clearly most labour leaders accepted the premise on which American Cold War foreign policy rested, and viewed the CIA as simply another institution which financed the extension of American-style corporate unionism overseas.

Even so, it was apparent that even in 1949 the CGT still had the support of the great majority of the French working class. So Brown urged that because the FO and other free unions suffered from lack of leadership, union leaders who had supported the Vichy government during the Nazi occupation be removed from the black-list and allowed to hold office in the CGT, while Communists who had held posts in the CGT at the time of the Nazi–Soviet pact be banned. Much the same story was true of the AFL's activities in Germany, Greece and Italy, where anti-Communist forces, even those severely implicated in Fascism and Nazism, were given full support providing they were opposed to the Reds. The CIA was fully implicated in deals with top Nazis who agreed to help them resist further Communist advances in Europe. Moreover the AFL felt that the WFTU had fallen completely under Soviet and Communist domination, and Irving Brown suggested holding an international conference on the Marshall Plan which could be used as a pretext for American unions to quit the WFTU.

In fact by 1949 a pretext was barely needed. The CIO had become convinced of the necessity of leaving the WFTU and the British TUC was persuaded to take the lead. A conference was called representing the new, breakaway trade unions of France and Italy plus most of the non-Communist West European ones still affiliated to the WFTU. Significantly, both the AFL and the CIO sent delegations, with free transportation and sixty dollars a day expenses paid by the Federal government, whose policy they were enacting.

So in 1949 CIO unions left the WFTU, and soon both AFL and CIO took the lead in setting up the new, anti-Communist International Confederation of Free Trade Unions. Domestic and foreign policies had fused to form a consensus. Containment of Communism meant expulsion of Communists from unions in America, and resistence to the Soviet Union and Red China abroad, support for anti-Communist unions in Europe, even alliance with former Nazis and Fascists. It also meant the American government's massive rearmament programme would ensure high levels of public spending, prosperity and full employment for the United States. The Keynesian consensus had been reached, the military-industrial complex was in place, and unions were becoming part of that corporate liberalism which became its political expression in the 1950s.

6. The Emergence of Corporate Consensus

In the 1950s and early 1960s organized labour in the United States enjoyed its most prosperous and effective years. All the many strands of development since the New Deal came together in that decade and a half to form one powerful thread which ran right through the central pattern of the nation's life. The eruption of unions during the Depression, their co-option after into the controlling industrial bureaucracy in wartime, and the outcome of the great wave of strikes which occurred after victory had combined to determine labour's new status. Links with the Democratic Party were now powerful and influential. Equally, labour's activities took place within a transformed economic climate. Keynesian notions about demand management, government's role in the economy, and the importance of rising profits, wages and employment helped ensure there was no return to the Depression years, which most had feared would happen once the war ended.

So for a quarter of a century the system of industrial relations pioneered during the New Deal, perfected in the Second World War, and legitimised in the immediate postwar years worked. While the American economy dominated the world's economic and financial life, capital accumulation grew, productivity rose impressively, and profits increased spectacularly. Higher productivity and profits, in turn, enabled corporations like General Motors and US Steel to negotiate contracts with unions which ensured steadily rising real standards of living, shorter hours, better conditions. An abundant, booming agricultural sector made food cheaper and plentiful, doubling the nation's blessings. America's domination of the globe was dependent upon its financial influence and its military might,

125

which in turn legitimised higher levels of public spending and budget deficits which created more jobs. Keynesian economics might not have worked, nor been applied consistently in the 1930s. But before his death in 1946 Keynes had left his mark on the Bretton Woods conference, which shaped the world's postwar economic and financial systems. So in the 1950s the American economy, and its labour unions, operated within a world system increasingly based upon the revolution in thinking the British economist had pioneered.

American military might, as during the Second World War, was dependent upon industry and the working class it employed. America's geopolitical function after 1945 was to act as a counter-balance to Soviet power in Europe and Communist China in the Far East. Bretton Woods, the Marshall Plan, the Truman Doctrine and the North Atlantic Treaty Organizations were fundamental determinants to the American foreign policy. Labour's part in making this whole system work was broadly accepted within the boundaries established in the late 1940s. Free collective bargaining determined pay, hours and conditions; fringe benefits became more common and more generous; unions disciplined the workforce; management managed; foremen were not organized; and Communists were not allowed. The mood of hysteria during the McCarthy period after 1950 made this plain. Indeed the purge of Communists within their ranks, which unions had themselves already carried out so effectively, had in many ways been the most significant step which brought everything else together. What historians call 'the corporate consensus' or 'liberal corporatism' ran the nation, while foreign policy was shaped by an élite which included corporate lawyers like Dean Acheson and John Foster Dulles.

Domestic priorities fitted completely with America's resistance to Communism abroad. Containment of Communism first provided military and economic aid to Greece and Turkey, and then launched the Marshall Plan, NATO and the United Nations police action in Korea, which was controlled from Washington and the Pentagon in the name of the UN. Korean War expenditure boosted the economy significantly, just at the moment when the postwar boom was showing signs of flagging. Significantly, labour leaders were the most enthusiastic supporters of all these policies. Indeed the AFL in particular augmented United States foreign policy by launching a campaign in postwar Europe to discredit and crush Communist or left-wing influence on unions in France, German, Italy and elsewhere and put anti-Communist unions in place. At home American labour leaders agreed not to rock the boat by too vigorously urging adoption of a comprehensive national Welfare State of the kind Britain and other European nations built in the aftermath of war. Nor did they press nationally for action in the field of race relations and civil rights for blacks, which was the nation's most serious longterm domestic problem.

Instead union leaders accepted the system which was at the core of America's economy: the military–industrial complex. Vast outlays of public money, of the order of 10 or 12 per cent of Gross National Product (GNP) were made by the Federal government on the defence system needed to contain the clear and present danger posed by international Communism. Aviation, and later the space programme, electronics, motor manufacture, steel, power generation and transmission were the beneficiaries. Boeing, General Electric, Lockheed, General Motors, US Steel grew ever more powerful. The unions which organized these industries applied themselves diligently to the task of seeing that their members were beneficiaries too. Within this context Keynesian economics, based on the notion of controlled inflation, was used to ensure full employment and prosperity, and to justify the central significance of the military-industrial complex. American control of the world economy ensured the supply both of cheap energy and the raw materials on which this hegemony rested. The nation's enormous productive capacity, and the buoyant demand of its internal market, fuelled the rapid spread of consumer durables and services to all social classes which made American prosperity yearly more apparent in the 1950s. A labour movement largely created by insurgent, rank-and-file activism had come under the control of a new bureaucracy. Wages became the chief preoccupation of postwar unions, so that money took primacy over the older labour demand for industrial democracy and social reform. As long as it granted higher real wages, management was given a relatively free hand in controlling the labour process.

Historians have often ascribed this bureaucratization to the growing maturity of the American labour movement. Grass-roots activism may have been needed to establish unions, but once they had secured bargaining rights, the union shop, access to management and political influence, labour's bureaucratic leadership inevitably took command. But this view gets the priorities of the process in the wrong order. Far from being the product of this process of maturation, bureaucratization was its essential prerequisite. Keynesian-based corporate liberalism, where employers and labour leaders increasingly shared the same attitudes, values and objectives, could only come about once the initiative and leadership had passed from the rank and file to the bureaucrats. The process had been at work before 1914 but from the 1930s, in the work of Lewis and Hillman, and then throughout the war in the influence exerted by Hillman and Murray on war planning, it became systematised. The purge of the Communists after the war completed the process.

Finally, a new generation of leaders took command in the 1950s. Since 1940 Lewis had been increasingly isolated, a power in the coal industry but without influence in the labour movement as a whole. Hillman had died in 1946, and Lewis had taken the UMW out of the AFL again in 1948. When Bill Green and Philip Murray died within days of each other in November 1952 the 'Old Guard' of the New Deal had gone completely. George Meany became president of the AFL, Walter Reuther of the CIO. The contrast between them in background and personality was as striking as that twenty years earlier between Lewis and Hillman. Yet Meany and Reuther epitomised the new-style labour leadership. Meany had started in the New York building trade, got early on to the plumber's union staff, and risen bat-like to power in the AFL. As his biographer has written, he 'articulated a public philosophy of American exceptionalism, laborite Keynesianism, and adamant anti-Communism'.[1] Walter Reuther, who had worked in Soviet Russia in the early 1930s, had admired the system there and been a Socialist and a radical organizer with the UAW on his return, personified in the late 1940s and early 1950s the transition from rank-and-file activism to bureaucratic control.

This new leadership operated in an intellectual climate transformed by the Keynesian revolution in economic thinking. Experience of the Great Depression, the Roosevelt recession of 1937–38 and the war had led in the 1950s to widespread acceptance of those Keynesian notions which had seemed outlandish in the early 1930s. A whole generation of students, such as John Kenneth Galbraith and Paul Samuelson, had set out on a voyage of discovery which made economics as exciting as astronomy had been in the time of Copernicus or Kelper. As the English poet John Donne wrote in his *Anatomy of the World* in the early 17th century, 'The new philosophy calls all in doubt'. So did the philosophy of Keynes, and it spread quickly after 1940. Economists drafted to wartime government service, civil servants, people in banking, business and industry, labour union research departments and a whole cohort of graduate students shared a new set of economic ideas which provided the background of shared aims and beliefs against which the dialogue of corporate liberalism was played.

Another point needs making too: the path followed by American labour in its progress to maturity was not that adopted by other nations. West German industry achieved its postwar 'economic miracle' on the basis of a system of co-determination between management and labour largely imposed by the victorious Allies on the postwar rubble. This paralleled the industrial council plan for long favoured by Philip Murray. Yet the system evolved into a corporate, non-adversarial one similar to the American, but with a much lower strike rate than in the United States. In postwar Britain, rank-and-file shop stewards' movements placed far more initiative and power on the shop floor. In France and Italy large and influential Communist unions changed the whole mix of industrial relations. Japan's industrial growth, eventually even more impressive than the German, which came to challenge and even surpass its mentor the United States, stemmed from a system of parternalistic labour relations peculiar to Japanese history and culture. Moreover, whereas in Britain and Western Europe the prosperity generated by postwar Keynesianism was used to finance a comprehensive Welfare State, in America this prosperity was used to justify not constructing such a universal, national system. The huge size and inexorable expansion of America's GNP, it was argued, meant that prosperity would trickle down to everyone and end poverty. Yet poverty, along with racial discrimination, remained a persistent problem in the United States, largely unseen and certainly not confronted until it burst on stage again in the 1960s as it had in the 1930s.

II

One final obstacle seem to stand in the way of the kind of corporate consensus which came to characterize the 1950s. This was the Taft–Hartley Act. President Harry Truman's unexpected and dramatic re-election in November 1948 had raised labour's hopes that the law might actually be repealed. This was not to be. A conservative coalition of Republicans and southern Democrats was now largely in control of Congress, and it had little sympathy with organized labour. Yet one amendment was adopted. Elections for the union shop had shown such overwhelming worker support that they were dropped. Otherwise, every move to revise or repeal the law was beaten back. Taft–Hartley remained on the statute books.

Labour continued to attack the 'slave-labour' law, with inaccurate and ineffective rhetoric True, certain of its provisions, like Section 14(b) with its encouragement of State right-to-work laws, did impede union organization. Yet there was growth in the next few years and the proportion of the nation's workers covered by collective bargaining agreements rose steadily. More important, the act demonstrated the truth that the law cannot enforce industrial harmony.

Where Taft–Hartley proved most ineffective as an agent of industrial peace was in settling strikes that endangered the public welfare. Title II, which labour condemned as re-establishing 'the abhorrent principle of government by injunction', offered no real solution. Between 1948 and 1952 its provisions were invoked reluctantly and often served to confuse rather than clarify the issues in dispute. The first major strike that led President Truman to use injunction proceedings came in coal. Despite the settlement which had been reached in 1947, intermittent work stoppages continued, and a new controversy developed when Lewis and the UMW claimed that the operators had dishonoured their contract over the health and welfare fund. This dispute was finally ironed out; but in 1949 Lewis began to agitate for higher pay. He avoided directly calling a strike, but instead called a series of so called 'memorial' stoppages spotlighting scandalously high death and injury rates in the mines.

As these work stoppages continued, Truman finally felt compelled under public pressure to invoke Title II of Taft–Hartley and on 6 February 1950 he obtained a temporary injunction against any further strikes. Union instructions ordering the miners back to work were largely ignored so the government began contempt proceedings against the United Mine Workers on the grounds that orders calling off the strike had been given only 'token compliance'. A Federal court, however, refused to sustain this charge, arguing that the government had not proved lack of good faith by the union. Thus blocked, Truman turned rather desperately to Congress for authority

– as in wartime – to seize the coal mines. While Congress dithered, a new agreement was finally reached in March 1950 and work stoppages ceased, without further governmental intervention. Taft–Hartley had proved very inconclusive as a means of enforcing industrial discipline.

This impression was strengthened when a steel industry strike involving the law's emergency provisions took place in 1952. It lasted nearly two months – the longest and costliest work stoppage the industry had ever experienced. Against the background of the Korean War, it aroused public concern comparable only to the strike crises during the Second World War. As then, wages and hours had again been put under government control as a result of Korea. When contract negotiations between the United Steelworkers and the industry broke down at the end of 1951, the dispute was referred to a new Wage Stabilization Board.

The USW agreed not to strike until the Board made its report and when the Board did so three months later, the union agreed to accept it. However steel employers denounced the report for advocating recognition of the union shop, and linked the proposed pay settlement to compensatory increases in the price of steel too. This looked like 1946 all over again. When the Federal government's Economic Stabilization Director denied the price increase, the industry rejected the settlement as a whole and the union prepared to strike. Instead, on 8 April 1952, Truman took the drastic step of seizing the steel plants on his own authority as the only way to maintain production vital to the Korean war effort. 'I feel sure', he stated, 'that the Constitution does not require me to endanger our national safety by letting all the steel mills close down at this particular time.'[2]

This created a storm. Though the steelworkers remained on the job, employers promptly took the matter to the courts. The legal issue was fought out against a confused background of preliminary injunctions against government operation, temporary stays of court orders, and a final appeal to the Supreme Court. On 2 June 1952, the latter ruled that seizure of the mills was unconstitutional. When Truman returned the mills to private hands the 560 000 steelworkers resumed their strike and brought production to a complete halt.

Controversy raged, while the USW and the employers renewed contract negotiations. Not until 26 July did they come to terms. The settlement at last reached generally conformed to that originally proposed by the Wage Stabilization Board in March, but in the meantime the strike had cost the industry 350 million dollars and the workers 50 million dollars in lost wages. More important, the strike had not only crippled the steel industry itself but had also caused many steel-using plants and automobile assembly lines to halt. It had seriously endangered the flow of essential military materials to Korea, and only the gradual cessation of hostilities there had prevented an even graver crisis.

Truman, rebuffed by the Court when he used an injunction against the UMW, now flatly refused widespread public demands that he seek an injunction under Taft–Hartley. Further pressure, he argued, was unwarranted, since steel workers had refrained from striking for three months while the Board investigated, and had then accepted for the Board report. Truman also tried to work more closely with the USW than he had with the UMW earlier, and by his handling of this 1952 steel dispute Philip Murray became Truman's favourite labour leader.

A third major strike, which in this instance did lead to action under the Taft–Hartley Act, occurred in 1953 on the docklands of New York, where the issue was corruption. True, the International Longshoremen's Association and the New York Shipping Association had failed to agree terms over wages and hiring practices, but the dispute became much more complicated than the strikes in coal or in steel which had been about pay. With the work stoppage tying up all shipping in New York, the AFL expelled the ILA union on charges of racketeering and chartered a new, less gangster-ridden longshoremen's organization; the state authoritites of New York and New Jersey intervened in the interests of law and order; and a Senate investigating committee angrily reported that the waterfront had become a 'lawless frontier' plagued by corruption, Communism and hoodlums. President Dwight D. Eisenhower, the war-hero who had now succeeded Truman, finally invoked the emergency provisions of the Taft–Hartley Act. Yet despite a Federal injunction a series of wildcat strikes occurred, caused by the bitter fight between the old and new longshoremen's unions, between established racketeers and those seeking to clean up the union.

Elections supervised by the Nation Labor Relations Board ultimately confirmed the right of the original ILA union, in spite of all the justified charges of corruption that had been brought against it, to represent the longshoremen: the ILA may have been crooked, but it had a long history of bargaining rights on its side. Negotiations were then resumed and a settlement reached which barred both strikes and lockouts for a two-year period. Something like peace temporarily returned to the embattled waterfront. But once again government intervention under Taft–Hartley had proved wholly unsatisfactory.

Other strikes which occurred in the aftermath of Taft–Hartley also hit the headlines and revealed the weakness of the law in tackling the causes of industrial unrest rather than the symptoms. Communications workers, textile workers, car workers, construction workers and others all had relatively brief stoppages. Railwaymen staged a series of 'sick' walkouts in 1951 which led to government threats to dismiss all employees who did not stay on the job. In 1952 the coal miners fought yet another strike. Strikes made good copy in the press. What passed largely unnoticed, however, was that in spite of all the furore over the coal miners, steel workers, longshoremen and other restive unionists, there had actually been a rapid and steep decline in strike-rate. The annual total of man-days lost in the years between 1947 and 1951 averaged 40 million in comparison with 116 million in 1946. Industrial unrest was returning to the level common throughout the history of the United States.

Controversy over Taft–Hartley and headlines about a handful of so-called national emergency strikes masked even more significant developments in labour relations. For one thing, when times were good and labour was scarce, unions continued to grow. They reached their relative membership peak at the end of the Korean War in 1954 when 20 million workers, or 36 per cent of the non-agricultural labour force, belonged to unions. Even in the South, where Taft–Hartley probably had a more restrictive impact on labour than elsewhere, union membership grew proportionately more rapidly. More important, an entirely new pattern of bargaining agreements was starting to appear.

III

Once again, as with the 1936–37 sit-down strike for union recognition, and the 1945–46 challenge to management prerogative, the decisive initiative came from the UAW. General Motors had resisted the union's bid to link company pricing policy with a negotiated pay settlement in 1946, and refused to open its books, but only at the cost of a damaging 113-day strike. Yet GM president Charles E. Wilson was a sophisticated conservative, who realised that such large-scale, disruptive strikes must end. They hampered the company's long-term planning and embittered shop-floor relations. Since they were caused largely by acrimonious bargaining for annual wage increases which in turn had been prompted by the uncontrolled postwar inflationary surge, the solution was to offer the union long-term contracts which sought both to control inflation and to protect workers against its corrosive effects. So in 1948 GM offered the UAW a two-year contract which included what were to become the twin pillars of postwar industrial relations: first, an automatic cost-of-living adjustment, or COLA as it was called, triggered by any rise in the general price index; second, a two percent pay 'annual improvement factor' reflecting, if only partially, the still larger annual rise in GM worker productivity.

Walter Reuther, the new president of the UAW who was in hospital recovering from the attempt on his life, endorsed the 1948 proposal because it included ideas of his own. Two years later he took a more active role, negotiating an even more elaborate package with GM which included a 125 dollar-a-month pension, improved COLA and productivity rates, all of which, most remarkably, was included in an unprecedented five-year contract. Thus Reuther and Wilson helped lay the foundations for the impressively stable social compact between capital and labour, based upon low inflation, which was to govern class relations in the United States for a generation until the 1970s. Despite his radical past and flair for innovative thinking, Reuther was by 1950 moving to a more defensive position which sought to conserve the gains labour had already won. The turning point had come in 1946–47, when Reuther had defeated the Addes–Thomas–Frankensteen caucus to win the presidency of the UAW, failed to force GM to share its power on profit distribution, but gone on to drive the Communists out of both the UAW and the CIO. Passage of the Taft–Hartley Act, the fiasco of Henry Wallace's campaign for President in 1948, and the deepening Cold War crisis had convinced him and many other union activists by the end of the decade that only anti-Communism and a more cooperative approach to management in creating a corporate consensus could protect them from further political attack while the Dixiecrat/Republican caucus still ruled Congress.

Like many founders of the liberal reformist Americans for Democratic Action, Reuther was determined to make his social and political views, which stemmed from the New Deal experience, more acceptable in the vastly changed atmosphere of the late 1940s by making his anti-Communist credentials quite clear. But ADA's efforts to revitalize the old Roosevelt social reform coalition had been blunted by the defection of many of its constituent elements, by the rightward drift in domestic politics and the growing self-confidence of the business community who were constructing the military-industrial complex. Instead of using union power to widen the Welfare State and force government to alter its economic and political priorities, union leaders like Reuther increasingly sought their own narrow constituency interests. 'Though he still fought to make the UAW a vanguard of social reconstruction,' his biographer Nelson Lichtenstein has noted, 'Walter Reuther could not escape the political and economic logic of his era.'[3] Sensing that America was entering a period of unexpected economic prosperity, he now played a key role in advancing a uniquely American version of labour's destiny in a Keynesian capitalist economy. It both assured rising living standards for the organized working class, and set firm limits to the overall exercise of union power.

Following the UAW agreement with GM in 1948 and 1950, the union negotiated similar contracts with Chrysler and Ford, while unions in other industries followed suit. Not surprisingly the union which bargained for more than a million workers in the nation's most important manufacturing industry set the standard followed in steel, mining, rubber, chemicals, textiles and road transport. The concept of pace-setting agreements was emerging. Moreover, the fact that a comprehensive Welfare State, on British or European lines, failed for political reasons to emerge in the United States made pension and health benefits, and the supplementary unemployment benefit (SUB), a form of guaranteed annual income added to unions contracts in 1955, even more vital. The UAW programme amounted to a sort of privatized Welfare State that by some estimates virtually doubled the real standard of living of American motor industry workers in the quarter century after 1945.[4] The retreat which all this represented from earlier attempts to limit managerial authority, start economic planning and sustain social reform for all was explained by *Fortune* magazine. 'GM may have paid a billion for peace,' it said of the landmark 1950 Treaty of Detroit, 'but it got a bargain. General Motors has regained control over one of the crucial management functions ... long-range scheduling of production, model changes, and tool and plant investment.'[5]

The strength of this new consensus, which historians have come to call corporate liberalism, was such that it survived the return of the Republican Party to the White House. With Dwight D. Eisenhower's election victory in 1952 right-wing Republicans had hoped he would reverse the policies of government economic intervention begun during the New Deal, expanded during the war and continued afterwards. No such roll-back of the Federal government occurred, despite the continued dominance in Congress of the Dixiecrat/ Republican conservative coalition. Just as Taft–Hartley was proving an uncertain means of curbing union power, so Eisenhower's attempts to balance the Federal Budget, like FDR's in 1937–38, led to recession in 1954–55. However, wise and vigorous Keynesian fiscal policy helped control inflation, which in turn guaranteed rising real incomes, profits, consumer demand and employment. Like Reuther with unions, GM's Wilson (known as 'Engine Charlie') became the outstanding exponent on management's side of this Keynesian consensus. When Eisenhower made him Secretary of Defense he occupied the central position in the military–industrial complex now controlling the economy. He became notorious for saying that he had always believed that 'What is good for General Motors is good for America, and vice versa'. Despite cries of outrage, this was the central fact about the new prosperity. Its corollary was that what was good for GM was good for the UAW, and vice versa.

The ripples caused by the UAW's new approach to pay bargaining after 1948 within the context of Keynesian capitalism spread across the calm surface of the 1950s. In negotiating on behalf of its aircraft workers at North American Aviation the union faced a special problem. Even during the Second World War aircraft workers had been comparatively low-paid. When war ended the demand for aircraft declined sharply and further differentials developed between them and UAW members working in the booming car industry. Verbatim transcripts which have survived of union–management negotiation in 1948 and afterwards provide fascinating insights into the attitudes of both sides.[6] E. D. Stark-weather, chief negotiator for the company, told Ben Nathanson, the union spokesman, in August 1948, 'I thought the CIO had learned its lesson. For about three years now they have been wanting to tie wages to the cost of living. . . . That is a foolish way to try to control the economy.' Nathanson replied, 'You are arguing along with some economists that that perpetuates inflation. . . . Our argument is that the wages never pulled up with the cost of living and we are always behind the eight ball.'[7]

Employers constantly voiced fears of what inflation would do to the value of money and profits, as reams of propaganda produced by the National Association of Manufacturers in the postwar period testify. What they were slow to understand was that controlled inflation was the name of the game in the postwar economic era. It would boost demand, sales and profits, while increased productivity would more than pay for higher wages and better conditions. Fringe benefits, made acceptable as a way round the Little Steel formula and wartime pay freeze, became increasingly popular with management and union negotiators. At North American Aviation they discussed sickness, hospital, life insurance and retirement pension plans, and how to pay for them. Comparisons with the approach to fringe benefits at other companies – GM, Kaiser, Bell, Fairchild, Lockheed, Douglas and elsewhere – abounded on both sides.[8] The contract signed at the end of the summer of 1948 contained a clause which looked back to the setting up of the Fair Employment Practices Commission in 1941, and forward to the civil rights movement about to erupt in America during the next decade. 'In applying the terms of this agreement,' it read, 'the company agrees that it will not discriminate against employees because of their race, creed, color or national origin.'[9]

The real nub of the contract remained wages, however, and the new agreement announced in October 1949 brought an average gain of 11 cents an hour to aircraft workers. Before the next pay round, the Korean War broke out, and American leadership of the United Nations police action enhanced government regulation of industry. Inflation rose, and the Wage Stabilization Board was revived to try to control it. Determined to bring their wages into line with those in other basic industries, and particularly with the motor industry, UAW Local 887 prepared for a strike. The issue was about 'first class' wage rates paid by the car companies and 'second class' wage rates paid by North American. 'There is talk these days', the union noted, 'about what the Wage Stabilization Board will allow. . . . Certainly our union agreed there must be stabilization during a time

of national emergency. But wage stabilization is *not* a wage freeze
. . . it is designed to give wage equity.'[10]

The threatened strike would have stopped production of F–86
Sabre jets needed in Korea. So the Federal government intervened.
President Truman deplored the probable effects of the intended
strike and appointed a panel to arbitrate the dispute. 'Maturity
means the period between negotiations,' observed one union
negotiator during these discussions on 12 September 1950 – an
interesting gloss on notions of maturity and bureaucracy in the
labour movement. Truman had warned about the danger of creating
another wage/price spiral, management explained, and employers
feared automatic pay improvements by the use of COLA would tend
to do this. The GM contract, management argued, was inflationary,
while the cost of living alone did not justify pay increases. Seeking
increases beyond the cost of living would inevitably increase the cost
of living. 'Aircraft workers should be patient', the corporation
concluded, 'because they are indirectly working for the United
States government.'[11] This last point was, of course, crucial.
Moreover the company's whole argument neglected the way rising
profits were based upon rising productivity, which in turn funded
pay rises. Finally the union made it clear it could see advantage in a
five-year contract on the lines of GM's 1950 agreement with the
UAW.[12] Finally, the justice of a pay rise at North American was
clear.

According to government figures, 90 per cent of North American
employees earned less than the 2.80 dollars an hour the Wage
Stablization Board judged necessary for a 'modest but adequate
budget' for a family of four. Kaiser–Frazer had reorganized the vast
Willow Run plant in Michigan to produce both giant transporter
planes and passenger cars, with workers on both lines getting the
same 'first class' rates.[13] With the government spending 3 billion
dollars a year on aircraft orders, all major manufacturers were doing
the same. In an attempt to revive the organization of foremen, which
had petered out after the Taft–Hartley Act, the UAW made a
special appeal to all supervisors. 'We . . . ask you to think more
clearly about current wage negotiations,' the unions wrote. 'You
may consider yourselves in the middle. . . . You believe in the fight
for first class pay. Top management is trying to push you into their
camp. . . . They may have presented some arguments that sounded
reasonable. But remember this. All of that nonsense still adds up to

five cents an hour pay cuts for you and 40 000 other people at work.'[14] In the end Truman's panel reported in terms which favoured the union, not the company, and the Wage Stabilization Board settled the strike on the basis of a 10 cents an hour increase on 28 April 1952.[15]

This pattern continued as the 1950s progressed. The year 1954 saw fewer strikes than any since the Second World War. They were not just fewer in number, but mostly small and mostly short. The explanation, the *Wall Street Journal* suggested, was the steadier pace of business development, the Eisenhower administration's 'hands-off' policy in labour/management disputes, the remarkably stable cost of living after the post-1945 and Korean War experiences and 'preventive mediation' by the NLRB and other agencies nipping potential strikes in the bud.[16] On the union side there was a quest for security. The ugly conflicts on the New York/New Jersey waterfronts, dramatized in Elia Kazan's movie *On the Waterfront*, were caused by a conspiracy between gangsters and union racketeers. Both New York's Republican Governor Thomas Dewey and Eisenhower's Secretary of Labor John Mitchell agreed about that.[17] But President Eisenhower himself was unable to do anything effective about the situation by invoking Taft–Hartley, and relations between the AFL and CIO were soured by the whole situation.

Nevertheless unions as a whole were able to use the economic prosperity which characterized the 1950s to win significant advances in wages and benefits. Senator Paul Douglas, a former University of Chicago professor of economics and one of the most enthusiastic Keynesians in the Democratic Party, advised the CIO throughout this period on the way to present its case to the public. The vast profits being made by the nation's major manufacturers were the basis for union claims when the landmark 1950 five-year contract expired in the auto industry. As Reuther told Douglas in a briefing paper, 'General Motors profits before taxes during the second quarter of 1955 amounted to 734.4 million dollars – a rate of nearly 3 billion dollars a year. These profits were equivalent to an utterly fantastic 89.1 per cent of net worth on an annual basis. At this rate, profits before taxes would equal General Motors' entire net worth in less than 14 months.'[18]

After taxes, GM profits from April until June 1955 amounted to 351.6 million dollars, equivalent to more than 1.4 billion dollars a year. This represented an annual return on net worth at the rate of

42.1 per cent; enough to recapture the entire net worth of the corporation in 28 months. These figures did not include 41.6 million dollars set aside to pay bonuses to a handful of top executives. For every dollar GM's hundreds of thousands of hourly-paid workers earned, top executives took 85 cents in bonuses. 'Yet if the corporation raises its prices', Reuther pointed out, 'it will be the modest gains of the workers rather than the lavish handouts to top personnel that will be used as the excuse.'[19] The situation was similar at Ford, while US Steel reported an equally steep rise in profits in the second quarter of 1955, up 41.6 per cent on the first quarter to 209.2 million dollars, an annual rate of return of 17.9 per cent. Had the recent pay rises to steel mill workers been given to all the corporation's workers, the cost would have been less than 7.5 per cent of its total labour cost. Yet even without raising prices such an increase would still have yielded profits of 14.8 per cent, far higher than the 11.2 per cent reported in 1950.[20]

Profits had risen impressively across the board in American manufacturing industry throughout the 1950s. 'Unquestionably 1955 will be the most profitable year in the history of the Steel Industry,' the CIO reported in December. 'In fact, Net Profits for the *first nine months* of 1955 are already higher than for any full year in the history of the Steel Industry.'[21] Ford tried to blame its increased tractor prices on higher wages paid to car and steel workers, but the UAW responded by claiming that both industries had made 'scandalous profits'.[22] With industry booming, President Eisenhower tried to do what he had done in 1954–55 (and what FDR had done in 1937–38) by cutting public spending in order to balance the Budget. The consequence was the same: a deepening recession which put an estimated 11 per cent of the total workforce of 57 million either on short time or fully unemployed in 1957–58. The Senate Antitrust and Monopoly Committee, chaired by the Tennessee Democrat Estes Kefuaver with three members from each party, met to consider the problem of the Eisenhower recession.

The answer, Senator Paul Douglas told them, was to cut the prices of steel and cars and reduce taxes 'to stimulate purchasing power'. His argument was completely Keynesian, pointing out that such cuts would have a multiplier effect of three – a 6 billion dollar cut would bring an 18 billion dollar increase in Gross National Product.[23] The Senate Committee found that in the steel industry prices had risen 19.50 dollars a ton in the 12-month period before the enquiry began on 8 August 1957, and concluded, 'The steel industry was not justified in imposing recent price increases, since the increases substantially exceeded its cost increases.'[24] But Douglas went further, proposing cuts in steel prices and a reduction of the excise tax on cars from 10 per cent to 2.5 per cent, or by 150 dollars on a 2000 dollar model. 'Here is a perfect example', he pointed out, 'for the exercise of that "partnership" between industry and government which the present Administration has been urging so strongly.' It was all the easier, Douglas concluded, because 'It happens that this is an industry with only four major producing companies and with only one union'.[25]

The corporate consensus of the 1950s was, in short, based on corporations bargaining with one industrial union, like the UAW or the USW. Moreover, the pattern of the UAW picking one car company to strike on expiry of its contract, and then using the new agreement it won to bring the other three into line, was by now well developed. It was one of the political advantages unions gained from such contracts. The 1958 UAW strike at Chrysler on expiry of the 1955 contract was a case in point. Here too the union used Keynesian arguments about the need to stimulate demand during a recession, basing its claim on company profits and worker productivity. Reviving tactics he had used in 1946, Reuther wrote to GM management, urging 1958 models be reduced by at least 100 dollars from 1957 prices to help reduce inflation. Harlow Curtice, GM's president, replied that he found Reuther's concern with inflation hard to reconcile with the union's claim 'for the biggest pay hike in the history of the UAW, a shorter work week, bigger pensions, insurance welfare and SUBs, which would all fuel inflation'. Most important, GM was 'not willing to negotiate the prices of its products with any Union ... the prices of its products are not properly the object of collective bargaining'.[26]

By 1958 the UAW was negotiating a 35-hour week and talking of profit-sharing, while the United Steelworkers, under David McDonald's leadership, was doing the same.[27] Steel, like the motor industry, also had one union and a handful of corporations, which strengthened the USW's hand. In the summer and autumn of 1959 the USW fought a three-month strike. 'Despite unprecedented profits', Reuther argued on behalf of the CIO 'and the tremendous rise in productivity', steel management not only refused higher wages but threatened to undermine protection the CIO had won 'against erosion of your present wages'. While corporation profits as a whole rose 56 per cent in 1958–59, steel profits alone rose by an incredible 196 per cent. 'Steelworkers are only asking gains of approximately 300 dollars out of a profit of 4500 dollars per worker.' Other industries were equally well fixed, Reuther added. 'GM made a total profit of 1.2 billion dollars. Ford Motors could have sold every car for 100 dollars less and still made 21 per cent profit after taxes.' Yet President Eisenhower opposed a 1.25 dollar national minimum wage 'because it is inflationary'.[28]

The shock of the first Soviet sputnik in October 1957 came as a traumatic blow to American self-confidence, however, and transformed priorities in government spending. Budget appropriations were hastily made to catch up with Russia and it was significant that the UAW had been arguing the case for investing large sums of Federal money on developing a guided missile system in the early 1950s. Space spending was to help sustain economic prosperity right through the 1960s, a decade when fears of inflation were less commonly expressed by corporate and government leaders.

IV

The corporate compact which coalesced in the 1950s and helped shape the economy transformed the adversarial relationship of unions and management not only at the bargaining table but on the shop floor too. The UAW's tradition of being a 'bottom up' union, where local union autonomy and rank-and-file insurgency ruled, meant that the new bureaucratic stability could not be established at once. Still less did it mean that Reuther and other leading UAW officials sought directly to impose the kind of 'top down' autocratic internal regime which characterized mining under Lewis, steel under Murray and his successor David McDonald, or road haulage under Dave Beck and Jimmy Hoffa of the Teamsters Union. Reuther had pioneered grievance systems during the Second World War at GM and later throughout the motor industry. Despite this, shop floor conflict remained endemic during the prosperous 1950s and 1960s. At Chrysler and International Harvester wildcat strikes were actually more frequent in the 1950s than they had been in the previous decade. Even at GM, where tough management penalized unauthorized walkouts, the number of grievances filed increased significantly. The difference between the 1930s and the 1950s, however, was that the union came increasingly to control this discontent.[29] As one radical worker put it, 'When I was a kid, if somebody asked me to define a grievance, I'd say it was something we don't like. Today, a grievance is something not in accordance with standards of arbitration. We're even *told* what the hell to be dissatisfied with these days.'[30] Individual Locals remained militant, but the UAW as a whole no longer aimed at transforming shop-floor relations in the motor industry.

Perhaps the real difference between the 1930s and the 1950s was not so much a reduction in shop-floor conflict, but the ability of unionized workers to project their fight on to a nationwide bargaining agenda. Of course, from the point of view of the shop floor, this had its drawbacks as well as its advantages. National leaders increasingly concentrated on those elements of bargaining which could be monetized and quantified, such as wages and fringe benefits. Locals still had the right to strike over other things, like speed-ups, work assignments, job content and other classic causes of dispute; and they did so with mounting frequency in the 1960s. But such issues took an increasingly subordinate place on the bargaining agenda when a union's national leaders sat down with corporate management to hammer out nationwide settlements. After 1958 the UAW, for example, adopted an informal policy of authorizing stoppages on these local issues, but only after a national contract had been negotiated, which severely limited the power of local officials, which it was designed to do. Still, these strikes were politically useful. They gave the rank and file a chance to let off steam, while enabling local officers to trade off difficult shopfloor grievances before they started to fester during the remainder of the contract.[31]

Within the UAW Reuther had since 1947 consolidated his control of the union by purging his opponents, creating an efficient bureaucracy and cultivating a liberal reformist but nonetheless monolithic political culture. The elimination of unionwide opposition to the national leadership in such democratic unions as the UAW had, by the 1950s, greatly reduced the relative freedom local officials had enjoyed a decade earlier, when two factions – led respectively by Addes and Reuther – had competed for their support. Communists could no longer exploit or lead rank-and-file discontent. Shop-floor activists were by the end of the decade either isolated by clever use of the union's growing organizational strength, or co-opted on to the union staff and controlled by patronage. When opposition did erupt from below, as during the inflationary swell of the Korean War, Reuther had been able to use wildcat strikes to force the major motor employers to re-open the five-year contracts they had signed with the UAW in 1950. Later in the 1950s he faced insurgent opposition from skilled workers, who threatened to disaffiliate unless more attention was paid to their special position. Mindful of the problems Homer Martin's breakaway UAW–AFL union had caused in the 1930s, Reuther pushed through changes in the UAW constitution which gave craftsmen a veto over contract negotiations and a more secure status in the union.[32] With the largest and most influential of industrial unions giving power to craft workers, and other industrial unions following the UAW pattern, the time seemed ripe to do something to heal the breach between the industrial CIO and the craft-based AFL.

When Philip Murray and Bill Green had died in November 1952 the time had seemed auspicious. Reuther, still only 45, succeeded Murray as president of the CIO, after a sharp political struggle between contending factions. Yet there could be no doubting Reuther's qualifications, even amongst his enemies. Able, abstemious, ambitious, he was a skilful organizer and stubborn negotiator who was more articulate in presenting his views to the public than any labour leader of his time. Despising the 'nickel and dime' attitude of business unionism, his ideas still owed something to the Socialist theory of his early manhood; but his approach was now completely pragmatic. Labour should work within the existing economic and social structure and ally itself to the Democratic Party. The new AFL president, George Meany, was a Roman Catholic, committed anti-Communist and corporate Keynesian, who had spent his whole life within the comfortable ambience of craft unionism. Little known outside union ranks, he had made his name within them as AFL secretary-treasurer in 1947 by demolishing the argument of the formidable John L. Lewis at the federation's convention on the issue of compliance with Taft–Hartley over non-Communist affidavits. A large, cigar-smoking figure, he was nearly 15 years older then Reuther and looked like the old-style labour boss that he was. But he had worked hard at making the AFL respond to the CIO's organizational challenge; at backing anti-Communist unions in postwar Europe; and in launching the new International Confederation of Free Trade Unions.

Like Murray before him, Meany was a convinced anti-Communist, but a more fervent supporter of the Truman Doctrine, the Marshall Plan, the creation of NATO, the Korean War and the other foundations of American foreign policy during the Cold War. He had begun his working life as a plumber, but unlike Green, Lewis, Reuther or Murray, lacked the home base of a powerful union. He had never led a strike, or even walked a picket line. Yet for more than thirty years he had been an administrator, lobbyist and bureaucrat. No one knew the work of legislative committees, regulatory bodies or the inner workshops of union politics better. In short, he was perfectly qualified to lead the AFL in the emerging corporate consensus of the 1950s, a man whose strengths and weaknesses complemented Reuther's. As with Reuther, his rise to the top of the labour movement indicated that the torch had passed to a new generation of leaders.

V

Such new leadership was needed. Despite its expansion and growing prosperity in the 1950s labour had learned a bitter lesson from passage of the Taft–Hartley Act. Economic advances could be snatched away unless they were underpinned by solid strength on the political front. The campaign for repeal continued unabated, but was thwarted by the Dixiecrat/Republican conservative coalition which now controlled Congress, and moreover made further social reform or effective action on civil rights impossible. Republican victory at the polls in November 1952 had dashed all such hopes, yet revision still seemed possible. President Eisenhower's experience, like Truman's before him, showed that Taft–Hartley needed correction. Moreover Ike's Secretary of Labor, Martin P. Durkin, was a former building tradesman (it was said Eisenhower's Cabinet consisted of nine millionaires and a plumber) and keen to amend the law. But though Durkin drafted 19 proposed changes to Taft–Hartley nothing was done, and he resigned charging Eisenhower with dishonouring his promise of support.

With this final failure to get anything about Taft–Hartley, the leadership of both AFL and CIO realized again that they would have to consolidate their political strength if they were to resist the danger of further restrictive legislation. The AFL had already followed the example of the CIO's Political Action Committee by establishing its own League for Political Action. Both organizations had worked hard, if not successfully, for the Democrats in Adlai Stevenson's 1952 election campaign. They now co-operated fully with each other to bring pressure to bear on Congress in labour's interest. This lobbying helped extend the Social Security programme, first established in 1935, to cover a growing number of workers with old-age and survivor insurance benefits, where monthly payments were substantially increased. In 1954 the Supreme Court's decision in *Brown* v. *Board of Education* began the process of dismantling segregation for black Americans. Then in 1955 Congress raised the minimum wage under the 1937 Fair Labor Standards Act from 75 cents to a dollar an hour. Finally, on another front, union lobbies worked consistently for passage through Congress of the health-care programme for the elderly, which became known as Medicair when it finally bore fruit in the 1960s.

But the immediate challenge in the 1950s was for organized labour to reform itself. These years were marked by substantial union economic advance and increasingly successful counter-attack through lobbying on the political front, as well as progress in civil rights for all American workers. Yet the forces of American labour remained divided as they had been since the 1937 schism. Of the estimated total of something like 18 million union members in the mid-1950s, the AFL claimed some 9 million, the CIO around 6 million, with approximately 2.5 million belonging to the United Mine Workers, the railway brotherhoods, and other independent unions. There had been repeated efforts – in 1937, in 1939, in 1941–43 and 1946–47 – to establish 'organic unity' among these divided elements.[33] A number of committees had been set up to discuss the complicated jurisdictional issues involved. But despite agreement in general terms that 'the economic, social and industrial interests of labor can best be served through the establishment of a united labor movement',[34] no satisfactory formula for achieving this could be devised.

Yet the original conflict between the AFL and CIO over industrial unionism had subsided. Both federations had long accepted that industrial unions had their place alongside, not in opposition to, craft unions. Some of the leading craft unions in the AFL, such as the machinists and the carpenters, had organized certain branches on industrial lines. Industrial unions, like the UAW, now made special arrangements for their skilled workers. Both national federations had increasingly cooperated, from the time of the War Labor Board and the No Strike pledge in 1942 until the creation of the United Labor Policy Council during the Korean War. They were in complete accord in their opposition to Taft–Hartley. Only the persistence of old personal rivalries between their leaders had delayed the move towards an effective merger. Now the leaders who had conducted these battles – Lewis, Green, Hillman, Murray – had either died or been shunted to the sidelines. The new leadership of Meany and Reuther was bound to give fresh momentum to the drive for reunification.

Despite the stark contrast between them, Meany and Reuther complemented each other. Where Reuther was hard-hitting and dynamic, his idealistic view of labour's role tempered by pragmatism, Meany was a careful bureaucrat who agreed with Reuther that labour must work within the existing framework yet aim at greater goals. The new heads of the federations also epitomised the steady professionalization and bureaucratization of the labour postwar movement. By the 1950s union officials earned high salaries, received substantial fringe benefits and held office for long terms. Labour leadership was less of a calling, more a career. Postwar labour leaders now commonly had higher education and law degrees. Even in the days of Samuel Gompers, some labour leaders had seen themselves as labour bureaucrats or executives. But by the 1950s more union officials were better educated and increasingly met regularly with corporate executives and powerful Federal officials. This meant top union leaders were increasingly removed from the rank and file they represented and were becoming part of a corporate élite.

Nevertheless Reuther and Meany were committed to the cause of labour unity as a basis for enhanced political strength, and ready to settle the differences which had divided the AFL and CIO for nearly two decades. A first step, in June 1953, was a two-year 'no-raiding' agreement among constituent unions, ratified the following year by both AFL and CIO conventions. Union piracy and jurisdictional strikes had long been recognized as disruptive, and perhaps the greatest obstacle to reunification. Meany and Reuther had both the vision and the authority to tackle the issue head-on, and point the way forward to a settlement which would end this costly and futile inter-union warfare. 'The signing of the No-Raiding Agreement between our two organizations', they jointly announced, 'is an historic step. We are confident that the No-Raiding Agreement may function in the spirit of understanding and fraternal friendship.'[35]

In past discussions about merger the AFL had always charged that the CIO was influenced by Communists, while the CIO argued that the AFL tolerated too much racketeering and racial discrimination. There had been substance in both arguments. But by the 1950s the AFL could no longer point to the danger of Communist infiltration because the CIO had purged such unions from its ranks. However, events on the New York and New Jersey waterfront in 1953 revealed that within the AFL gangsterism was if anything growing.

'We in the CIO don't believe . . . we . . . can tolerate racketeering any more than we are willing to tolerate Communism in the leadership of our own movement,' Reuther declared.[36] Meany promised to act on the New York harbour situation, and told Joe Ryan, brutal president of the International Longshoremen's Association, that he must clean up the ILA as a prelude to merger. First, the traditional 'shape-up' system of hiring dock labour on a casual, day-to-day basis must be replaced by 'a clear and explicit system of hiring' supervised by the New York district council of the AFL. Next the system of payments, involving wholesale use of gifts and bribes, must be changed. Finally, union officials with criminal records 'bring the trades unions into disrepute' must never be employed.[37] These were reasonable requests, especially when a Communist record was regarded as a more serious disqualification for office than a criminal one, but the ILA was so strongly influenced by the underworld that it failed to comply and was duly expelled from the AFL later in the year.

Racketeering remained a chronic, deeply-rooted problem in other unions too, not just on the watefront but in coal mining, construction, clothing, the food industry, the service trades and most notably in road transport, where the gangster-ridden Teamsters became notorious before finally being expelled from the AFL in 1957. Nevertheless Dave Beck of the West Coast Teamsters, who succeeded Dan Tobin as president, had been highly regarded in many quarters in the mid-1950s. On a much publicized trip to Europe he was hailed in the British press and elsewhere as the very model of a modern labour leader. He met Arthur Deakin, his opposite number in Britain, and Labour Party leaders like Clem,

Attlee and Herbert Morrison, criticizing their recent trip to Red China as 'unfortunate'.[38] Posing as a labour diplomat abroad, at home Beck had opposed the no-raiding agreement. Worse, he had repeatedly worked with gangsters and used his union to break strikes. Moreover he had made a million-dollar loan from Teamster funds to the road haulage employer Fruehauf. 'This is certainly a disgrace,' commented a local UAW leader, 'particularly the kind of corporation the Fruehauf Corporation is.'[39]

Despite the problem of the Teamsters, which had surpassed the UAW as the largest labour unions in the United States, unity talks continued. Arthur Goldberg, later to become Secretary of Labor and Supreme Court Justice, handled the CIO side of the merger negotiations, but not without vociferous opposition from left-wing elements in CIO ranks. Mike Quill, leader of the Transport Workers' Union of America, voiced the doubts of many who thought like him. He feared that statements other labour leaders had made so far did not come out strongly enough against racial discrimination or gangsterism, which he saw as the real check on the growth of effective unions. He wanted an AFL promise that it would really stamp out racial discrimination among all its affiliates and guarantee that all gangster elements would be purged. Moreover he wanted the new organization to agree on a 'good, fighting organizational program' so that the 'fighting spirit of the CIO would not be swallowed up by the AFL'. Otherwise, Quill concluded, 'The newly merged organization should be called the Submerged Organization.'[40]

Despite Quill's complaints, and the long history of previous failures, discussions on the merger now made rapid progress. By early 1955, 80 affiliated unions of the AFL and 33 of the CIO had accepted the no-raiding agreement. While it was to prove impossible, then or later, to eradicate jurisdictional strikes entirely, their frequency sharply declined and a better atmosphere developed among rival unions. The AFL and CIO further set up a Joint Unity Committee, headed by Meany and Reuther, which explored practical ways of merging. Discussions were secret, and outside official labour circles little was known about their progress. But the no-raiding agreement had been a significant straw in the wind and on 9 February 1955 the AFL and CIO announced full agreement. This was dramatic news. The draft AFL–CIO constitution would preserve the identity of each affiliated union; the no-raiding agreement would be continued on a voluntary basis; and special departments within the old AFL would remain, supplemented by a new Industrial Union Department.

The merged federation promised vigorous action on the three other internal problems, spotlighted by Mike Quill's criticisms, which plagued the labour movement: corruption, racial discrimination and possible Communist infiltration. On racial discrimination, the civil rights movement, which was growing slowly in the 1950s and then rapidly in the 1960s, left much of the labour movement behind. Merger persuaded expelled racket-ridden unions to seek readmission to the AFL–CIO in search of protection from prosecution and a degree of respectability. Likewise, Communist-led unions sought the greater immunity membership would give them from attack under Taft–Hartley or the Smith Act.[41] CIO support enabled Meany to promise a sustained campaign against criminal influences in the labour movement and to insist that unions accept members regardless of race. Despite his provincial background in the racially discriminatory building trades unions, Meany had worked seriously with civil rights organizations since the 1930s, and not even his severest critics accused him of racial bigotry. Meantime, the CIO deferred to Meany's militant anti-Communism by consenting to a declaration which promised to protect the labour movement from 'the undermining efforts of the Communist agencies and all others who are opposed to the basic principles of our democracy and of free and democratic unionism'.[42]

Since the AFL was older, richer and larger than the CIO – outstripping it in membership by some two to one – it was no surprise that Meany was elected president at the first convention of the new AFL–CIO in December 1955, with another AFL leader as secretary-treasurer. Reuther had to be content with being vice-president in charge of the Industrial Union Department. To achieve unity, Meany had had to distance himself from old-time AFL leaders who still nursed grievances against the CIO, and had broken with tradition by suspending the racket-ridden ILA. His insistence that the merged federation have power to require members to comply with a stiff ethical code gave retrospective sanction to his action over the ILA, while enhancing his future powers as AFL–CIO chief executive. Labour's anti-Communism had also been reaffirmed, and Meany had cleverly exploited deep fractures latent in the CIO – especially those between Reuther's UAW and David

McDonald's steelworkers – to stimulate growing sentiment for re-unification. 'The merger of the AFL and CIO,' Meany later declared, 'reuniting the house of labor, was the accomplishment I take most pride in.'[43] Though already 61 at the time, he was to preside over AFL–CIO affairs for a further 24 years. Reuther's ambition to succeed Meany was thwarted; but his close ties with liberal Democrats like Paul Douglas, Hubert Humphrey, and G. Mennen ('Soapy') Williams were to pay handsome political dividends during the Kennedy–Johnson Administration of the 1960s. In Michigan the UAW virtually took over the State's Democratic Party machine. Reloaction of the AFL–CIO Washington headquarters to right opposite the White House was symbolic. As the turbulent 1960s beckoned, labour seemed to have arrived at the seat of power.

7. The Collapse of the Keynesian Economy

I

At the start of the 1960s American labour appeared to be in a powerful position. After eight years of Eisenhower the Democrats won the White House. They put together the old New Deal coalition of labour unions and political machines, such as those of Richard Daley in Chicago and G. Mennen (Soapy) Williams in Michigan, and the solid South. This gave John F. Kennedy his wafer-thin victory over Richard Nixon in the November race to the White House. Despite his Roman Catholic religion, Kennedy had managed to hold the Democratic South while carrying the vote-heavy industrial States of the Northeast and Great Lakes region (with the exception of Ohio), plus Texas.

Kennedy had promised to 'get America moving again' towards fulfilment of a high-wage, full-employment economy based on Keynesian economics. He was the first President to have come of age and matured when Keynesian notions were winning acceptance, and his Cabinet and staff brimmed with younger men who believed in those ideas. His Secretary of Labor, Arthur Goldberg, had served as counsel to the CIO during its merger negotiations with the AFL in 1955. Goldberg's later promotion to the Supreme Court showed that American labour now influenced the highest branches of the Federal government. Unions should have been able to build upon the consensus created in the 1950s to further their historic goals.

Kennedy's assassination in November 1963 appeared, paradoxically, to strengthen labour's position. His successor, Lyndon Johnson, was a Texan without any important links with the labour movement. As Senate majority leader he had orchestrated the activities of the Dixiecrat–conservative coalition in Congress. Indeed,

152

labour had opposed him vigorously as JFK's running mate in 1960 because he was associated with reactionary big business and had voted for Taft–Hartley. But Johnson had started in politics as a Roosevelt New Dealer and his greatest ambition was to complete his hero's reforming crusade. When he won the greatest popular victory in history in November 1964 the road seemed clear for him to do so. President Johnson's Great Society programme was the blue-print for civil rights, social reform, labour legislation, government spending and full employment – the kind of Welfare State labour had been struggling to achieve since the New Deal. Not only did Johnson have the votes in Congress: no President in history was more skilled at persuading Congress to vote the way he wanted. By 1965 America in the words of the influential Keynesian economist John Kenneth Galbraith, had become *The New Industrial State*, in which what Galbraith called 'the concept of countervailing power' would enhance union influence.[1] Organized labour could face the future with more confidence than ever.

Such hopes proved illusory. In reality, the 1960s and 1970s became a period of bitter disappointment for American labour. The confident expectations aroused by the Kennedy–Johnson Adminis-trations took no account of important underlying developments which pointed in other directions, nor of future events which undermined and destroyed the Keynesian consensus. Dominating everything else was the Vietnam War. This ultimate test of contain-ment of Communism sucked in half-a-million men, and billions of dollars. Some 50 000 Americans were killed and it aroused the most violent opposition at home, before ending in defeat, humiliation and more in 1974. It influenced all events, domestic and foreign, for fifteen years.

Next came the explosive demands of black Americans for the civil and economic rights denied them for a century and more. Starting with the Supreme Court decision in 1954, which declared segregated schools unconstitutional, the campaign spread to universities, public accommodation, transport, and then voting and ultimately econo-mic rights. This campaign disintegrated the politics of the 1960s. Revolutionary in its implications, black protest articulated the hopes and fears of the poorest and weakest sections of the working class. For this reason it should have been the prime concern of American labour. Instead, this great rebellion – nothing less than a second and more successful Reconstruction – largely passed labour by. Nothing could have demonstrated more dramatically the dangerously privileged, and in a sense marginal, position of American unions.

Allied to civil rights was the rediscovery of poverty. Michael Harrington's landmark book, *The Other America*, which greatly influenced President Kennedy,[2] told a wider audience what government statistics had shown for years: in the Affluent Society between a quarter and a fifth of all Americans lived below the official poverty line. There was nothing really new about this. It had been the case throughout American history. But this rediscovery shocked liberal Americans, who believed that since the New Deal poverty had somehow been abolished.

The struggle of American women to assert their right to economic, political and social equality with men also transformed politics in the 1960s and 1970s and exposed the limitations of organized labour. So did the rebellion of migratory workers in California, and the failure of President Johnson's Great Society to bring an effective Welfare State to America. The youth movement which rebelled in the 1960s in favour of its own Counter-Culture was completely alienated from labour unions. Finally, traumatic changes in the world economy and America's position in it, the 'energy shock' of the mid-1970s when the OPEC cartel quadrupled the price of oil, the cost of the Vietnam War and the ultimate collapse of the Keynesian political economy – all destroyed the postwar consensus within which labour had grown and prospered.

II

The struggle of black Americans for basic civil and economic rights was the first and most important of these fundamental changes. The battle began in earnest with the Supreme Court's landmark decision of May 1954 in the case of *Brown v. Board of Education*, overturning more than fifty years of legal precedent and declaring segregation in schools unconstitutional. This launched a long, bitterly fought campaign against centuries of racism. The Montgomery bus boycott in 1955 marked the beginning of the end of segregated city transport, while the sit-in movement integrated lunch counters and all public facilities. Next, freedom rides struck at segregation on inter-state transport. Marches, rallies, demonstrations all over the South and the Freedom March on Washington in August 1963 were followed by the rise of the Black Power movement and race riots later in the decade which devastated scores of cities, causing hundreds of deaths and billions of dollars of property damage. Clearly profound forces were at work.

Yet historians of this epic tale often neglect the fundamental fact that civil rights and Black Power were essentially movements of the black working class. Moreover the elemental nature of the struggle left the white working class, and most of their leaders, largely behind. In the 1930s the white working class had created the CIO by a similar eruption from below. But by the 1950s they were part of that comfortable, pervasive white power structure which blacks were seeking to overthrow. The fact was that black Americans were effectively excluded from positions of power and influence based on their numbers within the newly-merged AFL–CIO, while many American unions had actually institutionalized racism and segregation for half a century. In that respect the civil rights movement was a first indication of how the corporate consensus which had been put together in the 1940s and 1950s would eventually unravel.

Just as New Deal liberal reformers found that the McCarthy years forced them to demonstrate their loyalty by becoming the most aggressive anti-Communists, so American black leaders of the 1930s and 1940s now found themselves compromised by the fact that Communists had been their most effective supporters.[3] The consequent vacuum in leadership at this crucial moment in the 1950s sucked in a new generation of young leaders, such as Martin Luther King and Malcolm X, when they were still only in their twenties. Political pressure from the Federal government, the big corporations and the labour movement itself led in 1956 to the collapse of the National Negro Labor Council, which had been backed by such leading black Communists as Paul Robeson and W. E. B. DuBois. In consequence, black workers found themselves lacking an organization which could effectively fight labour's institutionalized racism. The International Association of Machinists was simply the most senior of AFL skilled craft unions which excluded black members; so too did building trades unions, musicians, papermakers and waterfront workers. While AFL unions were most prone to such exclusion, CIO unions were not immune: only 0.3 per cent of sheet-metal workers were black as late as 1968, while even the progressive UAW had few blacks in senior union positions.[4]

As we have seen, the founding convention of the AFL–CIO in 1955 had ratified Article II of the new federation's constitution. This declared it would 'encourage all workers, without regard to race, creed, color, national origin or ancestry, to share equally in the full benefits of union organization'. The task of implementing this aim was largely turned over to A. Philip Randolph, the 'Grand Old Man' of the black labour movement, who had organized the 1941 March on Washington which forced Roosevelt to set up the Committee on Fair Employment Practices.[5] Randolph was president of the Brotherhood of Sleeping Car Porters, an all-black union, while other railway brotherhoods commonly excluded blacks.

His attempts to break down the barriers of segregation took place against a background of significant and rapid demographic change for American blacks. The Great Migration after 1915 had begun the movement of blacks away from the rural South to the industrial North. This trend was accelerated and diversified during the Second World War. Between 1940 and 1960 the percentage of blacks working on farms declined sharply from 32 per cent to 8 per cent, while the proportion of blacks classified as blue-collar workers rose by 10 per cent to 38 per cent in twenty years. Between 1950 and 1960 the black civilian workforce rose from 5.8 to 6.7 million, with 83 per cent of all black adult males and 48 per cent of all black adult females actively seeking jobs by 1960. Blacks were effectively excluded from the best jobs: only 9 per cent of all construction workers, 7 per cent of all manufacturing workers, but 34 per cent of workers who provided personal services were black. Unions which practised racial exclusion thwarted black efforts to get suitable apprenticeships or training. Moreover, blacks in unions which kept them out of local and national leadership positions had little incentive to support their unions during strikes.[6]

Many rural black families left the South during the 1950s hoping to find a higher standard of living. Incomes for blue-collar jobs were higher in Northern States, but membership and apprentice positions in many unions were not readily available to all black workers. Still in the early postwar years, black families nationwide had experienced a rise in real incomes. Non-white median income in 1947 was 3563 dollars; by 1952 it had reached 4344 dollars, 57 per cent of white figures. But after 1952 the trend returned towards more unequal incomes: by 1959, the black median income of 5156 dollars was only 52 per cent of the white median income – roughly where it had been in 1948. By 1962 the median income of all non-white males was lower than it had been in 1960.

The AFL–CIO's refusal to desegregate unions added to the growing frustration and unemployment among black workers in the North in these years. During the Truman Administration non-white unemployment peeked at 9 per cent in 1950, dropping to 5.4 per cent by 1952. But under Eisenhower unemployment for non-whites reached new peaks. In the 1958 recession, 12.6 per cent of all non-white workers were unemployed, more than twice the level experienced by whites. Youth unemployment was much more. In 1960, 24.4 per cent of all non-white youth in the labour force were without jobs, 30 per cent of them for more than 15 weeks. A growing army of idle and desperate black men and women began to appear in the industrial centres of the nation, driven to the edge of poverty. In 1960, 55.9 per cent of all non-whites lived below the Federal government 'poverty level', an index of the income necessary to provide basic food, clothing and shelter. For the 1.5 million black families without a husband present, the situation was even more dire: 65.4 per cent of such families in 1959 were below the poverty level. Of all black female-headed households in rural areas, 82.2 per cent were also under the poverty level. Increasingly, as their economic situation worsened, blacks began to demand the inclusion of specific economic reforms within the overall goals of the civil rights struggle.[7] Martin Luther King's campaign for civil and voting rights had been aimed at the South. In the North, blacks wanted jobs and income, and it was here that Malcolm X and Black Power had more appeal.

Yet it was hard to make headway when the AFL–CIO was dominated by whites. Many black delegates led by Randolph fought to obtain a greater commitment to racial equality from labour bureaucrats. They pointed out that the AFL–CIO's constitution authorised the executive council to expel any labour affiliate which was 'dominated, controlled or influenced in the conduct of its affairs' by Marxists, yet made no comparable statement on unions which deliberately excluded blacks from membership. Yet AFL–CIO president George Meany opposed banning overtly racist unions, and the proposal was easily defeated. At the 1955 convention Michael Quill, president of the CIO Transport Workers' Union, condemned the constitution as a 'license for discrimination against minority groups'.[8]

Inside the AFL–CIO the lack of union support for desegregation led black members of the Civil Rights committee to resign. The AFL–CIO did nothing, they complained, effectively to combat union racism even in the North. In Detroit, for example, a major black working-class city, less than 2 per cent of all apprentices in craft unions were black. In Kansas City, Missouri, blacks were effectively barred from employment as steam fitters, plumbers, electricians, operating engineers, and sheet metal workers. In 1957 a black electrician in Cleveland, Ohio, was forced to sue Local 38 in an unsuccessful attempt to gain membership. Unions aggressively removed black activists on the grounds that they were Communists or subversives. In March 1952, for example, Walter Reuther, the most effective CIO anti-Communist but a liberal proponent of desegregation, purged five militant anti-racists from leadership of Detroit's UAW Local 600, and barred them from seeking re-election. Several industrial unions, including the Communications Workers of America and the United Steelworkers, drafted blatantly segregationist provisions in their contracts with employers. Unions such as the Brotherhood of Railroad Trainmen continued to exclude blacks from membership or deliberately kept black participation to a minimum.

At the 1959 San Francisco AFL–CIO convention, A. Philip Randolph urged that two railroad brotherhoods be ordered to remove anti-black exclusion clauses from their constitutions. Randolph also demanded that the AFL–CIO expand its civil rights committee. These and other anti-discrimination measures were promptly defeated and during the debate George Meany was so enraged with Randolph that he shouted, 'Who in hell appointed you as the guardian of the Negro members in America?'.[9]

In public many white leaders of the AFL–CIO paid lip service to desegregation. In April 1960, for example, Meany criticised the moderate Civil Rights Bill before Congress as an insult to 'the will of the vast majority of Americans who believe in, and wish to implement, the basic constitutional rights which properly belong to all Americans regardless of race or color or national origin'. Meany demanded that the Federal government 'press forward vigorously in the full enforcement of civil rights laws, both old and new'.[10] Privately, it was clear to black trade unions that Meany and many other white labour leaders would do nothing as effective as Reuther to support desegregation.

Meany's position on civil rights was that of an older generation, like Randolph himself, who insisted, 'I don't know anyone who is the head of an organization . . . who has fought as vigorously as he has to end discrimination.' No racist himself, he knew many of his members were, and as a white labour leader saw his first duty was to them.[11] Moreover Meany equated black struggles with those of earlier Irish or East European peasants. So for the new generation of activists coming of age in the 1960s and 1970s, Meany epitomized all that was wrong with American labour. Apologists for Meany argued that the AFL–CIO could not expel racist unions, because in the words of Socialist Gus Tyler, 'the power of the Federation is moral, resting on consensus and persuasion'. Even if this was the case – and total exclusion of Communists proved it was not – it did not explain the AFL–CIO's weak stance towards desegregation campaigns in the South during the 1950s. The only unions which actively assisted the Montgomery bus boycott of 1955–56 were Randolph's Brotherhood of Sleeping Car Porters, several small UAW Locals, the United Packinghouse Workers, District 65, and Local 1199 of New York. Southern union members played visible and active roles in the Massive Resistance by the white community. In Montgomery, the all-white Bus Drivers' Union and the Montgomery Building Trades' Council took part in vigilante attacks on civil rights leaders, while Southern Locals refused to process the grievances of black members. Alone among senior AFL–CIO leaders, Reuther took part in the triumphant August 1963 Freedom March on Washington, where Martin Luther King delivered his moving 'I have a dream' speech.

III

Black workers, by contrast, comprised the great majority of those who had sacrificed during local battles to destroy Jim Crow laws. They had been arrested, attacked by police with dogs and firehoses, intimidated, sacked from their jobs, and even killed. King's gradual recognition that the civil rights campaigns needed to address economic issues and social guarantees for jobs, housing and health care pushed the movement towards the premises of democratic socialism embraced by much of the working class in other advanced capitalist nations. Gradually the pressure for racial reform which black workers turned on the larger American society began to manifest itself within organized labour itself. By 1968 over two and a half million blacks were union members. Most unions had abandoned anti-black restrictions, and a few actively supported desegregation in the South. Yet Randolph's original goal of creating a powerful presence for blacks inside the House of Labor was not realised. Patterns of racist discrimination still existed, and black workers tended to occupy the most dangerous, lower-paid jobs inside unions. Within the United Steelworkers, for example, not a single black served as an officer in its 30 districts, and fewer than 100 black employees were on the union's staff. Less than 2 per cent of the members of the carpenters' union and the largest construction unions were black. Even after the 1964 Civil Rights Act, segregated Locals such as railway clerks, chemical and paper workers were still affiliated with the AFL–CIO. Bi-racial democracy and equality were still blocked by racist resistance and a deliberate policy of white supremacy fostered or condoned by most American labour leaders.

Impatient with decades of AFL–CIO apathy and inaction, black workers influenced by Black Power began to fight union racism by creating their own unions. In 1967 Detroit workers formed the Trades Union Local 124 to outflank white racists in the city's union bureaucracy, while black nationalists and young workers at Ford's major car plant in Mahwah, New Jersey, established the militant United Black Brothers. In 1968 Boston's black non-skilled workers formed the United Community Construction Workers; black steelworkers in Maryland created the Shipyard Workers for Job Equality to fight the racist practices of both unions and the steel corporation. In the spring of 1968 radical black workers and intellectuals created the Dodge Revolutionary Union Movement (DRUM) in response to the expulsion from the Dodge Main automobile plant of seven black workers. DRUM attacked the management's use of plant 'speed-ups', racist hiring policies, lack of adequate medical facilities in the factory, unequal pay between black and white workers of equal grade, and other long-standing grievances. DRUM co-ordinated pickets and unofficial strikes against Dodge, and criticised the UAW's leadership for bowing to capital's interests over those of all workers. Within a year other black radical labour organizations developed along DRUM's model: the Ford Revolutionary Union Movement (FRUM) the General Motors Revolutionary Union Movement (GRUM), and many others. In 1969 many of these militant formations coalesced into the League of Revolutionary Black Workers.[12]

The UAW's response to these black radicals was twofold: first, it attempted to depict DRUM as anti-working class and fanatical; second, it tried to divide older black workers from such independent movements through a combination of paternalism, co-option and patronage. UAW secretary-treasurer Emil Mazey attacked DRUM in March 1969 as a 'handful of fanatics ... black fascists whose actions are an attempt to destroy this union'. Mazey declared that the 'black peril' of Black Power was worse than the infamous 'red peril' of earlier years.[13] Philip Randolph was also instrumental in AFL–CIO efforts to quiet the black militants. Throughout the 1960s he had begun to move even further to the right politically, and had stopped criticizing the labour bureaucracy. In December 1965 Randolph told the AFL–CIO convention in San Francisco that racial bias was no longer a major problem within organized labour. The following year he resigned as president of the Negro American Labor Council, and he was followed by other black labour leaders, such as Bayard Rustin. At the September 1972 convention of the International Association of Machinists, Rustin blamed blacks themselves for labour's record of blatant discrimination. The leaders of the victims were blaming the victims for being victimized.

Rustin's and Randolph's attack on the black working class they had spent a lifetime leading did not go unanswered. In September 1972 a progressive conference of 1200 black workers held in Chicago, co-ordinated by five black national spokesmen of labour, formed the Coalition of Black Trade Unionists. At the Coalition's second convention in May 1973 they explained that:

A free and progressive trade union movement ... must reflect greater participation of black trade unionists at every level of its decision-making process ... if the goals of the overall labor movement are to be achieved on behalf of all workers. ... Today, blacks occupy key positions in the political machinery of the labor movement and hold the critical balance of political power in this nation ... it is our challenge to make the labor movement more relevant to the needs and aspirations of black and poor workers. The CBTU will insist that black union officials become full partners in the leadership and decision-making of the American labor movement.[14]

Despite growing black rank-and-file opposition, many unions continued to fight attempts to bring racial equality and justice within their ranks. Black workers in the Longshoremen's Association, founded by the left-wing Harry Bridges in the 1930s, protested to white union officials against a systematic pattern of segregated locals and racist job referral policies, but to no avail.

For example, when Lyndon Johnson established 'Project Build', an apprenticeship programme funded by the Department of Labor with the goal of increasing the number of blacks in the construction crafts unions, white unionists at the local level devised elaborate methods to circumvent the law. After ten years only 25 per cent of the minority workers had completed the apprenticeship programme and those who did finish usually found themselves assigned by unions to tasks as lowly-paid labourers. Black graduates of the apprenticeship programme of the Operating Engineers Union in Philadelphia, who were also excluded from full union membership and jobs appropriate to their training, sued the union in August 1970. During the case white engineers physically assaulted black apprentice graduates at work sites and in their union hall.

White union opposition to racial equality continued to fester, corroding the structure of the labour movement. A number of unions, especially the American Federation of Teachers (AFL–CIO), led by the social democrat Al Shanker, fought to oppose 'affirmative action' policies designed to increase the percentages of racial minorities and women within the labour force because the ethnic groups who backed Shanker opposed such initiatives. At local level many white trade unionists were prominent in projects to halt the desegregation of public schools. In Boston, for example, a former leader of the Sheet Metal Workers' Union, James Kelley, became affiliated with a white paramilitary group which terrorised black poor and working-class families.

In politics, this 'white backlash' against black equality translated itself into support for anti-working-class conservatives. In Southern cities with large white working-class populations, Governor George Wallace did well running for President in 1968. He polled 33 per cent of the popular vote in Little Rock, Arkansas, 23 per cent in Greensboro, North Carolina, 36 per cent in Jacksonville, Florida, and 38 per cent in Nashville, Tennessee. In the Democratic Party primaries of 1972 working-class whites gave Wallace victories in Florida, Michigan, and Maryland. Not to be outflanked, President

Richard Nixon also made direct appeals to the conservatism and racism of white trade unionists and reaped similar gains. By the 1970s, the AFL–CIO was part of this conservative stragegy, and did little to halt the political trend to the right. When the Democrats nominated a social democrat who opposed the Vietnam War, Senator George McGovern, as their Presidential candidate against Nixon in 1972, Meany and other labour leaders were so outraged they refused to endorse him. As a result a majority of white working-class voters supported the anti-labour candidate Nixon, whereas 85 per cent of black voters cast ballots for McGovern's losing effort.[15] Finally, the Democratic Party's commitment to Civil Rights and Voting Rights legislation in the 1960s had destroyed its political support in the South, so costly in Presidential elections.

Ironically labour's support for the corporate consensus and failure to confront white racism was crippling the labour movement. It had alienated black workers from unionization, and weakened working-class campaigns to secure Federal and State legislation which would benefit all industrial workers. So labour's ability to organize American working people declined. The proportion of the non-agriculture workforce in unions dropped from 36 per cent in 1960 to 20.9 per cent in 1980. Between 1973 and 1978 unions actually lost over three-quarters of all certified workplace elections. During the Nixon and Ford Administrations the absence of a strong unifed, labour movement encouraged Federal failure to tackle unemployment. Between 1969 and 1975 joblessness for married males increased from 1.4 per cent to 4.8 per cent for whites, and from 2.5 per cent to 8.3 per cent for non-whites. Overall unemployment during those years jumped from 3.1 per cent to 7.8 per cent for whites and from 6.4 per cent to 13.9 per cent for non-whites. More perhaps than anything else, racism undermined the political and economic coalition labour had put together since the New Deal.[16]

IV

Just as American labour found it impossible to adapt to revolutionary changes within the black community, so the postwar feminist revolution caused intractable problems. Increasing numbers of women entered the labour force after 1945. The Second World War had witnessed a dramatic increase in women's employment: from 25 per cent of the total workforce in 1940 to 36 per cent five years later. Wartime propaganda had stressed the temporary nature of women's work, and one out of four women employed in factories was fired or quit during the summer of 1945. Although highly paid, non-traditional work for women ended with the war, many women subsequently returned to other roles. They accepted jobs in lower-paid clerical and service fields. During the immediate postwar period – from September 1945 to November 1946 – only 600 000 women actually dropped out of the labour force. The nadir for female employment was reached in 1947, when only 29 per cent of adult women were working, but by 1960, 37.7 per cent of all women aged 16 and over were employed, constituting one-third of the total workforce.

More important than this overall increase was the permanent change in the age and marital status of women workers. Until 1940 women's participation in the labour force had been highest between the ages of 20 and 24. After the war, instead of a continuous decline in employment after the age of 24, a new pattern emerged. Women still left paid employment to bear and rear children, but they returned to work after their children reached school age. By 1960 the highest work rates were occurring between the ages of 45 and 49, when 47.4 per cent of all women were working. The typical pattern until the late 1960s was for women to leave work when their first child was born and then return when their last child started school. In the early 1960s, 41.5 per cent of married women with children aged 6 to 17 were working, and by 1962 married women comprised 60 per cent of the female workforce.[17]

Class and race remained important factors in determining not only women's participation in the workforce, but also the kinds of jobs they held. Between 1940 and 1962 the number of professional women workers increased from about 1.6 to 2.9 million, but the proportion of women in professional fields remained the same at 13 per cent. Women operatives represented a smaller percentage in 1962 than in 1940 – 15 as compared to 18 per cent. The proportion of women in private household service declined from 18 per cent in 1940 to 10 per cent in 1962. The greatest expansion occurred in the clerical field, where 21 per cent of all women workers were located in 1940 and 31 per cent in 1962.[18]

Racial differences remained important. Between 1940 and 1960 clerical work replaced domestic service as the leading occupational field for white women, but not yet for black. While 41 per cent of white women in 1960 were clerical or sales workers, only 9 per cent of black women filled these occupations. Although the percentage of black women employed as private household servants had declined between 1940 and 1960, a disproportionate number were still in this category – 36 per cent, compared to only 4 per cent of white women. In 1960, 48 per cent of black women were in the labour force as compared to 37 per cent of white women. Black women were the lowest paid workers, earning in 1960 a median income of 1391 dollars compared to the white female median income of 2245 dollars. In that same year, black men were earning 3737 dollars and white men, 7150 dollars.[19]

Labour unions, which had done little to protect women's wartime jobs, did not organize women workers in the expanding clerical and service sectors in the postwar years. The traditional sexism of union men, and the essentially conservative nature of the postwar consensus they had struck with management and government, made unions timid about organizing new fields and anxious about their own political respectability. The union bureaucracy became pre-occupied with wages and hours, fighting the Cold War, keeping the Communists out and lobbying Congress once the merger had been accomplished. The united AFL–CIO did endorse the principle of equal pay for equal work in the mid-1950s but, as with equality for blacks, did little about it. Moreover, women's groups favoured a Federal pay law because they thought collective bargaining too slow. In 1957 only a quarter of those women workers with union contracts had agreements containing equal pay clauses. More important, unionized workers were at best barely a third of the labour force, and women were far less organized than men. Unionized women were concentrated in a small number of indus-tries: the needle trades, electrical goods and communications.

The predominantly female clerical and sales workers had been poorly organized before 1940, and union organizing efforts did not keep pace with the postwar expansion in employment. Even by 1960 only 9 per cent of all clerical workers, male and female, were in unions. The estimated total of 3 million women union members in 1957 comprised little more than one-sixth of the total union mem-bership and accounted for less than one-seventh of the women in the labour force. So union conservatism not only perpetuated women's status as marginal workers, but also helped marginalize the labour movement itself. The sectors of the economy growing most rapidly in the 1960s, especially the 'tertiary' or service sector – transportation, communications, wholesale and retail trade, finance, insurance, real estate services and public administration – tended not to be unionized, and they were employing more women than men in the economy as a whole. In 1965 median annual full-time earnings were 2719 dollars for women and 4254 dollars for men. Women by then were earning 64 per cent of what men did. Despite growing job opportunities for women, this wage gap widened a little of the next twenty years, from 61 per cent of men's in 1960 to 58.8 per cent in 1975. Moreover, black men and women were (and still are) more likely to be unemployed than white workers. Women, black or white, were also more likely to be unemployed than men. The unemployment rate for black women stood slightly below that for black men between 1954 and 1960, but after 1965 it rose. White women's unemployment remained consistently higher than white men's and moreover the differential in the male–female unemployment rates grew in the 1960s and 1970s.

In 1984, 50 million women were in the American labour force, compared to 32 million in 1971. Women contributed more than 62 per cent of the total growth in the civilian workforce between 1975 and 1984. Thus in 1960, 37.7 per cent of women aged 16 and over were in the workforce; ten years later, 43 per cent were either working or seeking employment. By 1984, 54 per cent of all women were in the labour force, with 70 per cent of those between the ages of 25 and 54 either employed or looking for work. In 1970 women had made up 38 per cent of the civilian workforce; by 1984, they were close to 44 per cent.[20]

Employment opportunities for women in the 1970s came mainly, as we have seen, in the expanding service sector, including clerical work, where low wages, high turnover and part-time employment were common. So a close relationship became established between the growth of the service sector, the increasing participation of women in the workforce and what historian Rochelle Gatlin has called 'the feminisation of poverty'. Service industries now became increasingly significant in the American economy. Between 1970 and 1980 they absorbed close to 86 per cent of all private sector employment growth, while goods-producing industries showed a 13.6 per cent decline in employment. Service industries are more labour-intensive and poorly paid than manufacturing industries, especially when they are not unionized, and in the 1980s the wage differential widened dramatically. In 1970 workers in retail trade earned 62 cents for every dollar earned by manufacturing employees; by 1980 sales workers had fallen a further 10 cents behind. Employees in the service sector had twice the turnover rate of those in manufacturing and a substantially higher rate of part-time employment. While only 17 per cent of manufacturing employees worked part-time in 1977, over 29 per cent of service workers did. In short, the economist Joan Smith explained, 'the contemporary economy had moved to centre stage a labor force that must be continually endowed with marginal characteristics'.

Most of this marginal labour force was female. Between 1970 and 1980 women workers comprised over three-quarters of the increased employment in financial, real estate and insurance firms, and more than 60 per cent in both the service and retail food store industries. Most of these new jobs also paid the lowest wages. Between 1970 and 1980 close to 90 per cent of the women entering the labour force found jobs which paid only 63 cents for every dollar paid elsewhere in the private sector. It appeared that women's comparative poverty was no longer the result of their relative exclusion from the labour force, but rather had become built into the very conditions under which they were being recruited into paid work.[21]

The most important of these conditions was that most of these women's jobs were not unionized, partly because American unions had done so little to organize the predominantly female clerical and service sectors. Male union leaders focused on traditional workplace issues, such as maintaining the 'family wage' for male workers, and claimed that women were only 'temporary' workers, which they were more likely to be if unions ignored them. Yet the decline of the unionized manufacturing sector after 1960 meant that the survival of the labour movement depended increasingly on organizing white-collar and service workers, the majority of whom were women. The fastest-growing unions after 1960 were those in the public and health care sectors. Women accounted for half the increase in union membership in the 1970s and by 1990 comprised close to one-third of all unionized workers. However, although the number of women in unions doubled between 1958 and 1978 from 3.3 to 6.6 million, keeping pace with the expansion of the female workforce, only about 16 per cent of all employed women by 1990 were labour union members, and women's workplace organizing often occurred outside established union structures.

The pattern of employment for women since the 1960s had, in short, been similar to that for blacks. An advantaged minority obtained good jobs in expanding sectors of the economy. A disadvantaged majority was left behind. Neither group tended to be organized. In addition, women who moved up to executive and white collar work tended to deny such jobs to black men. Women such as Jane Addams, Elizabeth Gurley Flynn, Mother Jones, Belle Moskovitz, Rose Schneiderman and Rose Porter Stokes had played a prominent part in the history of reform, labour and the working class movement. But by the 1970s few women were prominent in the local or national leadership and bureaucracy of unions, although Joyce Miller, of ACTWU and the coalition of Labour Union Women, became the first woman to sit on the executive of the AFL–CIO.

V

The third factor, after blacks and women, which broke up the postwar consensus in the 1960s and 1970s was the revolt of the young. Those who protested most vociferously against the Vietnam War, for civil rights and for Black Power, or for equal rights and pay for women, were likely to be in their teens or twenties. This was no accident. One of the problems for a modern, technocractic society is how to get people from the age of 14, when they are clearly not ready to take on adult responsibilities, to the age of 24, when they usually are. They are the people who cause most trouble in society. They are also the people who are the most interesting, most attractive, brightest, healthiest, liveliest. In a sense the whole elaborate American system of school, college and university education exists to make the transition as painless as possible. Yet there was something unusual about that age-group in America in the 1960s. Between 1890 and 1960 its size had grown a bit each decade: ten per cent, eight per cent, sometimes not at all. The total increase of that 'cohort', as sociologists say, in those seven decades was 12.5 million. Then in the 1960s *alone* it grew by 13.8 million, an increase of 58 per cent in one decade, five times the average rate of the preceding 70 years, more in one decade than the previous seven added together. D. P. Moynihan has argued that this alone was enough to explain the turbulence of the 1960s.[22]

Even without Vietnam, civil rights, the women's movement and so on there would have been a wave of protest welling up from young America. But this explanation underestimates the importance of the issues themselves in fuelling discontent, and neglects the fact that for the first time since the New Deal, protest and the demand for reform in the United States took a clearly left-wing, social democratic direction in the 1960s and 1970s. At all events, the youth revolution, the counter-culture, was in many ways the most obvious surface feature of American society between about 1964 and 1972. It consisted almost entirely of young American men and women, many of them college-educated. Much of it was outrageous, designed to shock, and superficial, based upon sexual promiscuity, drug abuse, long hair, untidy dress, bare feet and incessant playing of loud rock music. Much of it, too, was clearly fraudulent, since 'dropping out' of society was always based upon the certain knowledge of being able to live off it on the fringes and return to it at will. The prosperity of the 1960s was taken completely for granted: as Scott Fitzgerald said of the excesses of the Jazz Age in the 1920s, they were based upon the bedrock of absolute confidence.

Yet much that was more serious came out of the Youth Revolution in the 1960s. Starting with the Port Huron statement of 1962, and moving through the struggle for civil rights and against the atrocities of the Vietnam War, a genuine youth political culture did for a time emerge based upon European-style social democracy, which challenged the whole white power structure of corporate America: its industry, its universities, its values, its 'life-style', to use a popular phrase of the time. Little of this had anything to do with the working class. But as with the politics of blacks and women, the escalating demands of Young America sought to overthrow a system in which labour unions formed a central part of the corporate consensus. 'Never trust anyone over 30' was one of the watchwords of the youth culture. In labour unions it was impossible to find anyone in a position of power under 30 or, it sometimes seemed, under 60.

Wider educational opportunities, which gave millions of bright young Americans the chance to demonstrate at universities across the nation, were taking them away from blue-collar or lower-middle-class backgrounds. They despised the labour movement and its leaders, and this feeling was returned with interest. When student anti-war demonstrators marched down Wall Street in the spring of

1970, to protest against the American bombing of Cambodia, unionized building workers, carrying American flags, shouting patriotic slogans and wearing hard hats, clubbed and beat the young Vietnam protestors. Almost alone among spokesmen of corporate liberalism, George Meany believed the Chicago police who took part in the notorious and horrifying police riot in Chicago during the 1968 Democratic Party convention had not over-reacted. The protestors they beat up so brutally and indiscriminately were in his words 'a dirty-necked, dirty-mouthed, group of kooks'.[23] Observing all this, the journalist Theodore H. White wrote, 'The Democrats are finished'. He might have added that the labour unions which formed a central part of the Democratic New Deal coalition were finished too.

VI

The fact was that American unions were losing the support of a whole generation of potential labour leaders, as well as support among blacks and women. Unions had offered an attractive career to the young in the years between 1935 and 1960, but this was no longer true. Moreover the proportion of the non-agricultural workforce belonging to unions had never amounted to much more than a third. The great majority had remained unorganized. Semi-skilled and unskilled workers, migratory workers, those in service industries, government employees, white-collar workers, those in the South and Southwest had long proved resistant to unionization. Demographic, economic, social and technological change was from the mid-1960s rapidly transforming the nature of the labour force. Automation was reducing the need for workers in basic industries: by 1963 car companies were producing more cars than in 1955 with 17 per cent fewer workers. The following year President Johnson forecast that by the end of the 1970s the United States would be able to equal the industrial output of the 1960s with 22 million fewer workers and warned of the need to keep employment buoyant. When Harlow Curtice, president of General Motors, took Walter Reuther on a tour of the new, automated plant he told him, 'Walter, in the future the UAW will not be able to call the machines out on strike'. Reuther's response underlined the Keynesian nature of the corporate consensus under threat: 'Will the machines be able to buy your automobiles?'[24]

Reuther could see the need for energetic action by the AFL–CIO. He argued that organized labour must reach out to help the poor by creating community unions and launching aggressive organizing campaigns. Meany's response to this proposal to embrace the unorganized, the unemployed and the sporadically employed, like that of Hutcheson and Tobin in the 1930s, was contemptuous: 'Well, good luck on that one,' he told Reuther.[25] As late as 1972 Meany still spoke for the majority AFL–CIO leadership when asked, 'Why should we worry about organizing groups of people who do not want to be organized?'[26] Frustrated by this, and by the AFL–CIO's refusal to moderate its strident anti-Communism or its support for the increasingly unpopular Vietnam War, Reuther took the UAW out of the federation in 1967. 'The AFL–CIO, in policy and program,' he explained, 'too often continues to live in the past. It advances few new ideas and lacks the necessary vitality, vision, and imagination and social invention to make it equal to the challenging problems of a changing world. It is sad but nevertheless true that the AFL–CIO is becoming increasingly the comfortable, complacent custodian of the status quo.'[27]

Reuther wanted the UAW to fight for more democracy in the labour movement, a more aggressive campaign to organize the unorganized and an expanded Welfare State. But his next step revealed his isolation in the labour movement. In 1968 he invited the Teamsters to join the UAW in what he called an Alliance for Labor Action. The ALA united the nation's two largest labour unions, but in all other respects they were fundamentally different. The UAW, the most democratic, cleanest, reformist union, which had always backed the Democratic Party, was merging with the most autocratic, corrupt and successful exponent of business unionism which had always supported the Republicans. The Teamsters had long been the most notorious and boastful exponents of racketeering, extortion, underworld links and corrupt collusion with employers. But the same pattern occurred in smaller unions in construction, the docks, service trades, textiles and increasingly in the coal industry after John L. Lewis retired in 1960. The Landrum–Griffin Act of 1959 had been designed to put an end to this corrupt unionism, but had done little effectively.

So the image of union racketeering remained in the public mind to further damage labour as its power and influence declined. The ALA achieved nothing. Jimmy Hoffa, the Teamster boss, frequently faced Congressional investigation or legal indictment, and in 1967 began a term in Federal prison. His handpicked successor, Frank Fitzsimmons, carried on in the same old way. Then in 1971 Teamster political support for the Republicans paid off when the President Richard Nixon paroled Hoffa on condition that he abstained from union activity. In 1975 he showed signs of returning to politics, but was kidnapped and almost certainly murdered, probably by the underworld.[28] In 1970 Reuther, by then tired of waiting for the 76-year-old Meany to retire and give him a chance to return, and perhaps run for president of the AFL–CIO, was killed in a plane crash. American labour had lost its most dynamic and creative postwar leader while still in his early sixties. Hopes for the kind of effective, European-style social democratic union movement that he had long espoused died with him.

The direction Reuther had wanted American labour to go towards social reform and organizing the unorganized was revealed not by the ALA and the absurd link with the Teamsters but by a totally unexpected breakthrough which occurred in the late 1960s among the farm workers of the Southwest and California. The grape, lettuce and market garden harvests were produced here by intensive farming in what were essentially 'factories in the fields'. The Mexican-American, or Chicano, workers who toiled in them were among the most degraded and depressed sections of the American working class. This had always been so. Earlier attempts to organize them, by such radical movements as the Industrial Workers of the World, had always failed. Campaigns to awaken the public conscience to their plight, such as John Steinbeck's novel *The Grapes of Wrath* in 1939, or Edward R. Murrow's famous 'Harvest of Shame' programme on CBS television in 1961, had got nowhere. Faced with the choice between social justice and cheap wine and salad, the great American consumer had always chosen the latter. But in the 1960s these hitherto powerless workers for the first time started to build a successful union. Finding a leader in the charismatic Cesar Chavez, himself a Mexican-American of farm-worker origins, the migrant farm workers of California formed the United Farm Workers' Organizing Committee, which later became the United Farm Workers.

A dedicated idealist, which itself made him an unusual figure in American labour politics, Chavez also had great tactical insight. 'Alone, the farm workers have no economic power,' he explained, 'but with the help of the public they can develop the economic power to counter that of the growers.'[29] Conventional strikes and picket lines were useless in the countryside. Instead, Chavez perfected the technique of the consumer boycott of Californian grapes which soon became national and international in scope. The AFL–CIO provided 1.6 million dollars in funds, the UAW lent organizational assistance, and such influential politicians as Robert F. Kennedy and Roman Catholic prelates and priests gave moral support. The boycott strategy was so effective that in 1967 California grape growers began signing contracts with their farm workers – a victory no previous organization had achieved for such workers. Encouraged by the UFW's success in the vineyards, in 1969 and 1970 Chavez pushed ahead with demands for similar contracts from other California commercial farmers, notably lettuce growers.

The same technique of national and international boycott was pursued, but this time without success. For a time, it is true, backing the lettuce boycott became the height of 'radical chic' amongst the intellectual middle class of New York and San Francisco. But this time the situation was different. Salad products were consumed by everyone across the nation, and it was thus much more difficult to enforce an effective boycott. Following their earlier defeat, the growers had been able to regroup and retaliate. The real problem was that Chavez was more radical than anyone else on the union side. 'I'm very convinced', he told a boycott organizer in Toronto, 'that political power for the minority groups, in particular the farm workers, is a myth; that our votes really don't count for much unless they're backed by some economic force ... that without real economic power ... we will develop a small, élite group of workers, with a lot of benefits surrounded by mass unemployment, welfare, war on poverty, old people etc which will not be able to participate simply because they are not members.'[30]

This was a perceptive insight into the state of the American labour movement in the 1970s. In the end what really destroyed Chavez and the UFW was the brutal strength of the Teamsters. Since their truck drivers transported all the agricultural products, they had the power of life and death over the boycott. Moreover, they quickly started to move in, organize the farm workers themselves and sign collusive, kick-back contracts with the growers. Teamster tactics were the usual ones of using hundreds of beefy goons to conduct a reign of terror throughout the region, while AFW activists were arrested in thousands for violating court orders prohibiting every form of resistance and protest the UFW could devise. Pickets were shot, wounded and killed while, under the long-term contracts the Teamsters signed, hiring halls, grievance procedures and protection against dangerous pesticides disappeared along with the worker's right to a union of their own choice.

Meany described the Teamsters' raids as 'the most vicious strikebreaking, union-busting effort I've seen in my lifetime'.[31] When Ronald Reagan was Governor of California between 1966 and 1974 his Republican Administration's policies were anti-union and backed the grape and farming magnates, as well as the Teamsters, against the radical Farm Workers. His successor, the young and unconventional Democrat Jerry Brown, raised UFW hopes because he had supported the grape boycott as a student, but his Administration did nothing decisive to help the farm workers achieve their goals.

Still, the campaign to organize the farm workers did manage to salvage something. The 1975 Federal Agricultural Labor Relations Act established a five-man Agricultural Labor Relations Board, which acted much as the NLRB had for industrial workers done in the 1930s and 1940s by guaranteeing the right of farmworkers to organize and bargain collectively through representatives of their own choosing. Yet even this fell far short of what Chavez had dreamed. He wrote:

As a continuation of our struggle, I think we can develop economic power and put it in the hands of the people so they can have more control of their own lives, and then begin to change the system. We want radical change. Nothing short of radical change is going to have any impact on our lives or our problems. We want sufficient power to control our own destinies. This is our struggle. It's a lifetime job. The work for social change and against social injustice is never ended.[32]

Once again, as with the Knights of Labor or the Industrial Workers of the World in earlier times, Cesar Chavez and the UFW had tried to combine the immediate purposes of labour unions with the ultimate ambition of transforming the fundamental structure of American society. At a time when most labour leaders were striving simply to ensure the survival of their own organizations and their patronage machines, it was not altogether surprising that they failed.

VII

Another means of transforming society, indeed arguably the most effective means of helping the poorest sections of the American working class, might have been by improving the Welfare State. American labour had aimed at doing this for a generation. The problem in the postwar period was that the *ad hoc* system put in place during the New Deal had not been converted, as it had in Britain after 1945, into a fully comprehensive and nationally funded system. Prosperity in the postwar years, as we have seen, owed much to acceptance of Keynesian economics and the influence of the military-industrial complex. In Britain full employment and prosperity in the postwar years had been used to fund a Welfare State along the lines of William Beveridge's epoch-making Report. In America nothing comparable occured. In Britain Keynesian prosperity was used to fund welfare spending; in the United States such prosperity was used as a pretext for not doing so.

True, Congress had extended aid to dependent children and the disabled in the 1950s, expanding social security to cover both widows and disability insurance. But nothing had been done about Beveridge's basic assumptions as in Britain. No Health Service or family allowances were set up, no commitment made to a policy of full employment, while rising standards of living for the fortunate were used as a pretext for 'benign neglect' of welfare and refusal to tackle the problems of urban poverty. Though a far greater proportion of Americans than Britons enjoyed higher education, no comparable free system was established in the United States, while public housing provision, so crucial in ending urban degradation, fell far behind. The so-called 'trickle-down' theory argued that if GNP were kept large and expanding, enough wealth would percolate through the system to satisfy the poor.

Yet benign neglect and trickle-down economics did not work in this way, as Booth and Rowntree had demonstrated so decisively in Britain decades before. Far from withering away, poverty remained a serious problem until it was rediscovered in the 1960s. Some 39 million people, or 21 per cent of the population were officially estimated as being poor by the Federal government in 1962. Though the farm population had shrunk dramatically since the 1930s, the new American poor were in other respects much like the old: the aged, ethnic minorities and blacks, female-headed households, migratory workers, farm labourers driven from the land. So the great surge of self-confidence and prosperity which characterized the early 1960s, before the corrosive effects of the Vietnam War set in, led to the much trumpeted War on Poverty of the Kennedy–Johnson years. In fact it was more like a skirmish than a war. The Office of Economic Opportunity, set up under Lyndon Johnson amidst great ballyhoo, funded a variety of useful programmes: loans to small farmers and businessmen, aid for needy college students, VISTA (a sort of domestic Peace Corps), a Job Corps to develop skills and Community Action Plans. More than a thousand such CAPs were launched on the basis of 'maximum feasible participation' by the poor themselves. Yet they failed to give the poor what they most needed – jobs and income – and tried to offer local solutions to nation-wide economic problems. 'Maximum feasible misunderstanding', in D. P. Moynihan's phrase, often resulted.[33]

Despite this, in the period between 1965 and 1975 three major developments changed the face of American poverty and social welfare. First, the number of poor dropped steeply as a result of the economic boom created by the Vietnam War. Second, welfare programmes, especially social security, were greatly enlarged. And third, an explosive growth in the size of welfare rolls led to worried talk of a 'welfare crisis'. Real economic growth in the 1960s enabled millions of hitherto-poor workers and their families to climb out of the poverty trap. Numbers defined by the government as poor fell from 39 million in 1959, or 21 per cent of the working-age population, to 23 million, or 11 per cent of an enlarged population in 1975. Left-wing critics argued that this poverty line was too low, but could not deny that the gains were real. Yet those left behind were still minority groups: small farmers, farm labourers, the old, the disabled and female-headed families. Second, despite the intense opposition of the American Medical Association to anything which smacked of 'socialized medicine', Medicare and Medicaid were in the 1960s and 1970s added to social security, thus achieving a long-standing goal of American labour. Medicair, or health insurance for the aged, became a vital but expensive part of the welfare system. Medicaid, a matching Federal/State programme, extended medical help to those on categorical assistance, and by 1975 gave nine billion dollars in benefit to 23 million people. The American Welfare State had come of age.

Equally important in tackling hunger, food stamps were introduced to help the poor. Still the emphasis remained on providing opportunities, not handouts. Despite this there was a concerted attempt in Congress to put floors as well as doors in the system through a guaranteed income system of negative Federal income tax. The idea was that those below the poverty line would have their income automatically raised to pass it. Hailed by such arch-conservatives as Milton Friedman as an alternative to 'the welfare mess', negative income tax almost passed Congress in 1972.

Liberals, suspicious of Friedman's support, believed income levels were far too low and would simply encourage employers to cut wages for the poor. Yet the failure of negative income tax was in some ways an important turning point. After that the tide rushed out rapidly for welfare programmes. Under Richard Nixon and Ronald Reagan they were wound up with a vigour, which, had it been applied to making them work, might have ended poverty in America. Of course, their cost worried taxpayers fearful of inflation, and also worried by the nation's relative economic decline after OPEC's 400 per cent price hike, precipitated by the 1973–74 oil crisis. The need for action was clear. In 1972, 33 per cent of all blacks, compared with 9 per cent of all whites, lived in poverty, while 43 per cent of all poor families were headed by females. Yet 'the welfare mother' became an American stereotype to equal Britain's 'social security scrounger', and was used to justify cuts in social security benefits in both countries. Few worried about those who still fell through the welfare net, nor about tax evasion by the rich which actually cost the nation far more in lost revenue.

VIII

Social and political change was isolating organized labour. Yet underlying economic change, and relative economic decline, was at the base of all the problems unions faced. Unions had grown powerful since the 1930s as part of the Keynesian economy. But from the 1960s onwards there were increasing signs that this economy was no longer working as it once did. America's relative

position in the world economy was slipping. The financial dominance which had provided the basis for the Bretton Woods agreement, when Germany and Japan had been reduced to rubble in
1945, had long gone. Germany and Japan, with generous aid from
the United States, had restructured their economies in the postwar
years and by the 1960s were emerging as major competitors, while
the European community was emerging as a new economic force.
Just as the full implications of this were starting to sink in, the full
cost of the Vietnam War began to show. Lyndon Johnson had been
determined to fight the war without raising taxes: the inevitable
consequence was inflation, which began to bite in the 1970s, rising
to two figures by the middle of the decade.

The rapid closing down of many of Johnson's Great Society
programmes, and the ending of the War on Poverty by President
Nixon, was a direct result of the cost of the war. The Smithsonian
agreement, in August 1971, which devalued the dollar by 16 per
cent, showed the real trend of events. For America, in many ways, it
marked the end of the postwar period. Then came the oil shock of
1973–74, when the OPEC cartel raised the cost of oil by 400 per
cent. All of this had a devastating effect on the American domestic
economy. German and Japanese cars began to outsell those made in
the United States: in 1981–82 the American motor industry sold
fewer cars than in any year since 1955. Japanese steel began to
undercut the domestic product. In electronics, computers and other
high-tech industries which America had traditionally dominated,
leadership began to pass to Japan. High government spending on
defence and the Moon Race for a time sustained the Keynesian
approach to the role of government spending in managing the
economy. But when the Moon Race ended in the 1970s the economic
spin-off from such expenditures declined.

In any case, the labour force was starting to diversify again in
ways which were not helpful to labour unions. Expansion in high-
tech sectors of the economy was matched by growth in service
industries, sales, fast foods and the like, which were low-wage jobs
with great insecurity. In neither case were unions able to organize
effectively. Rapidly growing white-collar and government employment was transforming the labour movement.

This growth in government influenced union membership too.
Union membership among state and local government workers
almost tripled in 1978 to 2.2 million, while another 2.4 million

public workers belonged to employee associations, which effectively operated like traditional trade unions. Teachers, nurses, social workers and public servants began to unionize and strike. Membership of the American Federation of Teachers tripled to 500 000, while by 1978 the American Federation of State, Country and Municipal Employees, with 1.7 million members, had become the largest AFL–CIO affiliate.

Public workers and white-collar unions had increased their membership by more than 2 million, but their 36 per cent share of all state and local public employees only kept pace with the growth of jobs in this area and barely made up for AFL–CIO losses in declining sectors elsewhere. Then other things began to inhibit even this growth. The financial crisis of New York and other cities, taxpayers revolts and Federal retrenchment in the 1970s meant that government employment stopped expanding. Then the courts effectively ended the right of the public employees, and indeed any union with a contract or arbitration procedures, to strike. Finally, growth in the public sector was not matched by growth in the much more buoyant private sector. Companies like IBM in the Dallas/Fort Worth area of Texas, or California's 'silicon valley', practised 1920s-style welfare capitalism and company unionism with great success in the 1970s and 1980s.

Finally, the long-term demographic shift of population from the Northeast to the Southwest, from 'frost-belt' (or 'rust-belt' as it was sometimes called) to 'sun-belt', meant that employment was expanding in a section of the United States which had long been stony ground for union organizers. Here, Taft–Hartley 'right to work' laws controlled recruitment to the shopfloor. The population of traditional industrial States, such as Ohio and New York, remained static or actually declined, while that of States such as California and Florida rose rapidly. Moreover, there was for the first time a worrying decline in America's famed productivity. The 'oil shock' and other things led to an economic depression. Supply outpaced demand, inflation replaced price stability, and mass unemployment again became a reality in the 1970s and 1980s in most advanced industrial nations, including the United States. Steel centres such as Pittsburgh or Youngstown fell on hard times. Key industrial states like Illinois, Ohio and Michigan had unemployment rates far above average. Between 1974 and 1978 alone unions in manufacturing lost 11 per cent of their members. Detroit, the capital of motor manufacture, which throughout the years of Keynesian consensus had been the bell-weather of American prosperity, experienced unemployment rates not seen since the Great Depression.

As industry declined, unions found it harder to win new recruits in an expanding labour force switching to other sectors. The 1960s began well, when the Kennedy administration raised the minimum wage to 1.25 dollars an hour and then acted decisively to extend to the Federal government's 2.4 million civilian workers collective bargaining rights guaranteed by law to employees in private industry. Yet by mid-decade only about 10 per cent of white-collar workers (2.3 million out of 22 million) belonged to unions. Though total membership remained relatively stable, it continued to decline as a proportion of the civilian labour force, dropping to 25 per cent in 1965, the lowest level since 1950. The economic boom stimulated by the impact of the Vietnam War, and the Johnson administration's loose fiscal and monetary policies, made skilled labour suddenly scarce. As unemployment fell unions were operating in the most favourable climate since the Korean War, and membership rose. Even so, this rise only managed to keep pace with the increasing labour force. By 1970 the size and strength of unions was static again, and labour's market penetration had fallen a quarter in 25 years. By 1980 only 34 per cent of basic manufacturing, mining, transport and skilled crafts – the most completely organized sector of the economy – remained organized: the smallest proportion for more than fifty years.

By then, too, the cost of the Vietnam War, and America's declining position in the world, was becoming clear. When the dollar was devalued in August 1971 President Nixon introduced a draconian wage-price policy which froze all existing pay deals, but failed to freeze prices. Bitterly antagonized, the AFL–CIO complained that this 'inequitable and unworkable freeze' had been imposed 'suddenly and with no advance warning' after two years during which the AFL–CIO had warned 'there is a growing danger of recession'.[34] Phase II of Nixon's game plan, launched in November 1971, set 5.5 per cent guidelines enforced by a Pay Board with the aim of reducing annual price increases to between two and three per cent by the end of 1972. Neither goal was reached, but as 1972 began the nation moved for the first time in its history into a situation where economic controls were in effect during peacetime.[35] This artificial dam simply pent up demand for pay and price increases, which eventually after 1974 burst upon Nixon's luckless successor, Gerald Ford.

When Jimmy Carter regained the White House for the Democrats in 1976, the AFL–CIO looked forward to restoring the cosier relationship with the Federal government they had enjoyed in the Kennedy–Johnson years. They were to be bitterly disappointed. Carter and his Georgian mafia may have gone through the motions of consulting organized labour. But their first aim was to distance the administration from Washington's traditional power brokers, which included George Meany. This deliberate provincialism was in the end disastrous for the Carter White House, but it also effectively prevented labour from regaining any of the ground it had steadily lost in the previous fifteen years.

The Committee on Political Education was unable to stop the drift of the Democrats to the right. Candidates, including Carter himself, whose liberal credentials were at best marginal, refused to support labour on issues dearest to its heart. Taft–Hartley was not repealed, the NLRB became more reactionary, restrictions on construction and public employees' unions were not lifted, nor unions protected from punitive laws. Most worrying, AFL–CIO unions which in 1946 had won 90 per cent of NLRB supervised elections to establish their right to represent workers, won only 47 per cent of them in 1977. By 1980 total union membership had fallen below 25 per cent of the non-agricultural workforce and as the 1980s progressed it fell below 20 per cent.

Running against the honest but inept Carter for President in 1980, Ronald Reagan swept the nation, even taking almost half of all union members and their families. This triumph for the New Conservatism was based upon the fact, however, that United States economic and financial hegemony was being challenged by two nations, West Germany and Japan, who relied much less on defence spending and the military-industrial complex as the engine of their economies. Defeated in 1945, they had been stripped of war-making capacity and, in Japan's case, forbidden by the constitution the United States wrote from undertaking the kind of conventional military spending other sovereign states took for granted. West Germany was allowed military expenditure within NATO, but allotted only about 5 per cent of GNP for this purpose, while Japan spent less than 1 per cent in this way. By the 1980s the United States, by contrast, was spending 12 per cent of GNP on war-making capacity and thus crowding out more useful economic activity. Too much reliance upon a Keynesian approach dependent upon military expenditure was now becoming a liability.

The economic story of the Reagan Presidency, when America moved from being the world's greatest creditor to its greatest debtor, and ran huge Budget deficits, is beyond the scope of this book. But clearly the consequences for organized labour, as a central part of the Keynesian economic consensus, were significant. In this respect Reagan had one unique distinction: he was the only President in history to have been a member, indeed a leader, of a labour union. As president of the Hollywood Screen Actors' Guild he had denounced Communists in 1947.

The fact that he was also the first President since the creation of the Department of Labor in 1913 to appoint its Secretary without consulting union leaders showed the way his sympathies would be directed in the 1980s. His choice, Raymond Donovan, was a business executive with no links with labour, who was later involved in one of the scores of scandals which riddled Reagan's two Administrations. The new President's treatment of the Professional Airline Traffic Controllers' Organization in August 1980 seemed to symbolize labour's problems in the new decade. PATCO workers were employed by the Federal government. They were just the kind of white-collar, high-tech professional workers the AFL–CIO was most anxious to organize. After a long period of pay negotiations, PATCO called a strike in August 1981. But they had signed a No Strike agreement. Moreover, they had endorsed Reagan in the November election. With a strike threatening, the President made it clear he would not play favourites. When the union's members walked out, the President fired them, saying he had led a union himself and knew what such agreements meant.

The astonished PATCO members, who had believed right to the last that the President had been bluffing, lost their bargaining rights, their jobs and their union. They received only token support from the AFL–CIO, and from air traffic controllers abroad, as military personnel drafted by the President took over their work and kept America's planes flying. A large majority of union members, especially those employed in the private sector of the economy, whose taxes paid PATCO and other public sector salaries, endorsed the President's harsh policy.[36] In any case, they believed that by taking on the Federal government the union was bound to lose.

'The Feds have never lost a strike,' a senior AFL official explained. 'You can't beat Uncle Sam.' A generation earlier, unions had taken on the government and won. In that sense, the PATCO strike showed how much organized labour had weakened since the days of glory in the 1930s and 1940s, and the days of influence in the 1950s and 1960s. America might still be the world's most powerful nation, but the labour movement was no longer a power in the land.

8. Conclusion

In fifty years the American labour movement seemed to have come full circle. In 1929, on the eve of the Great Depression, the employers' counter-offensive against unions launched at the end of the war had been so successful that the AFL was near the point of collapse. In a period of unparalleled prosperity unions had been outflanked by welfare capitalism, company unionism and the open shop. To some it looked as if the United States, alone among Western capitalist nations, would develop an industrial economy without independent labour unions. Many perceptive observers spoke of unionism as 'a largely spent force' or 'having less and less impact on society'.[1] The doyen of labour relations experts, William M. Leiserson, believed that the 'labor problem', which had dominated serious discussion of industrial society since the 1870s, had been essentially solved. 'Scientific study of labor questions today', he concluded, 'is directed rather at understanding the nature of the relationship between employers, wage-earners, and the public, and finding the methods by which these labor relations may be organized, administered, and adjusted to the satisfaction of all concerned.'[2]

The upheaval of the next twenty years destroyed this cosy concept of 'industrial pluralism'. Depression, mass unemployment, reform, and war transformed the scene. The corporate hegemony and class collaboration of the 1920s was replaced in the 1930s by violent class conflict and radicalism. The 1935 Wagner Act threw the authority of the Federal government for the first time behind the worker's right to organize and bargain collectively. But the eruption represented by the sit-down strikes in the auto industry, the stealthy organization of steel and the creation of the CIO would almost certainly have occurred without the intervention of the law. It was more like a force of nature. The unionization of semi-skilled and unskilled workers in America's basic, mass-production industries was a chance for the weakest and most despised sections of the working class to stand up

184

and change their lives. Organization on the industrial, rather than craft, principle meant the end of craft-union hegemony, and a rift in the House of Labor. Alliance with the more rampant and reformist Democratic Party meant permanent political change. What was really happening in the 1930s was that the sons and daughters of the last great wave of immigrants who had flooded American shores in the first decades of the century were making their voices heard.

War continued the onward march of American unions. But where the New Deal had stimulated political advance, war caused an economic one. The acute labour surplus of the Great Depression was suddenly replaced by an even more acute labour shortage. The strong new unions were able to exploit the situation and bid up wages, while management and government, anxious to court organized labour, brought unions into partnership in running the war economy. The War Labor Board gave legitimacy to the union shop, and though the No Strike pledge and Little Steel formula inhibited union freedom of action, fringe benefits were used as a way round pay restraint and became a permanent part of bargaining.

The titanic struggles between unions and management in the immediate postwar years were an attempt by each side to seize the initiative. But they revealed what major changes had taken place within such a short time. They were not fought with the violence and loss of life which had characterized strikes after the First World War or during the New Deal. Their peaceful nature showed that organized labour had become an accepted part of the political economy. Moreover they had occurred because both sides feared a return to the economic depression which had characterized the 1930s. Instead the war had accelerated acceptance of Keynesian ideas about the role of government in managing a modern capitalist economy. Despite the anti-labour Taft–Hartley Act of 1947, a generation of prosperity followed and management quickly learned to work with labour. More, they co-opted unions into running industry by giving them the task of disciplining their workforce while they got on with management.

The expulsion of Communist unions, and labour's eager support for the Cold War, ushered in the period of corporate consensus based on Keynesian economics and the primacy of the military–industrial complex which characterized the 1950s and the 1960s. GM's Charles E. Wilson was succeeded as Defense Secretary by

Robert S. McNamara of Ford. A quiet revolution had occurred. In the 1920s America looked like an industrial society which could function without unions. By 1950 many agreed with the Harvard economist Sumner Slichter when he wrote that 'the United States is gradually shifting from a capitalistic community to a laboristic one – that is, a community in which employees rather than businessmen are the strongest single influence'.[3] The 1955 merger of the AFL and CIO, who had split in 1937 on the principle of industrial organization, should have enhanced the new power and influence of organized labour. Instead it marked its peak. Subsequent events were to reveal serious weaknesses in the House of Labor.

For even at their zenith American unions embraced little more than a third of eligible workers. The great majority remained unorganized. Unions were in part undone by the very prosperity they helped create. As they aspired to middle-class status, more affluent workers dropped blue-collar habits like union membership. Moreover, the failure to organize foremen in the 1940s had set the real limits of union growth. As the economy matured and diversified from an industrial to an increasingly service base, unions could at best barely keep pace with the growth of the new workforce. In the more dynamic sectors of the economy – service, white-collar, high-tech – new members gained failed to compensate for old ones lost in declining industries, like cars and steel. Political and demographic change exacerbated the problem. Blacks, Hispanics, women, migratory workers and the young were not proportionately represented by unions. When their demands for change took centre stage in the 1960s and 1970s the AFL–CIO found itself left out of, even in opposition to, these campaigns.

This was especially true of the campaign to end the Vietnam War, which dominated everything in those years. When the full cost of the war became apparent, the bills came in just as America's unchallenged dominance of the world economy was ending. West Germany and Japan, the defeated nations in 1945, with economies less dependent on the military–industrial complex, were starting to hurt American economic and financial interests at home and abroad. Dollar devaluation in 1971 was followed by the 400 per cent increase in oil costs in 1973–74, and further rises in 1979–80 and 1983. The triple scourges of inflation, recession and rising unemployment were the inevitable result. This marked the end of the postwar consensus. Ironically, just as President Nixon started saying in 1971 that 'We are all Keynesians now' the Keynesian era was coming to a close.

As major beneficiaries of the Keynesian era, labour unions were naturally among the big losers when the system began to break down in the 1970s. The forty years of dynamic growth, when American labour came to exercise significant economic and political influence, coincided with a period of American dominance of the world economy, cheap energy, through oil and electric power, the widespread purchase of consumer goods, Keynesian-style managed capitalism, and high productivity. All began to break down simultaneously. Likewise the old Democratic political coalition, put together during the New Deal, began to decay too. Though the Democrats still controlled Congress, they had by the end of the 1980s won only one Presidential election in 25 years. The commitment to civil rights under Kennedy and Johnson had destroyed the party's electoral base in the solid South. So the Dixiecrat–Republican coalition managed to frustrate labour liberalism. The AFL–CIO failed to repeal Taft–Hartley, the Landrum–Griffin Act and restrictions on the right to strike, or stop the return of injunctions apparently outlawed by Norris–La Guardia in 1932. Moreover, unions made no serious effort to organize the unorganized, as they had in the 1930s.

In a sense the great expansion between the 1930s and the 1950s was the exception to the rule of American history which set a subordinate role for organized labour. Yet what happened in the motor industry in the 1980s showed that in decline unions still had a part to play in organizing retreat. In the aftermath of the PATCO disaster the new president of the AFL–CIO, Lane Kirkland, realized labour unity was more vital than ever. He persuaded the UAW, which had left the AFL–CIO in 1967 over its refusal to organize the unorganized, to rejoin in 1981. Developments were already demonstrating the union's essential role in the motor industry. When the federal government acted to save the bankrupt Chrysler Corporation by subsidy in 1979–80, it had to have the cooperation of the UAW. In return for relinquishing some current benefits, Chrysler workers won a place on the board.

Even more revealing were the negotiations which opened between GM and the UAW in January 1982. Because of the motor industry's desperate economic plight, the union agreed to start bargaining well before existing contracts ended in September. Negotiators at once entered forbidden country. Unable to compete with lower-priced Japanese imports, GM bargainers asked the union to accept reductions in fringe benefits, paid holidays and vacations. The company also demanded other 'givebacks'. In response UAW leaders insisted that any reductions in labour costs must be passed on directly to the consumer. Management would then share equally in financial sacrifices. It was 1945–46 all over again, when Walter Reuther had first raised the question of the relationship between wages, prices, and profits, only this time within a shrinking market. In 1946 GM had refused to surrender managerial prerogatives and endured a long strike to defend them. In 1982, they quickly agreed to open company books and discuss prices and profits. Ford promised the same, modified their definition of managerial prerogatives, and opened new areas of policy to negotiation with labour. Then bargaining at GM collapsed, while Ford was in even more perilous economic plight than GM. So the UAW gave up several basic benefits: workers surrendered annual pay increases, deferred COLAs for nine months and lost six days of annual holiday. In return Ford promised to end plant closures and to maintain current employment. Soon GM did the same. Even so, by 1990 no cars were being made at Flint, Michigan, birthplace of both GM and the UAW. Yet the motor industry was not alone in suffering foreign competition. Steel, rubber, and petro-chemicals – the same mass-production industries the CIO had wept in the 1930s – now besieged by foreign competitors, demanded 'givebacks'. But in gaining union cooperation, they had to concede to labour a larger role in the making of corporate policy.

In some ways the 1980s were reminiscent of the 1920s. Unions again seemed on the defensive, without fresh ideas or strong momentum, unable to attract workers in the growth industries where employers practised the 'new welfare capitalism' and threatened by job losses in the declining older industries. Once again, the nation's rulers looked at unions without sympathy. Labour seemed to have lost its hold on affairs. Yet in the recession of the 1980s corporate leaders were prepared to give what they had refused forty years before and let unions look at their books while sharing responsibility for management decisions.

Even so, prospects in the 1980s offered haunting parallels with the 1920s. As new industries shifted with population from 'the frost-belt' to 'the sunbelt' the open shop flourished. Welfare capitalism and the anti-strike injunction reappeared after more than 50 years, while union membership was down to little more than 1920s levels. Facing this dispiriting picture, some historians blamed the decline of American labour on events in the 1930s. Had they wished, labour leaders could have used the tide of radicalism which created the CIO then to establish the kind of independent, social-democratic unions found in Western Europe. Or they could have broken away from the Democratic Party fold to set up an independent political party of their own. Such interpretations are ahistorical, and characteristic of the 'lost opportunity' approach favoured by some American historians in other fields of research. Neither the rank and file, nor responsible union leaders, had any serious intention of building Socialist unions in the 1930s or setting up some kind of farm–labour alliance behind Henry Wallace in 1948.[4] America was a capitalist democracy, and the Democratic Party could deliver rewards and protection to labour unions which Wallace's Progressive Party could not. When the crunch came in November 1948 Wallace's candidacy, far from providing labour with an opportunity, was seen as endangering Truman's re-election and thus repeal of the Taft–Hartley Act.

In short, the years between 1938 and 1948 reveal a major theme of American labour history: that the ambitions of the American working class were essentially pragmatic and mundane, unconcerned with millenial promises or the restructuring of society. As union members they would, for the most part, follow anybody who could deliver at contract time. The major leaders of American labour since the 1930s clearly fit that pattern. John L. Lewis was the great inspirational figure, but his vision was materialistic while he was also a great accumulator of union, and personal, power. Sidney Hillman may have been a social democrat, but he believed American workers must make the capitalist system act in their interests, not seek to change it. Philip Murray believed in co-determination, but in practice became one of the facilitators of the existing order. Walter Reuther was the most creative, dynamic and radical figure of his generation with a more idealistic vision than anyone, yet no one did more to create the corporate consensus. Finally, George Meany was both Keynesian bureaucrat and the archetypal AFL leader, who defended the privileges of the skilled and the organized during years of prosperity, while effectively blocking labour leaders like Reuther who wished to organize the unorganized.

Expulsion of Communists from CIO union in the late 1940s may have speeded acceptance of the consensus capitalism which characterized the 1950s. Yet in some ways this had been ironic. Indeed, the history of Communists in the American labour movement discloses the difficulties faced by those who seek to use the working class to restructure society. Communist support for the rights of the black working class cost them the support of much of the white working class. But aside from their determination to resist racism, in other ways American Communists accepted the capitalist system as readily as anyone else. They had been the most enthusiastic supporters of the wartime No Strike pledge and pay restraint policy. In major strikes they had always settled more quickly, and for less, than other CIO unions, and were even willing to sign longer contracts with employers. In short, the 'false promises' discussed in this book's introduction, and revived by the analysis of some labour historians, misses the central reality of American labour history. There was no real alternative to organized workers playing the kind of role they came to play between 1940 and 1970 within Keynesian consensus politics. Of course, with hindsight it may be possible to argue that the promise this kind of capitalism held out to American labour was essentially false; that in the 1980s unions found themselves back where they had been in the 1920s. Yet for a generation unions had been able to help their members obtain material, social and political benefits they would not otherwise have enjoyed.

Some observers were more hopeful about labour's situation as the 20th century drew to an end. They pointed out that unions were relatively stronger than in the 1920s. Then they had had a mere 3 million members, now they had 23 million, including women, nonwhites, professionals and others absent from the earlier labour movement. The American version of the Welfare State had proved more resilient under the attack of Reaganomics in the 1980s than some had believed it would. The Democratic Party's union support remained intact in most major industrial States, and though unable to win the White House, the party was still strong in Congress and in governor's mansions across the nation. Prematurely written off in the 1920s, labour had in fact been on the brink of a generation of dramatic growth triggered by the Depression and the New Deal. As the 1990s opened American Budget and trading deficits, structural weaknesses in banking, the stock market and the economy, meant that such an economic catastrophe could not be ruled out, especially given the dangerous imbalances in world trade and lending. If the 1987 Crash had been like a first heart attack, and the nation later succumbed to another Great Depression, so this line of argument ran, labour might benefit.

Yet is was hard to see labour being reborn, like a Phoenix from the ashes, as during the New Deal. Renaissance then had coincided with the rebirth of the Democratic Party and the revolutionary ideas of the economist J. M. Keynes. Its growth had depended on growth of the military-industrial complex. The destruction of the Berlin Wall, the collapse of Communism in Eastern Europe and the disintegration of the Soviet Union which occurred so rapidly in 1989–90 marked the end of the Cold War and thus the objective reason for the existence of the military-industrial complex. Another point is often overlooked. The end of unrestricted immigration in 1924 meant that in the 1930s the American working class was already becoming more homogeneous, and thus more easily organized and united. Following immigration reform in the 1960s, the American working class became much more ethnically, racially and culturally diverse, with Hispanics and Orientals in a sense playing the part Eastern and Southern Europeans did before 1914.

Yet the obituaries for American labour were no doubt being written prematurely. For all their caution, conservatism and bureacracy, unions had, in some sixty years of struggle, won more for the working class than any other institutions and played a central part in structuring modern American society. This answers, in part at least, the question posed by the historian Alice Kessler-Harris about why the American working class, or at least its leaders, colluded in the development of liberal capitalism rather than constraining it.[5] Well organized workers benefitted from the system, and by making it work more efficiently, for a time at least, understandably believed it was working more justly too. Thus labour helped shape the history of the contemporary United States.

Notes and References

INTRODUCTION

1.   Arthur M. Schlesinger, Jr. *Washington Post*, 1 January 1950; J. B. S. Hardman, 'The State of the Movement' in J. B. S. Hardman and Maurice Newfield (eds), *The House of Labor* (New York: Prentice-Hall, 1951) p. 53: Quoted in David Brody, *Workers in Industrial America* (Oxford: Oxford University Press, 1981) pp. 173 and 211 n.

1. LABOUR AND THE GREAT DEPRESSION

1.   George Schuyler, quoted in Gilbert Osofsky, *Harlem: the Making of a Ghetto: Negro New York, 1890–1920* (New York: Harper and Row, 1966).
2.   P. K. Edwards, *Strikes in the United States, 1881–1974* (Oxford: Basil Blackwell, 1981) Appendix A, Table A.6, p. 260.
3.   David Brody, *Workers in Industrial America*, (Oxford: Oxford University Press, 1981), p. 62. For a full treatment see Stuart Brandes, *American Welfare Capitalism 1880–1940* (Chicago: University of Chicago Press, 1976).
4.   For a succinct summary of the evidence, see A. M. Schlesinger, Jr, *The Crisis of the Old Order* (Boston: Houghton Mifflin, 1956) pp. 457–8.
5.   R. F. Kahn, 'The Relation of Home Investment to Unemployment', *Economic Journal*, XIV 1931, pp. 173–98.
6.   Robert Lekachman, *The Age of Keynes* (London: Allen Lane The Pilgrim Press, 1966) p. 107n.
7.   J. M. Keynes, *The Means of Prosperity* (London: Macmillan, 1933) p. 31.
8.   Irving Bernstein, *Turbulent Years* (Boston: Houghton Mifflin, 1969) p. 17, and Schlesinger, *Crisis*, pp. 189, 457–58. Harry Hopkins later suggested, only half-jokingly, that aggregate demand be raised by throwing money out of aircraft all over the country, as if in emulation of the 1930s popular song *Pennies from Heaven*.
9.   Schlesinger, *Crisis*, pp. 186–7.
10.   *Redbook*, December 1934, quoted in A. M. Schlesinger Jr, *The Politics Upheaval* (Boston: Houghton Mifflin, 1960) pp. 400–1.

11. Quoted in Raymond Moley, *After Seven Years* (New York: Harper and Brothers, 1939) p. 160.

12. F. Perkins to FDR, President's Secretary File (hereafter PSF) 77, Labor Department, March 1933 (italics in original).

13. PSF 77, 'Statistics for President's conference with the Governors' and memorandum marked 'Wolman'.

14. President's Official File (hereafter OF) 407 (1), Dept of Labor, 24 March 1933.

15. Letter in OF 407 (1), 19 April 1934. Signatories included Paul F. Brissenden, labour economist and historian of the IWW, Bruce Bliven, John Dewey and Reinhold Niebuhr. The Brookings survey had concluded that the nation's 631 000 richest families had a total income far higher than the total income of the sixteen million poorest families.

16. Quotes in Schlesinger, *Crisis*, pp. 185–6. Melvyn Dubofsky and Warren Van Tine, *John L. Lewis; a Biography* (New York: Quadrangle, 1977) is the definitive study. Matthew Josephson, *Sidney Hillman: Labour Statesman* (New York, 1948) is a more pedestrian life.

17. A. M. Schlesinger Jr, *The Coming of the New Deal* (Boston: Houghton Miflin, 1958) p. 141.

18. Ibid., p. 90.

19. Schlesinger, *Crisis*, p. 186.

20. Hillman to Lewis, Hillman Correspondence, 1930–46, H-O (hereafter Hillman Corr.) at New York Industrial and Labor Relations School Library, Cornell University, 13 December 1935.

21. Some of Hillman's members were scathing about his pretensions: 'He worked at parts for a couple of months,' a cloakmaker commented, 'and then he became right away a statesman.' Quoted in Bernstein, p. 84. For a perceptive picture of Hillman, see an essay by Steve Fraser, 'Sidney Hillman: Labor's, "Machiavelli" in Melvyn Dubofsky and Warren Van Tine (eds)., *Labor Leaders in America* (Chicago: University of Illinois Press, 1989), pp. 207–33.

22. FDR to Johnson, OF 407 (1), 19 October 1933.

2. NEW DEAL RENAISSANCE

1. Quoted in Schlesinger, *The Coming of the New Deal*, (Boston: Houghton Miflin, 1958) pp. 400–01. See also the National Labour Relations Act, Section 1, in H. S. Commager (ed.) *Documents of American History* (New York: Appleton-Century-Crofts 4th edition, 1948) p. 494.

2. Bernstein, *Turbulent Years* (Boston: Houghton Mifflin, 1969) pp. 330–5.

3. J. A. Gross, *The Reshaping of the National Labor Relations Board: National Labor Policy in Transition* (Albany: State University of New York Press, 1981) is the latest examination of the NRLB's work.

4. Schlesinger, *The Crisis of the Old Order* (Boston: Houghton Miflin, 1956) p. 401 and Bernstein, pp. 336–9.

5. Quoted in Bernstein, p. 349.

6. Bernstein, pp. 432–98, gives an excellent account of the SWOC drive in steel. For the historical background, see David Brody, *Steelworkers in America: the Non-Union Era* (New York: Harper and Row, 1960).

7. President's Official File, OF 407 (1), 6 September 1936.

8. Berry to FDR, President's Secretary File, PSF 77, 30 July, 18 August, 5 September, 26 October and 6 November 1936.

9. Lee Pressman 'Reminiscences', *Columbia Oral History Project* (hereafter COHP) 1977, p. 55.

10. Sidney Fine, *Sit-Down: the General Motors Strike of 1936–37* (Ann Arbor: University of Michigan Press, 1969) is the best account of these events. My own draws heavily on the excellent summary in Foster R. Dulles and Melvyn Dubofsky, *Labor in America* (Arlington Heights: Harlan Davidson, 1984, 4th edition) pp. 290–95.

11. Bernstein, pp. 482–3. Republic Steel alone spent 50 000 dollars in this way.

12. Schlesinger, *Coming.* p. 488.

13. For a perceptive discussion of this, see Steve Fraser, 'The Labor Question' in Steve Fraser and Gary Gerstle, *The Rise and Fall of the New Deal Order* (Princeton: Princeton University Press, 1989) pp. 72–4.

14. Dubofsky and Van Tine, *John L. Lewis: a Biography*, (New York: Quadrangle, 1977) pp. 288–9.

15. Since many CIO members did not pay dues, so membership figures have to be treated with some caution. Indeed, all general statistics on union membership are only approximate because of widely differing practices in reporting enrolment. See Dulles and Dubofsky pp. 259n and 288n.

16. Pressman, COHP, p. 94.

17. 'Labor's Long-Range Job' condensed from a CIO handbook, *Production Problems*, p. 1. Hillman Correspondence A–G in New York State School of Industrial and Labor Relations Library, Cornell University.

18. *Production Problems*, p. 2.

19. *Production Problems*, p. 3.

20. Dubofsky and Van Tine, *Lewis*, has a masterly discussion of this whole subject of Lewis in 1940, see pp. 339–70.

21. UAW Public Relations Department, Ford Motor Company Services. Box 2, Lewis File, WPR Library, 25 October 1941.

22. Melvyn Dubofsky, 'Not to "Turbulent Years": Another Look at the American 1930's', *Amerikastudien*, 24, pp. 5–20.

23. One of those most influenced by the Trotskyist Farrell Dobbs in the 1930s was, oddly enough, Jimmy Hoffa, who went on to become the most notorious racketeer in the American labour movement in the 1950s and 1960s. See Ralph and Estelle James, *Hoffa and the Teamsters: a Study in Union Power* (New Jersey, 1965) pp. 89–96.

24. David Brody, 'Labor and the Great Depression: the Interpretative Prospects', *Labor History* 13, 1972, pp. 231–44 and 'Radical Labor History and Rank-and-File Militancy', *Labor History* 16, 1975, pp. 117–26, survey the field and the literature.

25. Fine, *Sit-Down*, p. 307 and Brody, 'Radical Labor History', p. 125.

26. J. M. Keynes, 'The United States and the Keynes Plan', *New Republic*, vol. CIII (29 July 1940) p. 158.

27. Robert Lekachman, *The Age of Keynes* (London: Allen Lane, The Penguin Press 1966) pp. 127–29.

28. Report of the Heller Commission in Hillman Correspondence, A–G.

3. THE CRUCIBLE OF WAR

1. Manning Marable, *Race, Reform and Rebellion: the Second Reconstruction in Black America* (London: Macmillan, 1984) p. 14.

2. Fraser, 'The Labor Question' in Steve Fraser and Gary Gerstle (eds), *The Rise and Fall of the New Deal Order 1930–1980* (Princeton: Princeton University Press), pp. 72–3. See also Walter Reuther's perceptive views in 1937 in W. P. Reuther, UAW President's Office, Box 64, Folder 12.

3. The delegate, leading the 24-strong team from Local 174, was none other than W. P. Reuther. UAW President's Office, Box 1, Folder 9, UAW 4th Constitutional Election, Issues, March 1939.

4. See UAW Public Relations Department, Ford Motor Services Collection, Box 2, Homer Martin File, AFL 1939–1941, and affidavits, reports, stenographic transcript of UAW investigation and so on, March 1939.

5. Harvey Levenstein, *Communism, Anti-Communism and the CIO* (London: Greenwood Press, 1981) pp. 82, 97n.

6. United Automobile Workers of America, *Proceedings of Special Convention*, March 1939.

7. Ibid.

8. Ibid.

9. Levenstein, *Communism*, p. 83. As a rank-and-file delegate put it 'I respect R. J. Thomas. He was a member of my local. But I had more respect for Addes. In my book, R. J. Thomas was a plain bozo. Addes ... was a substantial guy. But Addes didn't have no leadership'. Nick DiGaetano, interview, 17 June 1968, Oral History collection, W. P. Reuther Library.

10. Fraser, *Labor*, p. 73.

11. Ibid., p. 77.

12. 'R. J. Thomas Repudiates Communist Endorsement', Association of Catholic Trade Unions (ACTU) Collection, Box 7, Folder 1, 16 July 1941.

13. FDR Official File (hereafter OF), 4245–E (Labor Division), 28 May 1940.

14. Sidney Hillman cuttings file, New York State School of Industrial

and Labor Relations Library, Cornell University, Vol. 8., 1940–41, p. 33.

15. OF 407, Box No. 3, Dept of Labor, 17 March 1941.

16. *New York Times*, 28 May 1940. In fact, the '500 planes a day' plan was not entirely novel: Reuther had, before the war, recognized that new techniques in car manufacture be applied to other industries. See letter from Walter E. Johnson, vice-president of a CIO technicians' union, to Reuther, 28 March 1938, in W. P. Reuther, UAW President's Office, Box 1, File 10, Correspondence 1938, WPR.

17. Nelson Lichtenstein, 'Walter Reuther and the Rise of Labor-Liberalism' in Melvyn Dubofsky and Warren Van Tine (eds), *Labor Leaders in America* (Chicago: University of Illinois Press, 1987) p. 287.

18. Quoted in Ronald W. Schatz, 'Philip Murray and the Subordination of the Industrial Unions to the United States Government' in Dubofsky and Van Tine, *Labor Leaders*, p. 248.

19. Text in OF 4245–E (Labor Division).

20. Howell Harris, *The Right to Manage: Industrial Relations Policies of American Business in the 1940s* (Wisconsin: University of Wisconsin Press, 1982) pp. 46–8.

21. OF 407, Box No. 3, Dept. of Labor. Correspondence between FDR, Hillman and other labour leaders lasted from 27 November until the end of December 1941; Dalrymple's letter is dated 24 February 1942.

22. Olds to FDR, OF 407 (2), 13 November 1941. See also Senate Document no. 114, 65th Congress, 1st Session, Vol. II.

23. FDR to Hillman, OF 407 (3), 10 October 1941.

24. UAW contract with North American Aviation, UAW Local 887 Collection, Series I, Box 1, File 1, W. P. Reuther Library.

25. Labor Dept, President's Secretary File (hereafter PSF), No. 152, Harry Hopkins.

26. Currie to FDR, OF No. 237 and PSF No. 147.

27. Henderson to FDR, OF No. 237, 19 and 23 June 1942, 8 April 1943, 24 June 1944.

28. UAW President's Office, Walter P. Reuther, Box 7, File 10.

29. Melvyn Dubofsky and Warren Van Tine, *John L. Lewis: a Biography* (New York: Quadrangle 1977) p. 419.

30. Ibid., p. 423.

31. F. R. Dulles and M. Dubofsky, *Labor in America* (Arlington Heights: Harlan Davidson, 1984) p. 426.

32. Here Lewis paraphrased, 'however inaccurately', a Department of Interior report: Dubofsky and Van Tine, *Lewis*, pp. 417. The authors give a masterly account of this dispute, pp. 415–40.

33. UAW President's Office, WPR, Box 7, File 7, 14 May 1943.

34. Special Meeting of UAW Executive, WPR, Box 7, File 23. Full text of Browder's speech reprinted as 'The Miners Strike and its Lessons', WPR, Box 8, File 1, excerpts in *Daily Worker*, 8 May 1943.

35. ACTU Collection, WPR, Box 15, File 1.

36. Mary Norton to FDR, OF No. 407, Box No. 3, Dept of Labor, 14 November 1941.
37. Francis Walter to FDR, OF No. 407, Box No. 3, Dept of Labor, 28 October 1941 and Section 1 HR 5218.
38. *New York Times*, 18 June 1943.
39. Quoted in Dulles and Dubofsky, *Labor in America*, p. 329.
40. Joel Seidman, *American Labor from Defense to Reconversion* (Chicago: University of Chicago Press, 1953) p. 190.
41. *CIO News*, 27 December 1943, quoted in Seidman, *American Labor*, pp. 203–4.
42. *Labor Action*, 31 May 1943 (caps. in original) in UAW President's File, Box 8, File 1, WPR.
43. Murray to FDR, OF 4245C, 16 March 1942.
44. Mark Ethridge, chairman of the Commission on Fair Employment Practices, to FDR, OF 4245–G, 27 October 1941 and 16 March 1942. The CFEP was established by Executive Order 8802 on 25 June 1941.
45. August Meier and Elliott Rudwick, *Black Detroit and the Rise of the UAW* (New York: Oxford University Press, 1979) *passim*, especially 37, 49–51, 61, 104, 108 and 109–19.
46. W. E. B. Du Bois, *The Philadelphia Negro: a Social Study* (Philadelphia, 1899) pp. 378–90.
47. Marable, *Race, Reform*, p. 14; Nelson Lichtenstein, *Labor's War at Home: the CIO in World War II* (Cambridge: Cambridge University Press, 1982) pp. 124–6.
48. Lichtenstein, *Labor's War, passim*, especially pp. 110–35, contains a revealing analysis of what he calls 'the ecology of shop-floor conflict'.
49. Brody, *Workers in Industrial America* (Oxford: Oxford University Press, 1981), p. 181.
50. Seidman, *American Labor*, pp. 129–30.
51. *The Times*, 8 November 1944 and President's Personal File (PPF) 8172.
52. FDR to Hillman, 25 November 1944, PSF File No. 152, Sidney Hillman.
53. For a perceptive discussion of this, see Steve Fraser, 'Sidney Hillman', in Dubofsky and Van Tine, *Labor Leaders*, pp. 229–30.
54. PPF 1017, 28 October 1944 (italics in original).
55. *Termination Report of the National War Labor Board I* (US Department of Labor, Washington DC 1949) p. 653.

4. RECONVERSION AND REACTION

1. CIO *Economic Outlook*, June 1945, and Joel Seidman, *American Labour from Defense to Reconversion* (Chicago: University of Chicago Press, 1953) p. 215.
2. Reuther to Anderson, 5 June 1929; Anderson to Reuther, 29 June 1945. Leo Fenster Collection, Series I, Box 2, File 25, WPR.

3. *CIO Economic Outlook* (October 1945) and Len De Caux, *CIO Public Relations Program 1945*, De Caux Collection, Series II, Box 2, File 8.

4. *CIO Economic Outlook* (June 1945). Employers were unable to answer this powerful argument about the postwar economy. Reuther wrote to Truman urging him to pay 1000 dollars severance pay to workers made redundant through termination of war contracts. Leo Fenster Collection, Series I, Box 2, File 25, 30 August 1945, WPR.

5. Philip Murray, *The CIO Case for Substantial Pay Increase* (November 1945) p. 5.

6. Broadcast quoted in *New York Time*, 31 October 1945.

7. UAW President's File, Box 10, File 17, WPR.

8. GM did however recover 52.9 million dollars of these loses as tax credits. David Brody, *Workers in Industrial America* (Oxford: Oxford University Press, 1981) pp. 183–4.

9. Accounts of the GM dispute of 1945–46 can be found in Howell J. Harris, *The Right to Manage: Industrial Relations Policies of American Business in the 1940s* (Madison: University of Wisconsin Press, 1982) pp. 139–41, 149–50, 252–3n; Seidman, *Defense to Reconversion*, pp. 224–30.

10. Seidman, *Defense to Reconversion*, pp. 229–30. Harris, *Right to Manage*, pp. 143–49 greatly expands Seidman's account.

11. Quoted in Brody, *Workers*, pp. 180–1.

12. Ibid.

13. Foster R. Dulles and Melvyn Dubofsky, *Labor in America* (Arlington Heights: Harlan Davidson, 1984) p. 340.

14. Philip Taft, 'Rank-and-File Unrest in Historial Prospective', in Joel Seidman (ed.), *Trade Union Government and Collective Bargaining* (New York: Praeger, 1970) p. 96.

15. Brody, *Workers*, p. 188.

16. Seidman, *Defense to Reconversion*, p. 244–5.

17. *CIO News*, 6 January 1947.

18. *CIO News*, 13 January 1947.

19. *CIO News*, 24 February 1947.

20. *The National Wage Stabilization Board, 1 January 1946–24 February 1947* (US Department of Labor, Washington DC 1947) p. 280.

21. Dulles and Dubofsky, *Labor*, and J. A. Gross, *The Reshaping of the National Labor Relations Board* (Albany: State University of New York Press, 1981), p. 347.

22. Quoted in Dulles and Dubofsky, *Labor*, p. 345.

23. Harry A. Millis and Emily Clark Brown, *From the Wagner Act to Taft-Hartley: a Study in National Labor Policy and Labor Relations* (Chicago: Chicago University Press, 1950) pp. 235–6, 244 and 265.

24. Steve Fraser, 'The Labor Question' in Steve Fraser and Gary Gerstle *The Rise and Fall of the New Deal Order, 1930–1980* (Princeton: Princeton University Press, 1989), pp. 72–4.

25. Seidman, *Defense to Reconversion*, p.4240.

26. Michael Goldfield, *The Decline of Organized Labor in the United States* (Chicago: University of Chicago Press, 1987) pp. 238–42, regards the

failure of operation Dixie and the related purge of the left as crucial in explaining the later decline of labour.
27. Harris, *Right to Manage*, pp. 72–4.
28. Brody, *Workers*, p. 204. See also pp. 206–7, 210–11.

5. PURGING THE COMMUNISTS

1. Harvey A. Levenstein, *Communism, Anti-Communism and the CIO* (Westport: Greenwood Press, 1981) p. 205. Much of the interpretation and information offered here is taken from Levenstein's book, which covers both the UAW and the CIO and is written in a more objective style than many other accounts. The subject of Communism in American unions is emotive, as well as important, and other books should be consulted. Bert Cochran, *Labor and Communism: the Conflict that Shaped American Trade Unions* (Princeton: Princeton University Press, 1977) covers much the same ground as Levenstein but in less detail, while Roger Keeran, *The Communist Party and the Auto Workers Union* (Bloomington: Indiana University Press, 1980) emphasises the constructive role Communists played in establishing the union in the 1930s and 1940s and, like Cochran, discusses the role of the Red Scare and Red-baiting in the decisive political conflicts among auto workers. The most recent and most completely documented study of the UAW is Martin Halpern, *UAW Politics in the Cold War Era* (Albany: State University of New York Press, 1988) which although it touches on the CIO more tangentially than Levenstein has the most comprehensive bibliography, is deeply researched and has a fresh viewpoint.
2. Levenstein, p. 190–1.
3. Earl Browder, *Columbia Oral History Project*, p. 409.
4. *Daily Worker* 24 May 1945.
5. Levenstein, *Communism*, p. 196–7.
6. Martin Halpern, *UAW Politics*, pp. 128–9, 309n.
7. See secret security report in UAW President's Collection, Box 64, File 10, War Dept: 10110–2666, Govt. Military Investigations 22 May 1940. The letter, signed Vic and Wal, with no date but probably 1934, was clearly written by Victor. Federal agents were cavalier with evidence when hunting Reds. By the end of the 1940s the CIA used Nazis and Fascists to hunt European Communists too. The intriguing aspect of the Intelligence report is that it unearthed little evidence of CP activity in Detroit between 1937 and 1940.
8. *UAW Minutes*, EC Meeting, 16 April 1946, UAW President's Collection, Box 5, WPR.
9. *UAW Minutes*, EC Meeting, 9 December 1946, UAW President's Collection, Box 7, WPR.
10. *UAW Minutes*, EC Meeting, 17 March 1947, UAW President's Collection, Box 7, WPR. See also accounts in Levenstein, *Communism*, pp. 199–201 and Joel Seidman, *American Labor from Defense to Reconversion* (Chicago: Chicago University Press, 1953), *passim*.

11. Levenstein, *Communism*, pp. 203, 207.
12. Walter Reuther, 'How to Beat the Communists', *Colliers*, 28 February 1948, and Reuther's report to the UAW Executive, Minutes, pp. 28–30, 33, Box 45, File 12, WPR.
13. *Detroit Free Press*, 20 November 1947.
14. Levenstein, *Communism*, pp. 140, 204–5. See Oral History Interviews with Horace Sheffield, 24 July 1968, WPR Archives, p. 8–11.
15. UAW President's Collection, Box 15, 'CIO Convention 1946' WPR.
16. *CIO Convention Proceedings 1946*, p. 233.
17. CIO EC meeting, November 1947, UAW President's Collection, Box 7, WPR.
18. Levenstein, *Communism*, p. 214.
19. *CIO Convention Proceedings 1946*, pp. 217–18.
20. Levenstein, *Communism*, pp. 216–17.
21. Arthur F. McLure, *The Truman Administration and the Problems of Post-War Labor, 1945–48* (Rutherford: Farleigh Dickinson University Press, 1969) p. 145. Murray pointed out that employers did not have to swear they did not belong to Fascist organizations, though some did. Lewis spoke contemptuously at the AFL's convention against signing affidavits, but was badly beaten in the debate by George Meany. See chapter 6.
22. *CIO Convention Proceedings 1947* p. 262.
23. Ibid. pp. 289–91.
24. Dulles and Dubofsky, *Labor in America* (Arlington Heights: Harlan Davidson, 1984), p. 355.
25. Levenstein, *Communism*, pp. 226–7, 232.
26. UAW Minutes, EC meeting, 15 March 1948, UAW President's Collection, Box 38, File 11, WPR. Wallace polled 1.15 million votes in November 1948 and failed to carry a single State, whereas Strom Thurmond, the 'Dixiecrat', took 1.16 million votes and carried Alabama, Louisiana and Mississippi.
27. *CIO Convention Proceedings 1949*, p. 252.
28. Ronald Radosh, *American Labor and United States Foreign Policy*, (New York: Athaneum Press, 1969) pp. 308–9. This book is the fullest exploration of this important topic, but an alternative view can be found in Roy Godson, *American Labor and European Politics: the AFL as a Transnational Force* (New York: Crane, Russak, 1976).
29. Radosh, *American Labor*, pp. 313–14, 320–1.
30. Ibid., p. 318.
31. Ibid., pp. 438–9.
32. Levenstein, *Communism*, p. 302.

6. THE EMERGENCE OF CORPORATE CONSENSUS

1. Robert H. Zieger, 'George Meany: Labor's Organisation Man' in Melvyn Dubofsky and Warren Van Tine, *Labor Leaders in America* (Chicago: University of Illinois Press, 1987) p. 324.

2. Quoted in F. R. Dulles and Melvyn Dubofsky, *Labor in America* (Arlington Heights: Harlan Davidson, 1984) p. 350. This book contains an excellent brief summary of the disputes involving Taft–Hartley, pp. 348–52, on which my text rests heavily.

3. Nelson Lichtenstein, 'Walter Reuther and the Rise of Labor–Liberalism' in Dubofsky and Van Tine, *Labor Leaders*, p. 293.

4. Ibid., pp. 293–4.

5. Ibid., p. 294.

6. UAW Local 887 Collection, Series IV, Box 10, 4137, WPR contains 9 folders of verbatim reports.

7. UAW Local 887 Collection, Series IV, Box 11, File 1, p. 1069, WPR.

8. Ibid., File 5.

9. Ibid., File 1.

10. Ibid., Box 15, File 2.

11. UAW Local 887 Collection, Series 1, Grievances, File 5, Minutes of Meetings, WPR. This contains an intriguing series of handwritten pencil notes made by a union delegate at meetings between union and management between 1950 and 1952. Though not easy to decipher, the series continues until 1965.

12. UAW Local 887 Collection, Series 1, Grievances, File 5, Minutes of Meetings, WPR.

13. UAW Local 887 Collection, Series V, Box 15, File 2, WPR.

14. Ibid., Series IV, Box 15, File 1.

15. Ibid., Series V, Box 15, File 1.

16. UAW Washington Office, Jacobs and Shifton, Box 57, File 21, WPR and *Wall Street Journal*, 8 April 1954.

17. UAW Washington Office, Jacobs and Shifton, Box 57, File 21, WPR.

18. Ibid., Box 55, File 2.

19. Ibid.

20. Ibid.

21. Ibid., Box 57, File 16 (capitals and italics in original).

22. Ibid., Box 55, File 2.

23. Ibid., File 7.

24. Ibid., Box 57, File 17.

25. Ibid, Box 55, File 7.

26. Leo Fenster Collection, Box 2, File 25, WPR. For the practice of isolating one car company, see Walter P. Reuther, UAW President's Office, Box 102, File 8, WPR.

27. *The Worker*, 18 January 1958; *New York Times*, 1 April, 13 May and 15 May 1958: in UAW Washington Office, Jacobs and Shifton, Box 55, File 5, WPR.

28. Address to 3rd Convention AFL–CIO, San Francisco, reprinted in UD *Digest*, Fall 1989, pp. 22–9, in W. P. Reuther, UAW President's Office, Series X, Box 567, File 5, WPR. Steel profits for 1959 are discussed in UAW Washington Office, Jacobs and Shifton, Box 57, File 19, WPR.

29. Lichtenstein, 'Walter Reuther', in Dubofsky and Van Tine, *Labor Leaders*, pp. 294–5.

30. Fred Thompson interview in Studs Terkel, ed. *Hard Times* (Chicago: Avon Books paperback, 1971) p. 357 (italics in original).

31. Lichtenstein, 'Walter Reuther', in Dubofsky and Van Tine, *Labor Leaders*, p. 295.

32. *Ibid.*, pp. 291–2.

33. Reuther used the phrase 'organic unity' in a speech to the UAW–CIO convention on 22 March 1953. See W. P. Reuther, UAW President's Office, Series VIII, Box 298, File 8, WPR.

34. *Ibid.*, File 17, WPR.

35. *AFL News Reporter*, 4 June 1953 (capitals in original).

36. Speech to UAW–CIO Convention, 22 March 1953 in W. P. Reuther, UAW President's Office, Series VIII, Box 298, File 8, WPR.

37. W. P. Reuther, UAW President's Office, Series VIII, Box 298, File 10, WPR.

38. See 'The AFL will absorb the CIO when . . .', *Colliers* magazine, 15 September 1951, and 'Dave Beck, Strikebreaker', *Minnesota Labor News*, 8 May 1953, in W. P. Reuther, UAW President's Office, Series VII, Box 300, File 10, WPR. For examples of Teamster raiding, see leaflets in Box 300, File 2.

39. *New York Times*, 29 January 1955, *Milwaukee Journal*, 7 February 1954 and Harvey Kitzman letter to Reuther, 9 February 1954, in W. P. Reuther, UAW President's Office, Series VIII, Box 300, File 10, WPR.

40. *Detroit Free Press*, 14 February 1955 and W. P. Reuther, UAW President's Office, Series VIII, Box 300, File 16, WPR.

41. A. H. Raskin, 'Too much labor Unity?' *New York Times*, 12 January 1956, in W. P. Reuther, UAW President's Office, Series VIII, Box 298, File 14, WPR. See also Box 333, File 5 and *CIO News*, 5 December 1955.

42. W. P. Reuther, UAW President's Office, Series VIII, Box 298, File 8, WPR.

43. Quoted in Zieger, 'George Meany' in Dubofsky and Van Tine, *Labor Leaders*, p. 335.

7. THE COLLAPSE OF THE KEYNESIAN ECONOMY

1. John Kenneth Galbraith, *The New Industrial State* (Boston: Houghton Miflin, 1962).

2. Michael Harrington, *The Other America: Poverty in the United States* (London: Penguin Books, 1962).

3. Manning Marable, *Race, Reform and Rebellion: the Second Reconstructions in Black America* (London: Macmillan, 1984) pp. 12–41. This excellent study has been a major source for the analysis I have attempted in this section.

4. Ibid, p. 129.

5. Philip S. Foner, *Organised Labor and the Black Worker, 1619–1973* (New York: International Publishers, 1974) pp. 314–15.

6. Marable, *Race, Reform and Rebellion*, pp. 57–8.
7. Ibid., pp. 58–9.
8. *AFL–CIO Convention Proceedings* (1955).
9. Robert H. Zieger, 'George Meany: Labor's Organization Man', in Melvyn Dubofsky and Warren Van Tine (eds), *Labor Leaders in America* (Chicago: University of Illinois Press, 1987) p. 344.
10. Gus Tyler, 'Contemporary Labor's Attitude Towards the Negro' in Julian Jacobson (ed.), *The Negro in the American Labor Movement* (Garden City, New York: Anchor Books, 1968) p. 367.
11. Zieger, *George Meany*, p. 344.
12. Marable, *Race, Reform and Rebellions*, p. 130.
13. Foner, *Organized Labor*, pp. 418–19.
14. Quoted in Foner, p. 435.
15. Marable, *Race, Reform and Rebellion*, p. 133. For a perceptive analysis of this process, see Ira Katznelson 'Was the Great Society a Lost Opportunity?' in Steven Fraser and Gary Gerstle, *The Rise and Fall of the New Deal Order, 1930–1980* (Princeton: Princeton University Press, 1989) pp. 185–211.
16. Marable, *Race, Reform and Rebellion*, p. 134.
17. Rochelle Gatlin, *American Women Since 1945* (London: Macmillan, 1987) p. 25. I have found this study most useful in obtaining facts and clarifying my own thinking.
18. Esther Peterson, 'Working Women' *Daedalus: Journal of the American Academy of Arts and Sciences*, XCIII (Spring 1964), p. 683.
19. Gatlin, *American Women*, pp. 28 and 262n.
20. Ibid, pp. 195–6.
21. Ibid, pp. 218–19 and 263n.
22. Daniel P. Moynihan, 'Why the 70s will be different from the 60s', *Insight USA*, No. 6 (November 1973) pp. 32–4.
23. Quoted in Zieger 'George Meany', p. 344.
24. Quoted in F. R. Dulles and Melvyn Dubofsky, *Labor in America* (Arlington Heights: Harlan Davidson, 4th ed., 1984), p. 365.
25. Zieger, 'George Meany', p. 342.
26. Ibid.
27. Dulles and Dubofsky, *Labor*, pp. 382–3.
28. Ibid., pp. 383 and 369n. Rumour had it that Hoffa's body had been buried in cement which built the pillar of a highway overpass, so that in death, as in life, truck drivers could depend on him.
29. Cletus E. Daniel, 'Cesar Chavez and the Unionization of Californian Farm Workers' in Dubofsky and Van Tine (eds), *Labor Leaders*, p. 367.
30. United Farm Workers, Office of the President, Box 33, File 6, Cesar Chaves to Marshall Ganz, 4 February 1970, WPR.
31. Quoted in Daniel, 'Cezar Chavez', p. 376.
32. Ibid, pp. 380–1.
33. David P. Moynihan, *Maximum Feasible Misunderstanding* (New York: Random House, 1969). The most useful discussion of the problems of poverty in postwar America can be found in James T.

Patterson, *America's Struggle Against Poverty 1900–1980* (Cambridge: Harvard University Press, 1981) and *The Welfare State in America, 1930–1980*, (British Association for American Studies, 1981).

34. AFL–CIO Convention, Bal Harbor, Florida, 18–24 November 1971, Call to the Ninth Constitutional Convention, UFW Office of the President, Series V, Box 71, File 15, WPR.

35. *Labour Relations Yearbook 1972* (Washington DC, 1973) foreword, p.v.

36. For a perceptive analysis, see David Morgan, 'Terminal Flight: the Air Traffic Controllers' Strike of 1981', *Journal of American Studies*, Vol. 18, No. 2 (August 1984) pp. 165–83.

8. CONCLUSION

1. F. R. Dulles and Melvyn Dubofsky, *Labor in American* (Arlington Heights: Harlan Davidson, 1984) p. 400.

2. William M. Leiserson, 'Labor Relations' in *Papers of William M. Leiserson*, Box 52, quoted in Christopher L. Tomlins, *The State and the Unions: Labor Relations, Law and the Organized Labor Movement in America, 1880–1960* (Cambridge: Cambridge University Press, 1985) p. xi.

3. Dulles and Dubofsky, *Labor in America*, p. 341.

4. See, for example, David Brody, 'Labor and the Great Depression: the interpretative prospects', *Labor History*, XIII, 1972, pp. 231–44, and 'Radical labor history and rank-and-file militancy', *Labor History*, XVI, 1975, pp. 117–26. In these articles Brody surveys the field and literature, especially the work of Alice and Staughton Lynd, Stanley Aronowitz, Loran L. Cary, James R. Green, James Weinstein and others. See also Melvyn Dubofsky, 'Not so "turbulent years": another look at the American 1930s', *Amerikastudien*, XXIV, pp. 5–20. For two book-length discussions, see Michael Goldfield, *The Decline of Organized Labor in the United States* (Chicago: University of Chicago Press, 1987) and Kim Moody, *An Injury to All: The Decline of American Unions* (New York: Verso, 1988).

5. Alice Kessler-Harris, 'A New Agenda for American Labor History' in J. Carroll Moody and Alice Kessler-Harris eds., *Perspectives on American Labor History: the Problems of Synthesis* (De Kalb: Northern Illinois University Press, 1989), pp. 223–4.

Bibliography

BOOKS (including books not mentioned in the chapter Notes)

Alinsky, Saul, *John L. Lewis: An Unauthorized Biography* (New York: Putnam, 1949)

Anderson, Karen, *Wartime Women: Sex Roles, Family Relations, and the Status of Women During World War II* (Westport, Connecticut: Greenwood Press, 1981)

Auerbach, Jerold S., *Labor and Liberty: The La Follette Committee and the New Deal* (Indianapolis: Bobbs–Merrill, 1966)

Bakke, E. Wight, *The Unemployed Worker: A Study of the Task of Making a Living without a Job* (Hamden, Connecticut: Archon Books, 1970)

Barbash, Jack, *The Taft–Hartley Law in Action* (New York: League for Industrial Democracy, 1954)

Barnard, John, *Walter Reuther and the Rise of the Auto Workers* (Boston: Little, Brown, 1985)

Baskerville Stephen and Willett, Ralph (eds), *Nothing Else to Fear: New Perspectives on America in the Thirties* (Manchester: Manchester University Press, 1985)

Beirne, Joseph A., *Challenge to Labor: New Roles for American Trade Unions* (Englewood Cliffs: Prentice–Hall, 1969)

Bernstein, Irving, *Turbulent Years: A History of the American Worker, 1933–1941* (Boston: Houghton Mifflin, 1970)

Bird, Caroline, *Born Female: The High Cost of Keeping Women Down* (New York: David McKay, 1968)

Bishop, C. E. (ed.), *Farm Labor in the United States* (New York: Columbia University Press, 1967)

Blum, Albert A. et al., *White-Collar Workers* (New York: Random House, 1971)

Bok, Derek C. and Dunlop, John T., *Labor and the American Community* (New York: Simon & Schuster, 1970)

Bonnifield, Paul, *The Dust Bowl: Men, Dirt, and Depression* (Albuquerque: University of New Mexico Press, 1979)

Bowen, William G., *Labor and the National Economy* (rev. ed., New York: Norton, 1972)

Brody, David, *Steelworkers in America: The Non-Union Era* (New York: Harper and Row, 1960)

Brody, David, *Workers in Industrial America* (Oxford: Oxford University Press, 1981)

Brooks, Robert R. R., *Unions of Their Own Choosing: An Account of the National Labor Relations Board and Its Work* (New Haven: Yale University Press, 1937)

Brooks, Thomas R., *Picket Lines and Bargaining Tables: Organized Labor Comes of Age, 1935–1955* (New York: Grosset & Dunlap, 1968)

Brown, Emily L., *National Labor Policy: Taft–Hartley after Three Years and the Next Steps* (Washington, DC: Public Affairs Institute, 1950)

Burdick, Eugene, *The Ninth Wave* (Boston: Houghton Mifflin, 1956)

Cain, Glen C., *Married Women in the Labor Force: An Economic Analysis* (Chicago: University of Chicago Press, 1966)

Cantor, Milton and Laurie, Bruce (eds), *Class, Sex, and the Woman Worker* (Westport, Connecticut: Greenwood Press, 1977)

Cantor, Milton (ed.), *Black Labor in America*, (Westport, Connecticut: Negro Universities Press, 1969)

Carr, L. J. and Stermer, J. E., *Willow Run: Industrialization and Cultural Inadequacy* (New York: Harper, 1952)

Cayton, Horace R. and Mitchell, George S., *Black Workers and the New Unions* (Chapel Hill: University of North Carolina Press, 1939)

Chandler, Lester V., *America's Greatest Depression, 1929–1941* (New York: Harper & Row, 1970)

Chernish, William N., *Coalition Bargaining: A Study of Union Tactics and Public Policy.* (Philadelphia: University of Pennsylvania Press, 1969)

Cochran, Bert (ed.), *American Labor in Midpassage* (New York: Monthly Review Press, 1959)

Cochran, Bert, *Labor and Communism: the Conflict that Shaped American Trade Unions* (Princeton: Princeton University Press, 1977)

Commager, H. S., *Documents of American History* (New York: Appleton-Century-Crofts, 1948)

Cooke, Morris L. and Murray, Philip, *Organized Labor and Production: Next Steps in Industrial Democracy* (New York: Harper and Row, 1940)

Cortner, Richard C., *The Jones and Laughlin Case* (New York: Random House, 1970).

Cronon, Edmund D., *Labor and the New Deal* (Chicago: Rand McNally, 1963)

Daniel, Cletus E., *The ACLU and the Wagner Act: An Inquiry into the Depression-Era Crisis of American Liberalism* (Ithaca: New York State School of Industrial and Labor Relations, Cornell University, 1980)

Davis, Mike and Sprinkev, Michael, *Reshaping the US Left: Popular Struggles in the 1930s* (New York: Verso, 1988)

Day, Mark, *Forty Acres: César Chavez and the Farm Workers* (New York: Praeger, 1971)

De Caux, Len, *Labor Radical: From the Wobblies to CIO* (Boston: Beacon Press, 1970)

Derber, Milton and Young, Edwin (eds), *Labor and the New Deal* (Madison: University of Wisconsin Press, 1957)

Dubofsky, Melvyn and Tine, Warren Van, *John L. Lewis: a Biography* (New York: Quadrangle, 1977)

Dubofsky, Melvyn and Tine, Warren Van (eds), *Labor Leaders in America* (Chicago: University of Illinois Press, 1987)

Du Bois, W. E. B., *The Philadelphia Negro: a Social Study* (Philadelphia: University of Pennsylvania Press, 1899)

Dulles, F. R. and Dubofsky, Melvyn, *Labor in America* (Arlington Heights: Harlan Davidson, 1984)

Dunne, John Gregory, *Delano: The Story of the California Grape Strike* (rev. ed., New York: Farrar, Straus & Giroux, 1971)

Edwards, P. K., *Strikes in the United States, 1881–1974* (Oxford: Basil Blackwell, 1981)

Ellis, Edward, *A Nation in Torment: The Great American Depression, 1929–1939* (New York: Coward–McCann, 1970).

Fernandez, John P., *Racism and Sexism in Corporate Life: Changing Values in American Business* (Lexington, Kentucky: Lexington Books, 1981)

Fine, Sidney A., *The Automobile under the Blue Eagle* (Ann Arbor: University of Michigan Press, 1963)

Fine, Sidney A., *Sitdown: The General Motors Strike of 1936–1937* (Ann Arbor: University of Michigan Press, 1969)

First, Edythe W., *Industry and Labor Advisory Committee in the National Defense Advisory Commission and the Office of Production Management May 1940 to January 1942* (Washington DC: US Civilian Production Administration, 1946)

Flynn, George Q., *The Mess in Washington: Manpower Mobilization in World War II* (Westport, Connecticut: Greenwood Press, 1979)

Fraser, Steve and Gerstle, Gary, *The Rise and Fall of the New Deal Order, 1930–1980* (Princeton: Princeton University Press, 1989)

Galbraith, John Kenneth, *The New Industrial State* (Boston: Houghton Mifflin)

Galbraith, John Kenneth, *The Great Crash, 1929* (New York: Avon, 1980)

Galenson, Walter, *The CIO Challenge to the AFL: A History of the American Labor Movement, 1935–1941* (Cambridge: Harvard University Press, 1960)

Garnel, Donald, *The Rise of Teamster Power in the West* (Berkeley: University of California Press, 1971)

Gatlin, Rochelle, *American Women Since 1945* (London: Macmillan, 1987)

Gerstle, Gary, *Working-Class Americanism: the Politics of Labor in a Textile City, 1914–1960* (Cambridge: Cambridge University Press, 1989)

Gillmer, Richard S., *Death of a Business: The Red Wing Potteries* (Minneapolis: Ross and Haines, 1968)

Glaberman, Martin, *Wartime Strikes: The Struggle Against the No-Strike Pledge in the UAW during World War II* (Detroit: Bewick, 1980)

Goldberg, Arthur, *AFL–CIO Labor United* (New York: McGraw Hill, 1956)

Goldfield, Michael, *The Decline of Organized Labor in the United States* (Chicago: University of Chicago Press, 1987)

Goldston, Robert, *The Great Depression: The United States in the Thirties* (Indianapolis: Bobbs-Merrill, 1968)

Goodman, Jack (ed.), *While You Were Gone: A Report on Wartime Life in the U.S.* (New York: Simon & Schuster, 1946)

Gouldner, Alvin V., *Wildcat Strikes: A Study in Worker-Management Relationships* (New York: Harper & Row, 1965)

Graham, Otis L., *An Encore for Reform: The Old Progressives and the New Deal* (New York: Oxford University Press, 1967)

Gross, J. A., *The Making of the National Labor Relations Board: A Study in Economics, Politics, and the Law* (Albany: State University of New York Press, 1974)

Gross, J. A., *The Reshaping of the National Labor Relations Board: National Labor Policy in Transition* (Albany: State University of New York Press, 1981)

Haber, William (ed.), *Labor in a Changing America* (New York: Basic Books, 1966)

Halpern, Martin, *UAW Politics in the Cold War Era* (Albany: State University of New York Press, 1988)

Hardman, J. B. S. (ed), *American Labor Dynamics in the Light of Post-War Developments: An Inquiry by Thirty-Two Labor Men, Teachers, Editors, and Technicians* (New York: Russell & Russell, 1968)

Hardman, J. B. S. and Neufeld, Maurice (eds), *The House of Labor* (New York: Prentice-Hall, 1951)

Harrington, Michael, *The Other America: Poverty in the United States* (London: Penguin Books, 1962)

Harris, Howell, *The Right to Manage: Industrial Relations Policies of American Business in the 1940s* (Wisconsin: University of Wisconsin Press, 1982)

Hoffman, Claude E., *Sit-Down in Anderson: UAW Local 663 Anderson, Indiana* (Detroit: Wayne State University Press, 1968)

Howe, Louise K., *Pink Collar Workers: Inside the World of Women's Work* (New York: Putnam, 1977)

Huberman, Leo, *The Labor Spy Racket* (New York: Modern Age Books, 1937)

Hutchinson, John, *The Imperfect Union: A History of Corruption in American Trade Unions* (New York: E. P. Dutton, 1970)

Huthmacher, J. Joseph, *Senator Robert F. Wagner and the Rise of Urban Liberalism* (New York: Athenaeum, 1968)

Jacks, Stanley M. (ed.), *Issues in Labor Policy* (Cambridge: MIT Press, 1971)

Jacobson, Julius (ed.), *The Negro and the American Labor Movement* (New York: Doubleday, 1968)

James, Ralph and James, Estelle, *Hoffa and the Teamsters: A Study of Union Power* (Princeton: D. Van Nostrand, 1965)

Johnson, Malcolm M. *Crime on the Labor Front* (New York: McGraw-Hill, 1950)

Josephson, Matthew, *Sidney Hillman, Statesman of American Labor* (Garden City: Doubleday, 1952)

Kampelman, Max M., *The Communist Party vs. the CIO: A Study in Power Politics* (New York: Praeger, 1957)

Keeran, Roger, *The Communist Party and the Auto Workers Unions* (Bloomington: University of Indiana Press, 1980)

Kennedy, Donald et al. (eds), *Labor and Technology: Union Response to Changing Environment* (University Park: Pennsylvania State University, 1982)

Kennedy, Robert R., *The Enemy Within* (New York: Harper & Row, 1960)

Kessler-Harris, Alice, *Out to Work: A History of Wage-Earning Women in the United States* (New York: Oxford University Press, 1982)

Kessler-Harris, Alice, *Women Have Always Worked: A Historical Overview* (Old Westbury: Feminist Press, 1982)

Keynes, J. M., *The Means to Prosperity* (London: Macmillan, 1933)

Kraus, Henry, *The Many and the Few* (Los Angeles: Plantin Press, 1947)

Kreps, Juanita, *Sex in the Marketplace: American Women at Work* (Baltimore: Johns Hopkins Press, 1971)

Lekachman, Robert, *The Age of Keynes* (London: Allen Lane, The Penguin Press, 1966)

Lens, Sidney, *The Crisis of American Labor* (New York: Sagamore Press, 1959)

Lester, Richard A., *As Unions Mature: An Analysis of the Evolution of American Unionism* (Princeton: Princeton University Press, 1958)

Levenstein, Harvey, *Communism, Anti-Communism and the CIO* (Westpoint, Connecticut: Greenwood Press, 1981)

Lichtenstein, Nelson, *Labor's War at Home: the CIO in World War II* (Cambridge: Cambridge University Press, 1982)

Lindblom, Charles E., *Unions and Capitalism* (Hamden, Connecticut: Archon Books, 1970)

Marshall, F. Ray, *The Negro and Organized Labor* (New York: John Wiley, 1965)

McClure, Arthur F., *The Truman Administration and the Problems of Postwar Labor, 1945–1948* (Rutherford: Fairleigh Dickinson University Press, 1969)

McDonald, David J., *Union Man* (New York: Duttan, 1969)

McFarland, Charles K., *Roosevelt, Lewis and the New Deal, 1933–1940* (Fort Worth: Texas Christian University Press, 1970)

McWilliams, Carey, *Factories in the Field: The Story of Migratory Farm Labor in California* (Boston: Little, Brown and Co., 1939)

Marable, Manning, *Race, Reform and Rebellion: the Second Reconstruction in Black America* (London: Macmillan, 1984)

Meier, August and Rudwick, Elliot M., *From Plantation to Ghetto* (rev. ed., New York: Hill & Wang, 1970)

Meier, August and Rudwick, Elliott, *Black Detroit and the Rise of the UAW* (New York: Oxford University Press, 1979)

Meltzer, Milton, *Brother Can You Spare a Dime: The Great Depression, 1929–1933* (New York: Knopf, 1969)

Miller, Donald L., *The New American Radicalism: Alfred M. Bingham and Non-Marxian Insurgency in the New Deal Era* (Port Washington, New York: Kennikat, 1979)

Miller, William D., *A Harsh and Dreadful Love: Dorothy Day and the Catholic Worker Movement* (New York: Liveright, 1973)

Millis, Harry, A. and Brown, Emily C., *From the Wagner Act to Taft–Hartley: A Study of National Labor Policy and Labor Relations* (Chicago: University of Chicago Press, 1950)

Mills, C. Wright, *The New Men of Power: America's Labor Leaders* (New York: Harcourt Brace, 1948)

Mitchell, Broadus, *Depression Decade: From New Era through New Deal, 1929–1941* (New York: Rinehart, 1947)

Mohr, Lillian H., *Frances Perkins: That Woman in FDR's Cabinet* (Groton-on-Hudson, New York: North River Press, 1979)

Moley, Raymond, *After Seven Years* (New York: Harper and Bros, 1939)

Moody, Kim, *An Injury to All: the Decline of American Unionism* (London: Verso, 1988)

Morris, George, *The CIA and American Labor: The Subversion of the AFL–CIO's Foreign Policy* (New York: International Publishers, 1967)

Morris, James O., *Conflict within the A.F. of L.: A Study of Craft versus Industrial Unionism, 1901–1938* (Ithaca: Cornell University Press, 1958)

Murton, Tom and Hyams, Joe, *Accomplices to the Crime* (New York: Grove Press, 1970)

Myer, Dillon S., *Uprooted Americans* (Tucson: University of Arizona Press, 1971)

National War Labor Board, *The Termination Report: Industrial Disputes and Wage Stabilization in Wartime, January 12, 1942–December 31, 1945*, 3 Vols. (Washington, DC: US Government Printing Office, 1948–9)

Okun, Arthur M. *The Battle against Unemployment* (rev. ed., New York: Norton, 1972)

Orren Karen, and Skowronec, Stephen (eds), *Studies in American Political Development*, Vols 1 and 2 (New Haven: Yale University Press, 1988 and 1989)

Osofsky, Gilbert, *Harlem: The Making of a Ghetto* (2nd ed., New York: Harper and Row, 1971)

Perkins, Frances, *The Roosevelt I Knew* (New York: Viking Press)

Perlman, Selig, *Labor in the New Deal Decade* (New York: Educational Department, International Ladies' Garment Workers' Union, 1945)

Perlman, Selig, *A Theory of the Labor Movement* (New York: Macmillan)

Peterson, Florence, *American Labor Unions: What They Are and How They Work* (2nd rev. ed., New York: Harper & Row, 1963)

Preis, Art., *Labor's Giant Step: Thirty Years of the CIO* (New York: Pioneer Publishers, 1964)

Purcell, Richard J., *Labor Policies of the National Defense Advisory Commission and the Office of Production Management, May 1940 to April 1942*, (Washington, DC: US Civilian Production Administration, 1946)

Quin, Mike, *The Big Strike* (Olema, California: Olema Publishing Co., 1949)

Radosh, Ronald, *American Labor and United States Foreign Policy* (New York: Random House, 1969)

Reuther, Victor G., *The Brothers Reuther and the Story of the UAWA* (Boston: Houghton Mifflin, 1976)

Roberts, Harold S., *Labor-Management Relations in the Public Service* (Honolulu: University of Hawaii Press, 1970)

Saposs, David J., *Communism in American Unions* (New York: McGraw-Hill, 1959)

Seale, Bobby, *Seize the Time* (New York: Vintage, 1970)

Schlesinger, Arthur M., Jr., *The Age of Roosevelt*; Vol. 1: *The Crisis of the Old Order*; Vol. 2: *The Coming of the New Deal*; Vol. 3: *The Politics of Upheaval* (Boston: Houghton Mifflin, 1957–60)

Scoville, James G., *The Job Content of the U.S. Economy, 1940–1970* (New York: McGraw-Hill, 1969)

Seidman, Joel, *American Labor from Defense to Reconversion* (Chicago: University of Chicago Press, 1953)

Seidman, Joel (ed.), *Trade Union Government and Collective Bargaining: Some Critical Issues* (New York: Praeger, 1970)

Spero, Sterling D. and Harris, Abram L., *The Black Worker: The Negro and the Labor Movement*, (Port Washington, DC: Kennikat Press, 1931)

Stanley, David T. and Cooper, Carole L., *Managing Local Government under Union Pressure* (Washington DC: Brookings Institution, 1972)

Stapp, Andy, *Up Against the Brass* (New York: Simon & Schuster, 1970)

Stinnett, T. M., *Turmoil in Teaching: A History of the Organizational Struggle for America's Teachers* (New York: Macmillan, 1968)

Stolberg, Benjamin, *The Story of the CIO* (New York: Viking Press, 1938)

Taft, Philip, *The A.F. of L. from the Death of Gompers to the Merger* (New York: Harper & Row, 1959)

Terkel, Studs, *Hard Times: An Oral History of the Great Depression* (New York: Pantheon Books, 1970)

Terkel, Studs, *Working* (New York: Pantheon Books, 1972)

Tomlins, Christopher L., *The State and the Unions: Labor Relations, Law and the Organized Labor Movement in America, 1880–1960* (Cambridge: Cambridge University Press, 1985)

Treckel, Karl F., *The Rise and Fall of the Alliance for Labor Action (1968–72)* (Kent, Ohio: Kent State University, 1976)

Tyler, Gus., *The Labor Revolution: Trade Unions in a New America* (New York: Viking Press, 1967)

Tyler, Gus, *The Political Imperative: The Corporate Character of Unions* (New York: Macmillan, 1968)

Uphoff, Walter H., *Kohler on Strike: Thirty Years of Conflict* (Boston: Beacon Press, 1966)

US Department of Labor, *The National Wage Stabilization Board, January 1, 1946–February 24, 1947* (Washington DC: US Government Printing Office, 1950)

US Department of Labor, Bureau of Labor Statistics, *Historical Studies of Wartime Problems*, Nos 1–78, (Washington DC: Bureau of Labor Statistics, 1941–45)

US Department of Labor, *Problems and Policies of Dispute Settlement and Wage Stabilization during World War II*, Bulletin 1009, (Washington DC: US Government Printing Office, 1950)

US Department of Labor, *Report on the Work of the National Defense Mediation Board, March 19, 1941–January 12, 1942*, Bulletin 714, (Washington DC: US Government Printing Office, 1942)

US Department of Labor, *Division of Labor Standards, The President's National Labor-Management Conference, November 5–30, 1945: Summary and Committee Reports*, Bulletin 77, (Washington DC: US Government Printing Office, 1946)

Walton, Richard, *The Impact of the Professional Engineering Union* (Boston: Graduate School of Business Administration, Harvard University, 1961)

Warne, Colston E. (ed.), *Labor in Postwar America* (Brooklyn: Remsen Press, 1949)

Warne, Colston E. et al. (eds), *War Labor Policies* (New York: Philosophical Library, 1945)

Weller, Jack E., *Yesterday's People: Life in Contemporary Appalachia* (Lexington, Kentucky: University of Kentucky Press, 1965)

Wertheimer, Barbara M., *Labor Education for Women Workers* (Philadelphia: Temple University Press, 1981)

Wertheimer, Barbara M. and Nelson, Anne H., *Trade Union Women: A Study of Their Participation in New York City Locals* (New York: Praeger, 1975)

Wertheimer, Barbara M., *We Were There: The Story of Working Women in America* (New York: Pantheon, 1977)

Westley, William A. and Westley, Margaret W., *The Emerging Worker: Equality and Conflict in the Mass Consumption Society* (Montreal: McGill-Queen's University Press, 1971)

Widick, B. J., *Labor Today: The Triumphs and Failures of Unionism in the United States* (Boston: Houghton Mifflin, 1964)

Wirtz, William W., *Labor and the Public Interest* (New York: Harper & Row, 1964)

Witney, Fred, *Wartime Experiences of the National Labor Relations Board, 1941–1945* (Urbana: University of Illinois Press, 1949)

Wolfbein, Seymour L. (ed.), *Emerging Sectors of Collective Bargaining* (Braintree, Massachusetts: D. H. Mark, 1970)

Wolters, Raymond, *Negroes and the Great Depression* (Westport: Greenwood Press, 1970)

Young, Jan, *Migrant Workers and César Chavez* (New York: Julian Messner, 1972)

Zelman, Patricia, *Women, Work and National Policy: The Kennedy–Johnson Years* (Ann Arbor: University of Michigan Press, 1982)

ARTICLES

Anderson, Karen Tucker, 'Last Hired, First Fired: Black Women Workers during World War II', *Journal of American History*, Vol. 69, No. 1 (June 1982) pp. 82–97

Ash, Philip, 'The Preriodical Press and the Taft–Hartley Act', *Public Opinion Quarterly*, Vol. 12 (1948) pp. 266–71

Antos, Joseph R. et al., 'Sex Differences in Union Membership', *Industrial and Labor Relations Review*, Vol. 33 (1980) pp. 162–9

Auerbach, Jerold S., 'Southern Tenant Farmers: Socialist Critics of the New Deal', *Labor History*, Vol. 7 (1966) pp. 3–18

Auerbach, Jerold S., 'The Influence of the New Deal', *Current History*, Vol. 47 (1965) pp. 334–9, 365

Babson, Steve, 'The Multinational Corporation and Labor', *Review of Radical Political Economics*, Vol. 5 (Spring 1973) pp. 19–36

Barnard, John, 'Rebirth of the United Automobile Workers: the General Motors Tool Diemakers' Strike of 1939', *Labor History*, Vol. 27, No. 2 (Spring 1986) pp. 165–87

Bartell, H. Robert, Jr., 'National Union Assets, 1959–61', *Industrial and Labor Relations Review*, Vol. 9 (1965) pp. 80–91

Bartol, Kathryn M. and Bartol, Robert A., 'Women in Managerial and Professional Positions: The United States and the Soviet Union', *Industrial and Labor Relations Review*, Vol. 28 (1975) pp. 524–34

Baskin, Alex, 'The Ford Hunger March 1932', *Labor History*, Vol. 13 (1972) pp. 331–60

Beffen, Neil, 'The Great Depression and the Activities of the Catholic Worker Movement', *Labor History*, Vol. 12 (1971) pp. 243–358

Bell, Daniel, 'The Next American Labor Movement', *Fortune* (April 1953)

Bell, Daniel, 'The Truman Administration and the Steel Strike of 1946', *Journal of American History*, Vol. 52 (1966) pp. 791–803

Bell, Daniel, 'Labor in the Post-Industrial Society', *Dissent*, Vol. 19 (1972) pp. 163–9

Bergquist, Virgina A., 'Women's Participation in Labor Organizations', *Monthly Labor Review*, Vol. 97 (1974) pp. 3–9

Bernard, Dan, 'The NLRB, the Courts, and Employer Free Speech', *Industrial and Labor Relations Forum*, Vol. 2 (1965) pp. 1–21

Bernstein, Barton J., 'The Truman Administration and the Reconversion Wage Policy,' *Labor History*, Vol. 6 (1965) pp. 114–23

Bernstein, Irving, 'The Growth of American Unions, 1945–1960', *Labor History*, Vol. 2 (1961) pp. 131–57

Biles, Roger, 'Ed Crump Versus the Unions: the Labor Movement in Memphis During the 1930s', *Labor History*, Vol. 25 (1984) pp. 533–52

Blackman, John L. Jr., 'Navy Policy Toward the Labor Relations of Its War Contractors', *Military Affairs*, Vol. 18 (1954) pp. 176–87; Vol. 19 (1955) pp. 21–31

Blum, Albert A., 'Sailor or Worker: A Manpower Dilemma during the Second World War', *Labor History*, Vol. 6 (1965) pp. 232–43

Blum, Albert A., 'Roosevelt, the M-Day Plans and the Military–Industrial Complex', *Military Affairs*, Vol. 36 (1972) pp. 44–6

Blum, Albert A., 'Soldier or Worker: A Revaluation of the Selective Service System', *Midwest Quarterly*, Vol. 13 (1972) pp. 147–67

Blum, Albert A., 'Working to Win World War II', *American Quarterly*, Vol. 30 (1978) pp. 39–53

Bolin, Winifred, 'The Economics of Middle-Income Family Life: Working Women during the Great Depression', *Journal of American History*, Vol. 65 (1978) pp. 60–73

Boyle, Kevin, 'Rite of Passage: The 1939 General Motors Tool and Die Strike', *Labor History*, Vol. 27 (1986) pp. 188–203

Braeman, John, 'The New Deal and the "Broker State": A Review of the Recent Scholarly Literature', *Business History Review*, Vol. 45 (1972) pp. 409–29

Braver, Carl M., 'Kennedy, Johnson, and the War on Poverty', *Journal of American History*, Vol. 69 (1982) pp. 98–119

Bremer, William W., 'Along the "American Way": The New Deal's Work Relief Programs for the Unemployed', *Journal of American History*, Vol. 62 (1975) pp. 636–52

Brody, David, 'Labor and the Great Depression: the Interpretative Prospect', *Labor History*, Vol. 13 (1972) pp. 231–44

Brody, David, 'Radical Labor History and Rank-and-File Militancy', *Labor History*, Vol. 16 (1975) pp. 117–26

Brooks, George W., 'Reflections on the Changing Character of American Labor Unions', *Proceedings of the Ninth Annual Meeting of the Industrial Relations Research Association*, December 28–29 1956, pp. 33–43 (Madison: IRRA 1957)

Brooks, George W., *The Sources of Vitality in the American Labor Movement*, Bulletin No. 41 (Ithaca: New York State School of Industrial and Labor Relations, Cornell University, 1960)

Brooks, George W. and Thomson, Mark, 'Multiplant Units: the NLRB's Withdrawal of Free Choice', *Industrial and Labor Relations Review*, Vol. 20 (1967) pp. 363–80

Burran, James A., 'The W.P.A. in Nashville, 1935–43', *Tenessee Historical Quarterly*, Vol. 34 (1975) pp. 298–306

Currigan, D. Owen, 'Martha Moore Avery: Crusader for Social Justice', *Catholic Historical Review*, Vol. 54 (1968) pp. 17–38

Chambers, John W., 'The Big Switch: Justice Roberts and the Minimum-Wage Cases', *Labor History*, Vol. 10 (1969) pp. 44–73

Chernow, Ron, 'All in a Day's Work: Housekeepers, Mostly Black Women, are the Last Frontier of Labor Organizing', *Mother Jones*, Vol. 1 (1976) pp. 11–16

Clive, Alan, 'Women Workers in World War II: Michigan as a Test Case', *Labor History*, Vol. 20 (1979) pp. 44–72

Cobb, William H. and Grubbs, Donald H., 'Arkansas' Commonwealth College and the Southern Tenant Farmers' Union', *Arkansas Historical Quarterly*, Vol. 25 (1966) pp. 293–311

Coode, Thomas and Fabbin, Dennis, 'The New Deal's Arthurdale Project in West Virginia', *West Virginia History*, Vol. 36 (1975) pp. 291–308

Cook, Alice H., 'Equal Pay: Where Is It?', *Industrial Relations*, Vol. 14 (1975) pp. 158–77

Cooney, Rosemary S., 'Changing Labor Force Participation of Mexican American Wives: a Comparison with Anglos and Blacks', *Social Science Quarterly*, Vol. 56 (1975) pp. 252–61

Cowl, Margaret, 'Women's Struggles for Equality', *Political Affairs*, Vol. 53 (May 1974) pp. 40–4

Darby, Michael R., 'Three-and-a-Half Million U.S. Employees Have been Mislaid: or, an Explanation of Unemployment, 1934–1941', *Journal of Political Economy*, Vol. 84 (1976) pp. 1–16

Davis, Howard, 'Employment Gains of Women by Industry, 1968–1978', *Monthly Labor Review*, Vol. 103 (1980) pp. 3–9

Derber, Milton, 'Labor–Management in World War II', *Current History*, Vol. 48 (1965) pp. 340–5

Di Bacco, Thomas V., 'Draft the Strikers (1946) and Seize the Mills (1952): the Business Reaction', *Duquesne Review*, Vol. 13 (1968) pp. 63–75

Dubay, Robert W., 'The Civilian Conservation Corps: A Study of Opposition, 1933–1935', *Southern Quarterly*, Vol. 6 (1968) pp. 341–58

Dubofsky, Melvyn, 'Not so "Turbulent Years": Another Look at the American 1930s', *Amerikastudien/American Studies*, Vol. 24 (1979) pp. 5–20

Duram, James C., 'The Labor Union Journals and the Constitutional Issues of the New Deal', *Labor History*, Vol. 15 (1974) pp. 216–38

Egolf, Jeremy R., 'The Limits of Shop Floor Struggle: Worker vs. The Bidaux System at Willapen Harbor Lumber Mills, 1933–35', *Labor History*, Vol. 26, No. 2 (Spring 1985) pp. 195–229

Erickson, Herman, 'WPA Strike and Trials of 1939', *Minnesota History*, Vol. 42 (1971) pp. 202–14

Felt, Jeremy P., 'The Child Labor Provisions of the Fair Labor Standards Act', *Labor History*, Vol. 11 (1970) pp. 467–81

Ferguson, C. E. and Stober, William J., 'Estimate of Union Membership from Reports Filed under the Labor–Management Reporting and Disclosure Act', *Southern Economic Journal*, Vol. 33 (1966) pp. 166–86

Fickle, James E., 'The Southern Pine Association and the N.R.A.: a Case Study of the Blue Eagle in the South', *Southwestern Historical Quarterly*, Vol. 79 (1976) pp. 253–78

Field, Jana, 'The Coalition of Labor Union Women', *Political Affairs*, Vol. 54 (1975) pp. 3–12

Fine, Sidney, 'Frank Murphy, the Thornhill Decision and Picketing as Free Speech', *Labor History*, Vol. 5 (1965) pp. 99–120.

Forkosch, Morris D., 'Workers' Councils and Worker Participation in Management in Theory and in Actuality', *Washburn Law Journal*, Vol. 10 (1971) pp. 339–55

Foster, James C., 'Why the American Labor Movement is Not Socialist', *The American Review*, Vol. 1 (1961) pp. 1–19

Fox, Bonnie R., 'Unemployment Relief in Philadelphia, 1930–1932: a Study of the Depression's Impact on Voluntarism', *Pennsylvania Magazine of History and Biography*, Vol. 93 (1969) pp. 86–108

Fraser, Steve, 'From the "New Unionism" to the New Deal', *Labor History*, Vol. 25, No. 3 (Summer 1984) pp. 405–30

Freeman, Joshua B., 'Delivering the Goods: Industrial Unionism During World War II', *Labor History*, Vol. 19 (1978) pp. 570–93

Gabin, Nancy, 'Women Workers and the UAW in the Post-World War II Period: 1945–1954', *Labor History*, Vol. 21 (1980) pp. 5–30

Gall, Gilbert J., 'Heber Blankenhorn, the La Follette Committee, and the Irony of Industrial Repression', *Labor History*, Vol. 22 (1982) pp. 246–53

Garber, Philip E., 'Taft–Hartley: Section 304. A Legislative History', *Industrial and Labor Relations Forum*, Vol. 7 (1970) pp. 59–102

Garraty, John A., 'The New Deal, National Socialism and the Great Depression', *American Historical Review*, Vol. 78 (1973) pp. 907–44

Garraty, John A., 'Unemployment During The Great Depression', *Labor History*, Vol. 17 (1976) pp. 133–59

Gillett, Alexander, 'Current Developments in Labor–Management Relations: Notes', *Industrial and Labor Relations Forum*, Vol. 5 (1969) pp. 328–32

Glazer-Malbin, Nona, 'Housework (a review essay)', *Signs*, Vol. 1 (1976) pp. 5–22

Goldberg, Joseph P., 'Government and Labor in the United States', *Current History*, Vol. 37 (1959) pp. 129–80

Goldberg, Joseph P., 'Labor–Management Since World War II', *Current History*, Vol. 48 (1965) pp. 336–52, 365–66

Gordon, R. A., 'Unemployment Patterns with "Full Employment".', *Industrial Relations*, Vol. 8 (1968) pp. 46–72

Gordon, Suzanne, 'Half-time Blues', *Working Papers for a New Society*, Vol. 8 (1981) pp. 36–41

Gray, Lois, 'Trends in Selection and Training of International Union Staff: Implications for University and College Labor Education', *Labor Studies Journal*, Vol. 5 (1980) pp. 13–24

Gray, Lois, 'Unions Implementing Managerial Techniques', *Monthly Labor Review*, Vol. 104 (1981) pp. 3–13

Green, James R., 'Working Class Militancy in the Depression', *Radical America*, Vol. 6 (1972) pp. 1–35

Green, James R., 'Fighting on Two Fronts: Working Class Militancy in the 1940s', *Radical America*, Vol. 9 (1975) pp. 7–48

Grodin, Joseph R., 'The Kennedy Labor Board', *Industrial Relations*, Vol. 3 (1964) pp. 33–45

Gujarati, Damodar, 'Labor's Share in Manufacturing Industries, 1949–1964', *Industrial and Labor Relations Review*, Vol. 23 (1969) pp. 65–77

Hanagan, Michael and Stephenson, C., 'The Skilled Worker and Working-Class Protest', *Social Science History*, Vol. 4 (1980) pp. 5–15

Harrington, Michael, 'Old Working Class, New Working Class', *Dissent*, Vol. 19 (1972) pp. 146–62

Haynes, John Earl, 'The "Rank and File" Movement in Private Social Work', *Labor History*, Vol. 16 (1975) pp. 78–98

Heinemann, Ronald, 'Blue Eagle or Black Buzzard? The NRA in Virginia', *Virginia Magazine of History and Biography*, Vol. 89 (1981) pp. 90–100

Hendrickson, Kenneth E., Jr., 'The Civilian Conservation Corps in Pennsylvania: a Case Study of a New Deal Relief Agency in Operation', *Pennsylvania Magazine of History and Biography*, Vol. 100 (1976) pp. 66–96

Herling, John, 'Change and Conflict in the AFL–CIO', *Dissent*, Vol. 21 (1974) pp. 479–85

Hicks, Floyd W. and Lambert, C. Roger, 'Food for the Hungry: Federal Food Programs in Arkansas, 1933–1942', *Arkansas Historical Quarterly*, Vol. 37 (1978)

Hirschorn, L., 'The Post-Industrial Labor Process', *New Political Science*, Vol. 2 (Fall 1981) pp. 11–32

Holland, Reid, 'Civilian Conservation Corps in the City: Tulsa and Oklahoma City in the 1930s', *Chronicles of Oklahoma*, Vol. 53 (1975) pp. 367–75

Hook, Sidney, 'Modern Quarterly, a Chapter in American Radical History: V. F. Calverton and his Periodicals', *Labor History*, Vol. 10 (1969) pp. 241–9

Hunter, John O., 'Marc Blitzstein's "The Cradle Will Rock" as a Document of America, 1937', *American Quarterly*, Vol. 18 (1966) pp. 227–33

Hurd, Rick, 'New Deal Labor Policy and the Containment of Radical Union Activity', *Review of Radical Political Economics*, Vol. 8 (1976) pp. 32–43

Hutchinson, John, 'Corruption in American Trade Unions', *The Political Quarterly*, Vol. 28 (1957), 214–35

Isserman, Maurice, 'Three Generations: Historians View American Communism', *Labor History*, Vol. 26 (1985) pp. 517–45

Jeansonne, Glen, 'Challenge to the New Deal: Huey P. Long and the Redistribution of National Wealth', *Louisiana History*, Vol. 21 (1980) pp. 331–9

Jennings, Ed., 'Wildcat! The Wartime Strike Wave in Auto', *Radical America*, Vol. 9 (1975) pp. 77–105

Johnson, Ralph Arthur, 'World Without Workers: Prime Time's Presentation of Labor', *Labor Studies Journal*, Vol. 5 (1980) pp. 199–206

Johnson, William R., 'Rural Rehabilitation in the New Deal: the Ropesville Project', *Southwestern Historical Quarterly*, Vol. 79 (1976) pp. 279–95

Kahn, Lawrence M., 'Unionism and Relative Wages: Direct and Indirect Effects', *Industrial and Labor Relations Review*, Vol. 32 (1979) pp. 520–32

Kahne, Hilda and Kohen, Andrew, 'Economic Perspectives on the Roles of Women in the American Economy', *Journal of Economic Literature*, Vol. 13 (1975) pp. 149–92

Kanier, R. M., 'Work in a New America', *Daedalus*, Vol. 107 (1978) pp. 44–77

Keezer, Dexter, 'Observations on the Operations of the National War Labor Board', *American Economic Review*, (June 1946)

Kessler-Harris, Alice, 'Organizing the Unorganizable: Three Jewish Women and Their Union', *Labor History*, Vol. 17 (1976) pp. 5–23

Kessler-Harris, Alice, 'Women's Wage Work as Myth and History', *Labor History*, Vol. 19 (1978) pp. 287–307

Kistler, Alan, 'Trends in Union Growth', *Labor Law Journal*, (Aug. 1977) pp. 539–45

Kleinberg, Susan J., 'Technology and Women's Work: The Lives of Working Class Women in Pittsburgh, 1870–1900', *Labor History*, Vol. 17 (1976) pp. 58–72

Klemesrud, Judy, 'Director of Hospital Walkout: Lillian Roberts', *New York Times*, August 5 1976, p. 52

Kochan, T. A., 'How American Workers View Labor Unions', *Monthly Labor Review*, Vol. 102 (1979) pp. 23–31

Koistinen, Paul A. C., 'Mobilizing the World War II Economy: Labor and the Industrial–Military Alliance', *Pacific Historical Review*, Vol. 42 (1973) pp. 443–78

Kolko, Gabriel, 'Working Wives: their Effects on the Structure of the Working Class', *Science & Society*, Vol. 42 (1978) pp. 257–77

Kornhauser, Ruth, 'Some Social Determinants and Consequences of Union Membership', *Labor History*, Vol. 2 (1961) pp. 30–61

Korstad, Robert and Bicktenstein, Nelson, 'Opportunity Found and Lost: Labor, Radicals and the Early Civil Rights Movement', *Journal of American History*, Vol. 75, No. 3 (1988) pp. 786–811

Koziara, Karen and Pierson, D. A., 'The Lack of Female Union Leaders: a Look at Some Reasons', *Monthly Labor Review*, Vol. 104 (May 1981) pp. 30–2

Krislov, Joseph, 'New Organizing by Unions During the 1950s', *Monthly Labor Review*, Vol. 83 (1960) pp. 922–4

Krislov, Joseph, 'Union Organizing of New Units, 1955–1966', *Industrial and Labor Relations Review*, Vol. 21 (1967) pp. 31–9

Lambert, C. Roger, 'Want and Plenty: the Federal Surplus Relief Corporation and the AAA', *Agricultural History*, Vol. 46 (1972) pp. 390–400

Larrowe, Charles P., 'The Great Maritime Strike of '34', *Labor History*, Vol. 11 (1970) pp. 403–51; Vol. 12 (1971) pp. 3–37

Leab, Daniel J., 'United We Eat: the Creation and Organization of the Unemployed Councils in 1930', *Labor History*, Vol. 8 (1967) pp. 300–15

Lens, Sidney, 'Labor Unity is No Panacea', *The Antioch Review*, (Summer 1955) pp. 180–94

Lens, Sidney, 'Will Merged Labor Set New Goals?', *Harvard Business Review*, Vol. 34 (1956) pp. 57–63

Lester, Richard A., 'Labor Policy in a Changing World', *Industrial Relations*, Vol. 2 (1962) pp. 39–52

Lichtenstein, Nelson, 'Ambiguous Legacy: The Union Security Problem During World War II', *Labor History*, Vol. 18 (1977) pp. 214–38

Lichtenstein, Nelson, 'Defending the No-Strike Pledge: CIO Politics during World War II', *Radical America*, Vol. 9 (1975) pp. 49–75

Longin, Thomas C., 'Coal, Congress and the Courts: the Bituminous Coal Industry and the New Deal', *West Virginia Magazine*, Vol. 35 (1974) pp. 101–30

MacDonald, Robert M., 'Collective Bargaining in the Postwar Period', *Industrial and Labor Relations Review*, Vol. 20 (1967) pp. 553–77

Malamont, B. C., 'British Labour and Roosevelt's New Deal: the Response of the Left and the Unions', *Journal of British Studies*, Vol. 17 (Sep. 1978) pp. 136–67

Marquart, Frank, 'From a Labor Journal: Unions and Radicals in the Depression Era', *Dissent*, Vol. 21 (1974) pp. 421–30

Marshall, F. Ray, 'Some Factors Influencing the Growth of Unions in the South', *Proceedings of the Thirteenth Annual Meeting of the Industrial Relations Research Association* December 18–19 1960, pp. 166–82 (Madison: IRRA, 1961)

Martin, Charles H., 'Southern Labor Relations in Transition: Gadsden, Alabama, 1930–1943', *Journal of Southern History*, Vol. 47 (1981) pp. 545–68

Meany, George, 'What Labor Means by "More"', *Fortune* (March 1955) pp. 1–12

Miller, John E., 'Progressivism and the New Deal: the Wisconsin Workers Bill of 1935', *Wisconsin Magazine of History*, Vol. 62 (1978) pp. 25–40

Miller, Richard, 'The Enigma of Section 8(5) of the Wagner Act', *Industrial and Labor Relations Review*, Vol. 18 (1965) pp. 166–85

Miller, Richard, 'Arbitration of New Contract Wage Disputes: Some Recent Trends', *Industrial and Labor Relations Review*, Vol. 20 (1967) pp. 250–64

Moore, William J. and Newman, Robert J., 'Determinants of Differences in Union Membership Among the States', *Proceedings of the Twenty-Sixth Annual Winter Meeting of the Industrial Relations Research Association*, December 28–29 1973, pp. 188–96 (Madison: IRRA, 1974)

Morgan, Thomas S., Jr., 'A "Folly, Manifest to Everyone": the Movement to Enact Unemployment Insurance Legislation in North Carolina, 1935–36', *North Carolina Historical Review*, Vol. 52 (1975) pp. 283–302

Nelson, Daniel, 'The Beginnings of the Sit-down Era: The Reminiscences of Rex Murray', *Labor History*, Vol. 15 (1974) pp. 89–97

Nelson, Daniel, 'Origins of the Sit-Down Era: Worker Militancy and Innovation in the Rubber Industry, 1934–38', *Labor History*, Vol. 22 (1982) pp. 198–225

Nelson, Daniel, 'The CIO at Bay: Labor Militancy and Politics in Akron, 1936–1938', *Journal of American History*, Vol. 71, No. 3 (December 1984) pp. 565–86

Nelson, Lawrence J., 'Oscar Johnston, the New Deal and the Cotton Subsidy Payments Controversy, 1936–37', *Journal of Southern History*, Vol. 40 (1974) pp. 399–416

Noble, Richard A., 'Paterson's Response to the Great Depression', *New Jersey History*, Vol. 90 (1978) pp. 87–98

Nye, Ronald L., 'The Challenge to Philanthropy: Unemployment Relief in Santa Barbara, 1930–1932', *California History*, Vol. 56 (1978) pp. 310–27

Ober, Michael J., 'The CCC Experience in Glacier National Park', *Montana: Magazine of Western History*, Vol. 26 (1976) pp. 30–9

O'Brien, David, 'American Catholics and Organized Labor in the 1930s'. *Catholic Historical Review*, Vol. 56, (1966) pp. 323–49

O'Brien, F. S., 'The "Communist-Dominated" Union in the United States', *Labor History*, Vol. 9 (1968) pp. 184–209

O'Neil, William L., 'Labor Radicalism and the Masses', *Labor History*, Vol. 7 (1966) pp. 197–208

Orren, Karen, 'Organized Labor and the Invention of Modern Liberalism in the United States', in Karen Orren and Stephen Skowrovek (eds), *Studies in American Political Development*, Vol. 2, (New Haven: Yale University Press, 1988), pp. 31–6

Ortquist, Richard T., 'Unemployment and Relief: Michigan's Response to the Depression during the Hoover Years.' *Michigan History*, Vol. 45, (1973), pp. 209–36

Patterson, James T. (ed.), 'Life on Relief in Rhode Island, 1934: a Contemporary View from the Field', *Rhode Island History*, Vol. 39 (1980) pp. 79–93

Pessen, Edward, 'A Young Industrial Worker in Early World War II in New York City', *Labor History*, Vol. 22 (1981) pp. 269–81

Plotkia, David, 'The Wagner Act, Again: Politics and Labor, 1935–37 in Karen Orren & Stephen Skowrovek (eds), *Studies in American Political Development*, Vol. 3, (New Haven: Yale University Press, 1989) pp. 105–56.

Pivar, David J., 'The Hosiery Workers and the Philadelphia Third Party Impulse, 1929–1935', *Labor History*, Vol. 5 (1964) pp. 18–28

Pomper, Gerald, 'Labor and Congress: The Repeal of Taft–Hartley', *Labor History*, Vol. 2 (1961) pp. 323–43

Pomper, Gerald, 'Labor Legislation: The Revision of Taft–Hartley in 1953–1954', *Labor History*, Vol. 6 (1965) pp. 143–58

Pratt, William C., 'Women and American Socialism, the Reading Experience', *Pennsylvania Magazine of History and Biography*, Vol. 99 (1975) pp. 72–91

Raphael, Edna E., 'Working Women and the Membership in Labor Unions', *Monthly Labor Review*, Vol. 97 (May 1974) pp. 27–33

Ratner, Ronnie, 'The Paradox of Protection: Maximum Hours Legislation in the US', *International Labour Review*, Vol. 119 (1980) pp. 185–7

Renshaw, Patrick, 'The Labour Movement' in Stephen Baskerville and Ralph Willett (eds), *Nothing Else to Fear: Perspectives on America in the Thirties* (Manchester: Manchester University Press, 1985) pp. 214–35

Renshaw, Patrick, 'Organized Labour and the United States War Economy, 1939–1945', *Journal of Contemporary History*, Vol. 21 (1986) pp. 3–22

Renshaw, Patrick, 'The United States of America' in Stephen Salter and John Stevenson (eds), *The Working Class and Politics in Europe and America* (London: Longman, 1990) pp. 241–72

Riche, Martha F., 'Union Election Challenges Under the LMRDA', *Monthly Labor Review*, Vol. 88 (1965) pp. 1–7

Rischin, Moses, 'The Jewish Labor Movement in America: a Social Interpretation', *Labor History*, Vol. 4 (1963) pp. 227–47

Rockoff, Hugh, 'The Response of the Giant Corporations to Wage and Price Controls in World War II', *Journal of Economic History*, Vol. 41 (1981) pp. 123–8

Rozenweig, Roy, 'Organizing the Unemployed: the Early Years of the Great Depression, 1929–1933', *Radical America*, Vol. 10 (Jul.–Aug. 1976) pp. 37–60

Rozenweig, Roy, 'Radicals and the Jobless: The Musteites and the Unemployed Leagues, 1932–1936', *Labor History*, Vol. 16 (1975) pp. 52–77

Rozenweig, Roy, 'Socialism in our Time: the Socialist Party and the Unemployed, 1929–1936', *Labor History*, Vol. 20 (1979) pp. 485–509

Samoff, Bernard L., 'The Impact of Taft–Hartley Job Discrimination Victories', *Industrial Relations*, Vol. 4 (1965) pp. 77–94

Schatz, Ronald W., 'Connecticut Working Class in the 1950s: a Catholic Perspective', *Labor History*, Vol. 25 (1984) pp. 83–101

Schatz, Ronald W., 'Labor Historians, Labor Economics, and the Question of Synthesis', *Journal of American History*, Vol. 71, No. 1 (June 1984) pp. 93–100

Seale, Bobby, *Seize the Time* (New York: Vintage, 1970)

Schwartz, Bonnie, 'New Deal Work Relief and Organized Labor: the CWA and the AFL Building Trades', *Labor History*, Vol. 17 (1976) pp. 38–57

Schweitzer, Mary, 'World War II and Female Labor Force Participation Rates', *Journal of Economic History*, Vol. 40 (1980) pp. 89–95

Seidman, Joel, 'The Sources for Future Growth and Decline in American Trade Unions', *Proceedings of the Seventeenth Annual Meeting of the Industrial Relations Research Association*, December 28–29 1964, pp. 98–108 (Madison: IRRA, 1965)

Seretan, L. Glen, 'The "New" Working class and Social Banditry in Depression America', *Mid-America*, Vol. 63 (1981) pp. 107–17

Shapiro, Edward S., 'Decentralist Intellectuals and the New Deal', *Journal of American History*, Vol. 58 (1972) pp. 938–57

Shister, Joseph, 'The Outlook for Union Growth', *Annals of the American Academy of Political and Social Science*, Vol. 35 (1963) pp. 55–62

Stein, Bruno, 'Labor's Role in Government Agencies During World War II', *Journal of Economic History*, Vol. 17 (1957) pp. 389–408

Stein, Bruno, 'Wage Stabilization in the Korean War Period: the Role of the Subsidiary Wage Board', *Labor History*, Vol. 4, No. 2 (Spring 1963) pp. 161–71

Tomlins, Christopher L., 'AFL Unions in the 1920s: Their Performance in Historical Perspective', *Journal of American History*, Vol. 65 (1979) pp. 121–42

Trey, J. E., 'Women in the War Economy, World War II', *Review of Radical Political Economics*, Vol. 4 (1972) pp. 40–57

Troger, Anne Marie, 'Coalition of Labor Union Women: Strategic Hope, Tactical Despair', *Radical America*, Vol. 9 (1975) pp. 85–110

Troy, Leo, 'Trade Union Growth in a Changing Economy', *Monthly Labor Review*, Vol. 92 (Sep. 1969) pp. 3–7

Troy, Leo, 'American Unions and their Wealth,' *Industrial Relations*, Vol. 14 (1975) pp. 134–44

Ulman, Lloyd, 'The Labor Policy of the Kennedy Administration', *Proceedings of the Fifteenth Annual Meeting of the Industrial Relations Research Association*, December 27–28, 1962, pp. 248–62 (Madison: IRRA, 1963)

Verba, Sidney and Schlozman, Kay Lehman, 'Unemployment, Class Consciousness, and Radical Politics: What Didn't Happen in the 1930s', *Journal of Politics*, Vol. 34 (1977) pp. 291–323

Weber, Arnold R., 'The Craft–Industrial Issue Revisited: A Study of Union Government', *Industrial and Labor Relations Review*, Vol. 16 (1963) pp. 381–404

Weiner, Lois, 'Women Trade Unionists Organize', *New Politics*, Vol. 9 (Winter 1974) pp. 31–5

Weir, Stan, 'American Labor on the Defensive: a 1950s Odyssey', *Radical America*, Vol. 9 (1975) pp. 163–85

Widick, B. J., 'New Trends in the Unions', *Dissent*, Vol. 20 (1973) pp. 281–83

Wolfson, Theresa, 'Women in the Labor Force', *Industrial and Labor Relations Forum*, Vol. 7 (Oct. 1971) entire issue

Wolfson, Theresa, 'Women in the Workplace: A Special Section', *Monthly Labor Review*, Vol. 97 (May 1974) pp. 3–58, 85–9

Zieger, Robert H., 'Towards the History of the CIO: A Biographical Report', *Labor History*, Vol. 26, No. 3 (Fall 1985) pp. 517–45

Index

223